Domestic Violence in Pakistan

CLARENDON STUDIES IN CRIMINOLOGY

Published under the auspices of the Institute of Criminology, University of Cambridge; the Mannheim Centre, London School of Economics; and the Centre for Criminology, University of Oxford.

Recent Titles in This Series:

Transforming Justice Responses to Non-Recent Institutional Abuses
McAlinden, Keenan and Gallen

Mafia Expansion: The 'Ndrangheta in Established Democracies
Hauser

Constructing Victimhood: Beyond Innocence and Guilt in the Transitional Justice
Lawther

Crime and Civilization: The Birth of Criminology in the Early Nineteenth Century
Kivivuori

Palestinian Political Organizations in Israeli Prisons
Bernstein

Victims and the Labour of Justice at the International Criminal Court: The Blame Cascade
Ullrich

Law and Personality Disorder: Human Rights, Human Risks, and Rehabilitation
O'Loughlin

Policing Sport Mega-Events: Security, Spectacle, and Camouflage in Rio de Janeiro
Pauschinger

Character, Circumstances, and Criminal Careers: Towards a Dynamic Developmental and Life-Course Criminology
Wikstrom, Treiber, and Roman

Children in Police Custody: Adversity and Adversariality Behind Closed Doors
Bevan

Victims and Criminal Justice: A History
Cox, Shoemaker, and Shore

Domestic Violence in Pakistan

The Legal Construction of 'Bad' and 'Mad' Women

Daanika Kamal

Lecturer in Law, Royal Holloway, University of London, UK

OXFORD
UNIVERSITY PRESS

OXFORD
UNIVERSITY PRESS

Great Clarendon Street, Oxford, OX2 6DP,
United Kingdom

Oxford University Press is a department of the University of Oxford.
It furthers the University's objective of excellence in research, scholarship,
and education by publishing worldwide. Oxford is a registered trade mark of
Oxford University Press in the UK and in certain other countries.

Published in the United States of America by Oxford University Press
198 Madison Avenue, New York, NY 10016, United States of America.

British Library Cataloguing in Publication Data
Data available

Library of Congress Control Number: 2025930987

ISBN 9780198953449

DOI: 10.1093/9780198953470.001.0001

Printed and bound by
CPI Group (UK) Ltd., Croydon, CR0 4YY

FSC www.fsc.org
MIX
Paper | Supporting responsible forestry
FSC® C013604

The manufacturer's authorised representative in the EU for product safety is Oxford University Press España S.A. of El Parque Empresarial San Fernando de Henares, Avenida de Castilla, 2 – 28830 Madrid (www.oup.es/en or product.safety@oup.com). OUP España S.A. also acts as importer into Spain of products made by the manufacturer.

This book is dedicated to Pakistani women who show extraordinary resilience in the face of gender-based violence and injustice, with the hope that their strength inspires a future where such resilience is no longer necessary.

Series Editors' Preface

The *Clarendon Studies in Criminology* series aims to provide a forum for outstanding theoretical and empirical work in all aspects of criminology and criminal justice, broadly understood. The Editors welcome submissions from established scholars, as well as manuscripts based on excellent PhD dissertations. The Series was inaugurated in 1994, with Roger Hood as its first General Editor, following discussions between Oxford University Press and Oxford's then Centre for Criminological Research. It is edited under the auspices of three centres: the Centre for Criminology at the University of Oxford, the Institute of Criminology at the University of Cambridge, and the Mannheim Centre for Criminology at the London School of Economics. Each supplies members of the Editorial Board and, in turn, the Series General Editor or Editors.

Domestic Violence in Pakistan: The Legal Construction of 'Bad' and 'Mad' Women by Daanika Kamal sensitively explores women's experiences in the courts and with the police. Drawing on documentary evidence that includes case files and judgments as well as interviews and observations, Kamal captures the challenges victims of domestic violence face in obtaining meaningful justice. In so doing, she illuminates the gendered nature of criminal justice processes and outcomes in Pakistan, a country on which Anglo-American criminology has, until now, had little to say.

This is a theoretically sophisticated account, in which Kamal reads her rich empirical detail through feminist and postcolonial theory. That conceptual literature also shapes the author's methodological choices and her style of writing. Through vignettes and storytelling, Kamal centres women's voices. She also plays an important role in the narrative herself, situating their stories, explaining them, raising questions, and drawing us in.

Arranged according to the criminal process, the chapters of the book follow the path a complainant would take, from the police to the courts. In each location Kamal finds that those who seek redress are often dismissed or humiliated, their legitimacy and standing drawn into question by highly gendered character allegations.

In many respects, *Domestic Violence in Pakistan* presents a depressingly familiar story. Kamal documents and describes a legal system that is not designed for women. Rather than delivering them justice, police officers and court officials all too often reproduce the kinds of gendered inequalities that led to their victimization, labelling the women as 'mad' or 'bad' and belittling their claims.

Yet, as with all good feminist accounts, the women are not passive and Kamal is not entirely pessimistic. Instead, as she argues powerfully in the conclusion, the task for critical feminist scholars remains clear—to document and call for change, and to produce sensitive depictions of the law in context, in order to identify its failings and to propose alternatives. To start this process of change, Kamal ends the book with a set of modest suggestions for the Pakistan courts: Ratchet down the adversarial nature of court processes, she suggests. Change how court proceedings are recorded to allow women greater freedom to speak and be heard. Adopt higher thresholds for the kinds of medical evidence that can be presented against them, to prevent them from being erroneously dismissed as mentally unwell.

This is an engaging and at times infuriating book where we see again and again a system stacked against women. The jurisdiction may be unfamiliar to some readers, but many of the issues are not. As such, it reminds us of the enduring need for feminist scholarship and action. We are pleased to include this rich study in the Clarendon Studies in Criminology series.

Mary Bosworth and Carolyn Hoyle
General Editors
Centre for Criminology, University of Oxford
November 2024

Acknowledgements

This book is based on my doctoral thesis, made possible by the funding I received from Queen Mary University of London through the Principal's Research Studentship, and the academic support of a supervisory dream team. Ruth Fletcher has been a phenomenal mentor, and I am hugely grateful for her ongoing dedication, curiosity, and guidance. Leila Ullrich and Jeffrey Kennedy have continued to provide invaluable encouragement from near and far, keeping me optimistic and motivated every step of the way. I am equally grateful to my PhD examiners, Vanessa Munro and Penny Green, for deeply and thoroughly engaging with this work, and for providing feedback that has significantly strengthened many parts of it.

This book has also benefited from the generous comments and insights of academic colleagues over the years, and I thank Raza Saeed, Kate Malleson, Maksymilian Del Mar, Roxana Banu, and Neve Gordon for their reflections. To those who were engaged with earlier drafts on chapters at conferences and workshops, especially Trever Hoppe, Lama Karame, Kelly Fong, and others at the Law and Society Association, thank you for helping to shape my approach to socio-legal scholarship. My gratitude also goes to Raich Frith, Ogulcan Ekiz, Abhijeet Kumar, Thomas Lehmann, and Uche Ani for their unwavering friendship as we navigate both the stresses and the rewards of being early career scholars. And to colleagues at the Department of Law and Criminology at Royal Holloway, University of London, thank you for providing such a welcoming and intellectually enriching work environment.

At Oxford University Press, I would like to acknowledge Fiona Briden for giving this work a nurturing home, the peer reviewers for their time and invaluable feedback, and Charlotte Kershaw for her excellent editorial support throughout the production process.

This book owes much to my colleagues and friends in Pakistan, who have been the hidden force behind the empirical work that underpins it. I am greatly indebted to them for their support, networks, and assistance in the field. Thanks particularly to Shameen Raza and to Rashid and Amna

Jahangir for opening their hearts and homes to me during various periods of fieldwork.

To my family, thank you for a lifetime of love and faith. I am grateful for Sameer and Stephanie's comforting reassurances, for Maazin and Anum's passion for storytelling, and for Imaani's warm laughter. My mother, Simi Kamal, is my voice of conscience. I am immensely proud to be her daughter and to witness first hand her resolute commitment to feminist principles. My brilliant father, Altamash Kamal, and my dear Nani, Syeda Asiya Jabbar Niazi, continue to watch over me from above. I am deeply thankful for their enduring light and guidance.

Most of all, I owe immense gratitude to my husband, Rodrigo Vaz da Silva. He has seen this work develop from a conceptual proposal into a research project, then into a doctoral thesis, and now into a monograph. His boundless love, companionship, and patience have carried me (and this manuscript) through. Amo-te.

*

This book is not mine alone; it is shared with all those who generously entrusted me with their stories. I have tried, to the best of my ability, to do justice to their voices.

Contents

Table of Cases

PAKISTAN

Table of Legislation

1
Domestic violence in Pakistan

> *Jooti tay runn see ikk missal ay, aie tay aie nai tan door hatai* [A wife, like shoes, deserves similar handling: carry on with them if they fit well, otherwise throw them away][1]

Introduction

Vignette 1.1 Fieldwork diary, 9 June 2022, Islamabad

There's something unsettling about this court complex. A self-contained little village in the heart of the capital with tiny weaving streets littered with empty juice boxes and peels of dried paint. I walk at brisk pace towards the security checkpoint which connects an overcrowded parking lot to a frenzied world dotted with specks of white shirts and black blazers. *Kachehri*, we call it. Walking briskly wasn't a conscious choice, rather almost robotic; something my body did out of habit, a rush that was prompted into motion simply by being here, by being *back* here. It was the first time I had returned to the district courts in a very long time, the last time being when I was there for my own divorce hearings. I recalled the many days I took time off work to drive from my office to F-8; rushing to find parking and then rushing to find my way to the family courts, only to be sent back because the hearing was rescheduled at the last minute to accommodate another case, or because the judge was no longer available. Other days, most days, I would wait for hours—with my mind continuing to rush even as my body stayed still—only for the hearing to be adjourned with no progress because the other party's lawyer asked for more time to file requisite

[1] A Punjabi proverb. See M Shahbaz, *Saday Akhaan [Our Proverbs]* (Aziz Book Depot 2004) 155.

Domestic Violence in Pakistan. Daanika Kamal, Oxford University Press. © Daanika Kamal 2025.
DOI: 10.1093/9780198953470.003.0001

replies, or because they did not show up at all. It was a repetitive cycle over a course of weeks, of months.

... But there is also something to be said about returning to the same court for fieldwork, to research the same ideas that began taking root when I was here last. To sit with the discomfort of vividly remembering my hands shaking as I held the court summons for the case he filed right after I initiated legal proceedings for divorce. A suit which boldly contended that I had left the marital abode against his will, having negated to perform my duties as a Muslim wife, and that requested the court to direct me to return to him and fulfil my obligations towards his conjugal rights under Islamic injunction. To sit with the unease of viscerally remembering my body trembling as I watched his lawyer tell the court that my cases relating to the dissolution of marriage should be dropped, because the reasons I had provided for divorce were frivolous and a figment of my imagination; claiming that I had a 'mental issue' and was therefore unable to recollect things said or done. And to sit with the disquiet of realizing that I was contending with two legal cases simultaneously: one for my rights, where I had been subjectivized as a 'mad' woman; and the other for what was claimed to be the restitution of his rights, where I had been subjectivized as a 'bad' woman.

I had long been grappling with how to begin this book. As reflected in Vignette 1.1, I know where the story starts, for me, but sharing it required me to revisit an unyielding pain of a life past lived that mercifully finds no place in my reality today. It required me to return to the agonizing ache of being momentarily suspended in time, haunted by scars that marked me and narratives that shamed me. And yet, I also know that this experience isn't specific to me; it is a reality shared by most Pakistani women who make the difficult decision to walk away from oppressive marriages and abusive domestic relationships. It is a reality marred by judicial tactics that bury her in legal paperwork, use frivolous excuses to prolong her case, and levy ceaseless allegations to discredit her experiences, dismiss her harms, and mask her truths. As a researcher, there's an incongruity in witnessing the same courts that I once approached for relief as a litigant, the same systems that I once grappled with for my rights, be animated by strategies that actively work to block that access for women.

Around the time of my own legal proceedings, I had been working alongside a team on a project that established and supported numerous legal aid centres in Sindh and Punjab through grants focusing on access to justice for women, children, and marginalized communities. During fieldtrips to those legal aid centres, managers and panel lawyers would regularly share details about ongoing cases to help ascertain that the legal needs of clients were being sufficiently met. It was during these conversations and in the related case notes that I started noticing a pattern, where in numerous instances, women's claims relating to domestic abuse and violence were being dismissed by the other legal party through several allegations. Two featured prominently. The first was that the complainant was of immoral character because she engaged in illicit affairs, wore immodest clothing, or was of 'bellicose' nature. Subjectivizing women in this manner was a familiar patriarchal technique, one that I was well accustomed to growing up in Karachi. Similar to the messaging conveyed by the gendered proverbs at the beginning of every chapter in this book, we frequently heard stories circulating through school corridors, tea parties, and television screens that were glittered with caveats about the '*buri aurat*' ['bad' woman]—almost as warnings to other women. Stories of women being physically and sexually assaulted in public spaces were seen as 'expected', because she was out and about in public spaces on her own. Stories of women being abused within their own homes were seen as 'normal', because she must have done something to deserve it. And stories of women being battered by intimate partners were seen as 'justified', because she shouldn't have had sexual relations outside of marriage.

The second prominent allegation, however, was a bit less familiar to me. It stated that the woman complainant, as a victim of domestic violence, was mentally unstable. This assertion was made through labels such as 'psycho', '*paagal*' [crazy], '*nafsiyati*' [mentally disordered], or '*zehni mareez*' [mental patient]. I refer to these labels as 'psy' labels because they either relate to or are adjacent to the disciplines of psychiatry and psychology. These labels were often accompanied by assertions that the complainant needed psychiatric treatment, and at times framed as a grave concern for her wellbeing. There was little to no provision of medical evidence that would speak to the complainant's mental incapacity in any way. Rather, these 'psy' labels were used subjectively to insinuate that her claims of abuse were a product of mental illness and should consequently be discredited. When I questioned this practice, I was told that the use of such 'character allegations' was simply a 'common practice' in the courts, particularly in response to cases which alleged domestic violence (or 'cruelty', as it's more commonly termed in Pakistan) that were filed by women.

When allegations become commonplace, they are so enmeshed within legal practices that it is sometimes difficult to differentiate one from the other. It also becomes more difficult to question those practices. In hindsight, I must admit that, like the legal actors I spoke to, my greater familiarity with the first set of allegations in comparison to the second made me question the latter more. During my own divorce hearings, I was warned by my lawyer that the other party may try to 'assassinate my character'. I was advised to dress and present myself in a certain way in the courtroom, so that I didn't fuel the spark the other party would likely light. It was *expected* that they would raise concerns about my inability to be a 'good Muslim wife'. Frustrating, but also normal. Just an everyday practice they adopt because, as my legal team put it, 'they have nothing else, you see'. And having prepared myself for this line of discourse, I was quite taken aback when the response from the other party not only claimed that I was of 'bad' character and unable to perform my 'duties' and 'obligations' under Islamic injunctions, but also claimed that I had a 'mental issue.' I remember thinking then, *it probably serves the same purpose*; but I fell short of identifying precisely what that purpose is.

It is against this background that this book took shape, as I questioned why and how the framing of victims of domestic violence as 'bad' and/or 'mad' was a 'common practice' in the Pakistani legal system. Broadly, the forthcoming discussions are inspired by perspectives and approaches commonly bracketed under feminist poststructuralism, drawing on theorizations relating to the interplay between power, meaning and subjectivity as they relate to gender. In questioning *why*, I explored and developed ideas relating to the use of gendering strategies in discursive spaces.[2] This includes engagement with interdisciplinary scholarship from South Asian postcolonial thought relating to the social control of women, as well as feminist perspectives of law and psychiatry.[3] And in questioning *how*, I turned to empirical work. Over a cumulative six-month period of fieldwork in the cities of Karachi, Lahore, and Islamabad, primary research materials include more than one hundred case files and judgments, seventy-two

[2] See C Smart, *Feminism and the Power of Law* (Routledge 1989); J Butler, *Bodies That Matter: On the Discursive Limits of 'Sex'* (Routledge 1993); N Fairclough, *Discourse and Social Change* (Polity Press 1992); V Munro, *Law and Politics at the Perimeter: Re-evaluating Key Debates in Feminist Theory* (Hart 2007); and C Weedon and A Hallak, 'Feminist Poststructuralism: Discourse, Subjectivity, the Body and Power' in J Angouri and J Baxter (eds) *The Routledge Handbook of Language, Gender and Sexuality* (Routledge 2021) 437.

[3] The conceptual framework through which the research materials are analysed is developed in Chapter 2.

semi-structured interviews with victims, lawyers, judges, police personnel, and victim support personnel, and ethnographic notes from multiple days spent in court observations.[4]

In short, I argue that character allegations function as a gendering strategy to construct victim-subjects of domestic violence. This book accordingly captures and offers empirical sociolegal insights into how these gendered constructs are produced and reinforced at various stages of the legal system. By shadowing women's experiences, it identifies and develops four main themes through which complainants are subjectivized, finding that character allegations are used by legal actors to (a) silence victims through gendered narratives, (b) police victims through gatekeeping approaches, (c) script victims through lawyerly practices, and (d) enact victims through anticipatory performances. This also allows for engagement with two areas that have relevance and applicability in legal contexts beyond Pakistan. The first is whether gendering practices and narratives are an inevitable product of adversarial legal processes (where challenging the accused's credibility is the default focus of defence strategies),[5] or whether the courtroom can be imagined as a space that recognizes and values stories grounded in lived experiences (rather than boilerplate 'bad' character tropes). The second addresses broader questions in relation to the expansion of domestic abuse definitions to include psychological and emotional abuse, as reflected in legislative developments in various parts of the world.[6] Such expansions are crucial to acknowledge the full scope of coercive relationships and speak to the complex relationship that often exists between domestic abuse and mental health.[7] However, it could arguably fuel narratives of 'mad' women, where the harms identified by complainants as outcomes of domestic abuse may simultaneously be used by the defence to position her as an unreliable and uncredible litigant.

[4] The methodological approach of this book is outlined in Chapter 2.

[5] D Smith, 'The Disordered and Discredited Plaintiff: Psychiatric Evidence in Civil Litigation' (2009) 31(3) Cardoza Law Review 749.

[6] For developments in England and Wales, for example, see C Wiener, 'From Social Construct to Legal Innovation: The Offence of Controlling or Coercive Behaviour in England and Wales' in M McMahon and P McGorrery (eds), *Criminalising Coercive Control: Family Violence and the Criminal Law* (Springer 2020) 159.

[7] See S Oram, H Khalifeh and LM Howard, 'Violence against Women and Mental Health' (2017) 4(2) Lancet Psychiatry 159; C Humphreys and R Thiara, 'Mental Health and Domestic Violence: "I call it symptoms of abuse"' (2003) 2(1) The British Journal of Social Work 209; T Afifi and others, 'Mental Health Correlates of intimate partner violence in Marital Relationships in a Nationally Representative Sample of Males and Females' (2009) 24(8) Journal of Interpersonal Violence 1398.

Further, while this book uses the framings of 'bad' woman and 'mad' woman to capture the two more prominent character allegations in the Pakistani legal system, I acknowledge the plurality and complexity of subjectivities that come to form through such allegations both within and outside of these framings. Using these framings as a stepping-off point was a choice rooted in the everyday vernacular of '*buri aurat*' ('bad' woman) and '*paagal aurat*' ('mad' woman), as a means to investigate and unpack the discursive embodiment of gendered allegations circulating within Pakistani society, and indeed, Pakistani courtrooms.

Mapping the legislative landscape

The Human Rights Commission of Pakistan (HRCP) states that only a fraction of cases relating to abuse and violence against women are officially reported, and those that are mostly relate to extreme cases where the victim is burnt, disfigured, raped, tortured, or murdered.[8] It is therefore incredibly difficult to cite accurate figures to determine the prevalence of domestic violence in Pakistan. Official government data estimates that 1 in 3 Pakistani women experience domestic violence in their lifetimes,[9] while approximations from independent studies commissioned by the National Commission of Human Rights (NCHR) find that this number is closer to 90 per cent, with the majority of perpetrators being husbands.[10]

Domestic violence is a contentious, sensitive issue in Pakistan, with societal discourse using religion, in part, to justify the use of physical and coercive acts to 'discipline' women in household settings.[11] This discourse stems from a particular interpretation of verse 4:34 of the Quran, which states:

[8] K Hayat, *State of Human Rights in 2001* (Human Rights Commission of Pakistan 2002).

[9] National Institute of Population Studies, 'Pakistan Demographic and Health Survey 2017–2018' (NIPS and ICF 2019) <https://dhsprogram.com/pubs/pdf/FR354/FR354.pdf> accessed 3 June 2023.

[10] K Ali and M Inam, *Domestic Violence Policy Brief* (National Commission of Human Rights Pakistan 2023).

[11] FF Fikree, JA Razzak and J Durocher, 'Attitudes of Pakistani Men to Domestic Violence: A Study from Karachi, Pakistan' (2005) 2(1) Journal of Men's Health and Gender 49; also see R Karmaliani and others, 'Understanding Intimate Partner Violence in Pakistan through a Male Lens' (Overseas Development Institute, March 2017) <https://cdn.odi.org/media/documents/11398.pdf> accessed 4 June 2023.

> Men are protectors and maintainers of women, because Allah has given the one more [strength] than the other, and because they support them from their means. Therefore the righteous women are devoutly obedient, and guard in [the husband's] absence what Allah would have them guard. As to those women on whose part ye fear disloyalty and ill-conduct, admonish them [first]. [Next], refuse to share their beds, and [last] beat them [lightly]. But if they return to obedience, seek not against them means [of annoyance]. For Allah is Most-High, Great [above you all].[12]

Shaheen Sardar Ali argues that this verse is not only interpreted by some Islamic schools of thought as giving women a 'lower status' than men, but, more problematically, has also been interpreted to legitimize violence against women in domestic settings.[13] The main point of contention in the above verse comes from the word *daraba*, which is commonly translated as 'striking' or 'hitting.' To counter this discursive reading, Ali offers alternate translations and understandings of the term, suggesting it could mean 'to prevent' or 'to set an example', contending that scholars have proposed various interpretations which indicate that at a time when 'men did not *need* permission to strike their wives, verse 4:34 could only be restrictive, rather than prescriptive'.[14]

These common interpretations, however, have led to backlash against legislative developments in the domestic violence realm in Pakistan. For example, the Council of Islamic Ideology (CII), a constitutional body, has deemed laws that serve to protect women in domestic settings as 'un-Islamic',[15] publicly citing verse 4:34 to state that beating women 'lightly' is justified.[16] Similarly, the federal domestic violence bill extending to the Islamabad Capital Territory (ICT) was passed by the National Assembly in

[12] Translation by Y Ali, as cited in SS Ali, *Modern Challenges to Islamic Law* (Cambridge University Press 2016) 33. In *Malik Tanveer Khan v Amber Liaqat* [2009] CLC 1210, it was stated that '. . . a righteous woman guards the sanctity of the bond of marriage and protects her and husband's chastity and virtues, guards her honour for him and to be faithful to him.'

[13] ibid 36.

[14] ibid 38 citing A Barlas, *Believing Women in Islam: Unreading Patriarchal Interpretations of the Quran* (University of Texas Press 2002) 188 [emphasis added].

[15] I Gabol, 'Religious Parties Denounce Law Protecting Women from Abuse as "Un-Islamic"' *Dawn News* (15 March 2016) <https://www.dawn.com/news/1245835> accessed 11 July 2023.

[16] R Khan, '"Lightly Beating" Wife Is Permissible, Says CII's Proposed Women Protection Bill' *Dawn News* (26 May 2016) <https://www.dawn.com/news/1260803> accessed 2 June 2018.

2021, but blocked by the Senate for further deliberations due to concerns that it 'contravenes the Islamic [injunctions] and way of life as enshrined in responsibility of the state'.[17] And while provincial domestic violence legislation has been instituted following devolution, societal concerns have led to a continual lack of prosecution through these laws. As such, most cases in Pakistan are not prosecuted through the existing provincial domestic violence legislation, but rather found across a spectrum of legal cases, ranging from other kinds of criminal offences on one end, to civil and family disputes on the other.

Over the following sections, I provide a summary of domestic violence definitions and legislations as per Pakistani law, as well as an overview of other relevant laws where acts of domestic violence prominently feature. Under the criminal ambit, this includes cases of murder and 'honour' killings, rape, and sexual assault, as well as cases prosecuted through the 'hurt offences' of the Pakistan Penal Code (PPC).[18] And under the civil and family ambit, cases of domestic violence frequently feature in cases relating to the dissolution of marriage (including divorce and *khula*), and in petitions for custody and guardianship of children.

Domestic violence laws

Following devolution in 2010, domestic violence fell under the domain of provincial governance.[19] Over the past ten years, each of Pakistan's four provinces have instituted laws pertaining to women's protection within the family and home,[20] starting with Sindh in 2013,[21] then Balochistan in

[17] Domestic Violence (Prevention and Protection) Bill 2021 [PAK]. 'Govt Recommends Referring Domestic Violence Bill to Council of Islamic Ideology' *Dawn News* (6 July 2021) <https://www.dawn.com/news/1633531> accessed 19 July 2023.

[18] Pakistan Penal Code (Act XLV of 1860) [PAK], hereafter 'PPC.' 'Hurt offences' is an umbrella term used to refer to s 332–s 337 of the PPC.

[19] See Constitution (Eighteenth Amendment) Act 2010 [PAK].

[20] It is pertinent to note that while domestic abuse can, of course, be perpetrated by both men and women, and similarly have both male and female victims, research has consistently shown that domestic abuse continues to be a predominantly gendered crime (see V Munro and R Aitken, 'From Hoping to Help: Identifying and Responding to Suicidality amongst Victims of Domestic Abuse' (2020) 26(1) International Review of Victimology 29). Given that women continue to endure the most prolonged and severe forms of domestic abuse at the hands of men, and reflective of legislative definitions of domestic abuse in Pakistan which primarily specify women as 'aggrieved persons', this book's focus is on women victims.

[21] The Sindh Domestic Violence (Prevention and Protection) Act 2013 [PAK], hereafter 'SDVA'.

2014,[22] Punjab in 2016,[23] and Khyber Pakhtunkhwa (KP) most recently in 2021.[24] There are slight variations in understandings and definitions of which acts of domestic violence are covered under each provincial law. Broadly, these acts can be categorized as follows: physical abuse, psychological and emotional abuse, sexual abuse, and financial abuse.

In line with Pakistani culture, legislative developments have accommodated joint family structures by expanding the definition of what constitutes a 'household', thereby also expanding definitions for who can be a perpetrator of domestic violence. The language used in the respective laws accordingly reflects that offences can be committed by a person who is living or has lived in the same premises as the victim, when they are related to one another through marriage, adoption, employment, blood kinship, or 'other' family relationship. Further, while the Punjab laws limit the scope of 'aggrieved persons' to females (which includes both women and girls),[25] Sindh expands it to specify women and children (regardless of sex) as well as other 'vulnerable persons'.[26] Balochistan is the only province to include adult men within the definition of 'aggrieved persons', and additionally extends the law to live-in domestic staff.[27] And unlike other provinces, the KP law specifies that the 'complainant' can only be a woman (clarified as a female over the age of 18).[28] This presents a major loophole for girls who are coerced into child marriages, as their exclusion means they would be unable to seek remedies for acts of spousal or domestic violence through this law.[29]

All provincial laws similarly have slight differences in the scope and definitions of acts of domestic violence provided. For physical violence, Sindh

[22] The Balochistan Domestic Violence (Prevention and Protection) Act 2014 [PAK], hereafter 'BDVA'.

[23] The Punjab Protection of Women against Violence Act 2016 [PAK], hereafter 'PPWAVA.'

[24] Khyber-Pakhtunkhwa Domestic Violence against Women (Prevention and Protection) Act 2021 [PAK], hereafter 'KPDVA'. At the time of writing, the federal Domestic Violence Bill (extending to ICT) that was passed by the National Assembly but blocked by the Senate for further deliberation still has not come into force. See Dawn News (n 17).

[25] PPWAVA, s 2(1)(a).

[26] SDVA, s 2(1)(a); A 'vulnerable person' is defined as 'a person who is vulnerable due to old age, mental illness or handicap or physical disability or for other special reason'. See SDVA, s 2(1)(s).

[27] See BDVA, s 2(a). As of the time of writing, the author is unaware of any domestic abuse cases in Balochistan where a man has filed a petition as an aggrieved person (or victim) under this legislation.

[28] KPDVA, s 2 (1)(c).

[29] It has been argued that this exclusion was intentional, in order to 'avoid any controversy by religious circles'. See WA Shah, 'View from Courtroom: KP Domestic Violence Bill a Diluted Version of Previous Drafts' *Dawn News* (11 January 2021) <https://www.dawn.com/news/1600820> accessed 13 February 2022.

and Balochistan primarily rely upon the PPC for definitions, specifying acts of physical abuse in domestic settings as assault, criminal force, intimidation, and wrongful confinement.[30] Punjab laws have opted for a more general provision, where violence means 'any offence committed against the human body of the aggrieved person',[31] while the KP law does not provide an explanation for physical violence at all. Psychological and emotional abuse, on the other hand, have been specified in the Sindh and Balochistan laws as 'a pattern of degrading and humiliating conduct',[32] whereas Punjab and KP have defined it on the basis of the impact it has on the victim (that is, acts resulting in mental health illnesses or disorders such as 'suicidal attempts, or clinically proven depression').[33] The provincial laws also specify acts of economic abuse to mean the deprivation or denial of financial resources that are entitled to the aggrieved person, with Punjab and KP further specifying the withdrawal of provision of food, clothing, and shelter as financial abuse.[34]

Additionally, Sindh and Balochistan laws define sexual abuse as 'any conduct of a sexual nature that abuses, humiliates, degrades or otherwise violates the dignity of the aggrieved person', and also include penalties for 'compelling the wife to cohabit with anybody other than the husband'.[35] On the other hand, both the Punjab and KP laws contain 'sexual abuse' in the text of their respective domestic violence laws but do not provide an explanation for what that stipulates. However, in order to safeguard against complaints of marital rape being brought forth through this legislation, the KP law specifies that it 'does *not* include ordinary and natural relationships amongst husband and wife so committed in accordance with injunctions of Islam'.[36] This is in spite of the ambiguous wording of Pakistan's rape laws, which do not explicitly exclude marital rape from falling under section 375 of the PPC.[37]

It is perhaps not surprising, given the societal and institutional backlash against domestic violence laws, that despite the existence of provincial legislation, implementation has been slow in some provinces, and stagnant

[30] See SDVA, s 5; BDVA, s 4.
[31] PPWAVA, s 2(1)(r).
[32] SDVA, s 5(f); BDVA, s 4(m).
[33] PPWAVA, s 2(1)(r); KPDVA, s 2(1)(p)(ii).
[34] See SDVA, s 5(o); BDVA, s 4(e); PPWAVA, s 2(1)(r); KPDVA, s 2(1)(p).
[35] SDVA, s 5(l); BDVA, s 4 (l).
[36] KPDVA, s 2(1)(p)(iii) [emphasis added].
[37] Rape is covered under s 375 of the PPC. I discuss this further in the section titled 'Rape and sexual assault' in this chapter.

in others. For example, data from the Punjab police finds that no case of domestic violence was registered under the Punjab Protection of Women against Violence Act of 2016 in the years that followed.[38] This is because the Act includes a clause which states that it will come into effect after notices have been issued in the various provincial districts, and it has, to date, only been notified in one district.[39] And in Sindh, the Domestic Violence Act was passed in 2013, but it was only in 2019—six years after it came into effect—that the first case was petitioned under it. Additionally, the percentage of cases of domestic violence that make it to criminal proceedings is reported to be a staggering 0.4 per cent,[40] with many cases being prosecuted not under the domestic violence laws, but under the PPC. In cases of extreme violence leading to death, the murder and 'honour' killing offences are used, whereas for sexual offences perpetrated by family members, the rape offences are used. Less serious physical acts of domestic violence, too, are prosecuted under the 'hurt offences'.

Murder and 'honour' killings

A report presented to the National Assembly of Pakistan in 2022 finds that as per police data, close to 4,000 women were killed as a result of domestic abuse and 'honour' violence between 2019 and 2021 across the country.[41] This number does not account for deaths that were unreported, nor does it account for those that were considered 'non-suspicious' and therefore not investigated by police officials and instead filed as natural deaths or suicides.[42] The reported cases referred to here are those that were prosecuted

[38] Ali and Inam (n 10).

[39] PPWAVA, s 1(2), s 1(3).

[40] S Mehboob, 'Where Pakistan's domestic violence law fails' *The Express Tribune* (7 August 2022) <https://tribune.com.pk/story/2369842/where-pakistans-domestic-violence-law-fails> accessed 18 July 2023.

[41] R Mushtaq and SB Haider, 'Why Violence against Women Continues Unabated Despite Presence of Laws' *Geo News* (24 October 2022) <https://www.geo.tv/latest/448066-why-violence-against-women-continues-unabated-despite-presence-of-laws> accessed 10 June 2023.

[42] For example, in the case of Samia Shahid, the Pakistani police had originally treated her death as non-suspicious and only later was the case fully investigated to find that she had been murdered on the pretext of 'honour'. Her father and ex-husband were subsequently arrested. See F Perraudin, 'Alleged "Honour" Killing Victim Was Murdered, Pakistani Police Confirm' *The Guardian* (3 August 2016) <https://www.theguardian.com/uk-news/2016/aug/03/alleged-honour-killing-victim-samia-shahid-murdered-pakistani-police-confirm> accessed 26 June 2023.

under the *qatl-e-amad* (murder) offences, which are regulated by Section 300 and Section 301 of the PPC:

> ... Whoever, with the intention of causing death or with the intention of causing bodily injury to a person, by doing an act which in the ordinary course of nature is likely to cause death, or with the knowledge that his act is so imminently dangerous that it must in all probability cause death, causes the death of such person, is said to commit *qatl-e-amd*.
>
> ... Where a person, by doing anything which he intends or knows to be likely to cause death, causes death of any person whose death he neither intends nor knows himself to be likely to cause, such an act committed by the offender shall be liable for *qatl-i-amd*.[43]

In 2004, the Criminal Law (Amendment) Act, also referred to as the 'Honour Killings Act', amended Pakistan's Criminal Procedure Code (CrPC) and the PPC to include the offence of *qatl-i-amd* under 'the pretext of honour'.[44] However, the laws are compoundable and therefore allow the heirs of the victim the right to pardon the accused, or to enter into a compensatory compromise known as *diyat*. In 2016, following the widely reported 'honour' killing of a social media personality known as Qandeel Baloch by her brother, parliament revisited these procedural loopholes with an aim to eliminate the availability of family pardons.[45] Yet, in 2022, Baloch's brother was acquitted after their parents pardoned him for the offence.[46]

Further, it is pertinent to note that as per a recent judgment of the Supreme Court, 'in incidents of domestic violence, more so in the event of homicidal death of a wife in the house of her husband, a heavy onus is cast upon the latter to satisfactorily explain the circumstances leading to the tragedy'.[47] This indicates that the burden of proof in cases where women are

[43] PPC, s 300, s 301.

[44] Criminal Law (Amendment) Act 2004 [PAK].

[45] M Asad, 'Loopholes Persist in "Honour Killing" Bill' *Dawn News* (24 July 2016) <https://www.dawn.com/news/1272833> accessed 10 July 2023; also see *Muhammad Wasim v The State* [2019] LHC (Criminal Appeal) 917.

[46] SM Baloch, 'Pakistan Court Acquits Man Who Killed Sister after Parents' Pardon' *The Guardian* (14 Feb 2022) <https://www.theguardian.com/world/2022/feb/14/pakistan-court-acquits-man-waseem-azeem-who-killed-sister-after-parents-pardon> accessed 1 June 2023.

[47] *Shaukat Hussain v the State* [2022] SCMR 1358. Similarly, in *Saeed Khan v The State* [2015] SCMR 710, it was stated that, 'With regard to vulnerable members of society, such as children, women and the infirm, who were living with the accused or were last in his company (before their death), the accused ought to offer some explanation as to what happened to them.'

found dead in their own households falls on their husbands. In many cases, this burden of proof has led to claims by husbands and family members that the death of the woman was not due to domestic violence, but self-inflicted and a result of suicide.[48] Explanations provide for this claim include that the deceased took her own life due to 'depression',[49] or because she was 'not mentally stable'[50] or 'under tremendous mental strain'.[51] Such narratives are also found in cases where women have been killed by family members under the pretext of 'honour'. In *Muhammad Farooq v the State*, for example, the judgment reads that 'the accused persons while sharing their common intention, committed the murder of the sister of the complainant under the pretext of honour . . . whereas the appellant came forward with the stance that it was suicide committed by the deceased'.[52] These examples are indicative of domestic violence instances being found and contested in cases of murder and 'honour' killings, but that are not necessarily always filed or reported using that terminology.

Rape and sexual assault

Sexual offences are primarily regulated by Section 375 to Section 377 of the PPC, which were added through an Amendment to the Criminal Laws in 2006[53] and defined rape as follows:

> A man is said to commit rape who has sexual intercourse with a woman under circumstances falling under any of the five following descriptions, (i) against her will, (ii) without her consent, (iii) with her consent, when the consent has been obtained by putting her in fear of death or of hurt, (iv) with her consent, when the man knows that he is not married to her and that the consent is given because she believes that the man is another person to whom she is or believes herself to be

[48] See for example: *Punoon v The State* [2016] YLR Note 44; *Muhammad Hanif v Add. Sessions Judge* [2016] PCrLJ 756; *Riaz Ahmad v The State* [2016] PCrLJ Note 95; *Muhammad Ibrahim v The State* [2017] PCrLJ 1130; *Papoo v The State* [2018] YLR 120; *Hikmat Shah v Bakhtiar Khan* [2018] YLR 1168; and *Noor Alam v The State* [2018] PCrLJ Note 134.

[49] See for example, *Syed Tahir Shah and others v The State* [2018] CrLJ 242; and *Muhammad Hanif v Add. Sessions Judge* [2016] PCrLJ 756.

[50] *Hakim Zada v The State* [2015] PCrLJ 1171.

[51] *Manzoor Elahi v Sessions Judge* [2016] PCrLJ 211.

[52] *Muhammad Farooq v The State* [2019] PCrLJ 609.

[53] See Protection of Women (Criminal Laws Amendment) Act 2006 [PAK].

married; or (v) with or without her consent when she is under sixteen years of age.[54]

Pakistani organization War on Rape (WAR) estimates that 82 per cent of perpetrators in rape cases are family members such as fathers, brothers, uncles, and in-laws.[55] As such, there are numerous cases of domestic violence that surface through these sections of the PPC. Examples include a 2017 case where a father raped his adult daughter in Multan,[56] a 2019 case from Larkana where charges had been brought against a man for attempting to rape his daughter-in-law,[57] and a 2022 case where a man was prosecuted for raping his two minor nieces in Rawalpindi.[58]

It is important to note that the statistic cited above is not reflective of instances of marital rape by husbands, which is an offence that continues to be unclear in Pakistani law. This lack of clarity is despite the addition of sexual abuse offences under domestic violence laws, as discussed above, and the lack of an explicit exclusion of marital rape under section 375 of the PPC. Prior to the 2006 amendment of criminal laws, sexual offences were

[54] PPC, s 375. The offence of rape has recently adopted more gender-neutral language through s 2 of the Criminal Law (Amendment) Act 2021 [PAK] where: 'A person A is said to commit "rape" if A — (a) penetrates his penis, to any extent, into the vagina, mouth, urethra or anus of another person B or makes B to do so with A or any other person; or (b) inserts, to any extent, any object or a part of the body, not being the penis, into the vagina, the urethra or anus of B or makes B to do so with A or any other person; or (c) manipulates any part of the body of B so as to cause penetration into the vagina, urethra, anus or any part of body of B or makes B to do so with A or any other person; or (d) applies his mouth to the vagina, anus, urethra or penis of B or makes B to do so with A or any other person, under the circumstances falling under any of the following seven descriptions, — firstly, against B's will; secondly, without B's consent; thirdly, with B's consent, which has been obtained by putting B or any person in whom B is interested, in fear of death or of hurt; fourthly, with B's consent, when A knows that A is not B's husband and that B's consent is given because B believes that A is another man to whom B is or believes herself to be lawfully married; fifthly, with B's consent when, at the time of giving such consent, by reason of unsoundness of mind or intoxication or the administration by A personally or through another of any stupefying or unwholesome substance, B is unable to understand the nature and consequences of that to which B gives consent; sixthly, with or without B's consent, when B is under sixteen years of age; or seventhly, when B is unable to communicate consent.' However, for the majority of relevant cases discussed in this book, the prior provision of s 375 was being used, as the date of the registered offence predates that of the amendment.

[55] 'Over 82 Per Cent of Rapists are Fathers or Brothers of Victim: PTI MNA' *Naya Daur* (15 September 2020) <https://nayadaur.tv/2020/09/over-82-per-cent-of-rapists-are-fathers-or-brothers-of-victim-pti-mna/> accessed 28 July 2023. Also see *Altaf Hussain Shah v The State* [2021] YLR 2107; *Zulfiqar Ali v The State* [2012] YLR 847; *Muhammad Latif v The State* [1981] PLD FSC 317; and *Feroz Khan v The State* [2015] YLR 703.

[56] *Khursheed Ahmad v The State* [2017] PCrLJ 1664.

[57] *Sajjan v The State* [2019] YLR 2442.

[58] *Iftikhar Ali v The State* [2022] PCrLJ 1396.

regulated by the Offence of Zina Ordinance of 1979, which defined *zina-bil-jabr* (rape) as a man or woman having sexual intercourse with whom he or she is not validly married, against the will of the victim, or without the consent of the victim.[59] This wording therefore explicitly excluded the possibility of a man raping his wife. Current laws, however, are silent on the issue. While ambiguity in the provisions of current rape laws could be interpreted as allowing marital rape to fall under its ambit, there are no reported judgments which clarify the position of the law in this matter. Interestingly, a woman in Multan did bring a case against her husband for marital rape in 2018,[60] but the case was heard not under Section 375 ('rape') but under Section 377 ('unnatural offences') of the PPC, which reads: 'whoever voluntarily has carnal intercourse against the order of nature with any man, woman or animal . . .'[61]

Other relevant sections of the PPC where acts of domestic violence may feature in relation to sexual offences include Section 509, 'insulting modesty or causing sexual harassment', and Section 511, which regulates attempts of sexual assault.[62]

'Hurt offences'

In Pakistan, physical acts of domestic violence are typically filed under the 'hurt offences'. 'Hurt offences' is an umbrella term used to refer to Sections 332 to 337 of the PPC, which reads: 'Whoever causes pain, harm, disease, infirmity or injury to any person or impairs, disables, [disfigures, defaces] or dismembers any organ of the body or part thereof of any person without causing his death, is said to cause hurt.'[63] In *Asad v The State*, for example, a woman was beaten up by her husband on the instigation that 'she has made him eunuch' and sustained injuries on her lips, nose, left eye, and abdomen.[64] This case falls under domestic violence laws as per definitions provided by way of current legislation, but was instead filed and prosecuted under the 'hurt offences' of the PPC.

[59] Offence of Zina (Enforcement of Hudood) Ordinance 1979 [PAK].

[60] 'Woman Files Case of "Marital Rape" against Husband' *The News* (16 September 2018) <https://www.thenews.com.pk/print/369113-woman-files-case-of-marital-rape-against-husband> accessed 20 July 2023.

[61] PPC, s 377.

[62] PPC, s 509, s 511.

[63] PPC, s 332 (1).

[64] *Asad v The State* [2017] YLR Note 295.

As of 2011, 'hurt offences' also include specific sections criminalizing acid crimes. Acid crimes are defined as any act of assault which uses acid, with legislative definitions using the mode of assault, rather than the motivation behind it, for prosecution.[65] Such acts typically result in 'severe pain, permanent disfigurement, subsequent infections, and blindness in one or both eyes'.[66] The Acid Survivors Foundation (ASF) in Pakistan reports that acid attacks are overwhelmingly employed in acts of domestic violence towards women and girls.[67] These acts are an attempt to maim and permanently scar victims. Through an assessment of the cases on which the organization has worked, ASF finds that where the primary target is a woman, the main identifiable reasons for acid attacks include: an escalation of preexisting domestic abuse by the husband; a broader family dispute (such as disagreements with in-laws); and acts of retaliation when women decline marriage proposals.[68]

Given the high incidence rates of acid attacks, activists spearheaded legislation to specifically criminalize acid and burn-related violence. The Acid Crime Prevention Act of 2011 accordingly added Sections 336-A and 336-B to the PPC.[69] In addition to outlining penalties for acid crimes, the law outlines a process for conducting trials to ensure cases are concluded within sixty days. Implementation, however, remains a challenge. Recent statistics from 2018 indicate that fifty-four cases of acid violence were registered with the police in Pakistan, of which only thirteen were prosecuted, and only five led to convictions.[70]

The lack of prosecution through existing criminal laws means that only a small fraction of reported cases of domestic violence find their way to criminal proceedings.[71] The rest either end up in the family courts, or simply

[65] United Nations, 'Good Practices in Legislation on "Harmful Practices" against Women' (2009) EGM Meeting, Department of Economic and Social Affairs <https://www.un.org/womenwatch/daw/egm/vaw_legislation_2009/Final%20report%20EGMGPLVAW.pdf> accessed 20 July 2023.

[66] UN Women, 'Acid Attacks' (27 January 2011) <http://www.endvawnow.org/en/articles/607-acid-attacks.html> accessed 2 June 2023.

[67] Acid Survivors Foundation, 'Acid Violence in Pakistan: A Situational Analysis' (ASF, 2015) <https://asfpakistan.org/wp-content/uploads/2017/02/SAAV-report-2015.pdf> accessed 2 June 2023.

[68] ibid 11.

[69] Criminal Law (Second Amendment) (Acid Crime Prevention) Act 2011 [PAK].

[70] Acid Survivors Foundation, 'Acid/Burn Violence Statistics 2018' (ASF, 2018) <https://asfpakistan.org/wp-content/uploads/2020/07/ASF-Data-2007-2018-FINAL.pdf> accessed 2 June 2023.

[71] M Tanwir, S Fennell, HR Lak and S Salman, 'Not Accepting Abuse as the Norm: Local Forms of Institutional Reform to Improve Reporting on Domestic Violence in Punjab' (2019) 20(7) Journal of International Women's Studies 129, 140.

disappear from the system. Some scholars posit that this is because 65 per cent of the Pakistani population believes that domestic violence is a family's 'personal' problem and a 'justifiable response' to the behaviour of the wife.[72] As such, domestic violence cases are often directed to the family courts by police officers. Not only does this mean that elements of domestic violence crimes are found in family cases, but the categorization of these cases under the civil ambit as opposed to the criminal one may contribute to the exclusion of these cases when identifying the prevalence of domestic violence in Pakistan. The two main areas of family law where domestic violence is cited as the main reason for litigation are dissolution of marriage cases and custody and guardianship cases.

Dissolution of marriage

As per the Muslim Family Laws Ordinance (MFLO) of 1961, a husband has an unconditional right to divorce his wife and may do so without any cause. By exercising his right to *talaq* (divorce), a man may inform his wife of his decision either verbally or in writing. It has been argued that judicial involvement is undignified, because the privacy and secrecy of the home must be preserved.[73] Men in Pakistan can therefore dissolve their marriages without involving the courts, simply by 'pronouncement of *talaq* in any form whatsoever', provided that he informs his wife and the chairman of the Arbitration Council of the same.[74] Women, on the other hand, do not have an unrestricted right to dissolve a marriage. Islamic scholars have argued that this was instituted to prevent women from recklessly using the right to divorce, given their 'highly emotional and irrational' natures.[75]

In Pakistan, the *nikkahnama* or marital contract, enacted under the MFLO, provides legal evidence of the marriage and must be signed by both Muslim partners. It additionally lays out various marital rights and obligations of both parties. For example, Section 18 of the *nikkahnama* specifies

[72] TS Ali and others, 'Intimate Partner Violence in Urban Pakistan: Prevalence, Frequency, and Risk Factors' (2011) 3 International Journal of Women's Health 105. Also see, Gilani Research Foundation Survey, 'Opinion Poll: Social Behaviour and Others' (*Gallup Pakistan*, 2 March 2017) <http://gallup.com.pk/wp-content/uploads/2017/03/2-March-2017-English-1.pdf> accessed 3 November 2020.

[73] Y Qassem, 'Law of the Family (Personal Status Law)' in N Bernard-Maugiron and B Dupret (eds), *Egypt and Its Laws* (Kluwer Law International 2002) 19, 25.

[74] See s 7, Muslim Family Laws Ordinance 1961 [PAK], hereafter 'MFLO'.

[75] N Hamadeh 'Islamic Family Legislation: The Authoritarian Discourse of Silence' in M Yamani (ed) *Feminism and Islam: Legal and Literary Perspectives* (Ithaca Press 1996) 331, 337.

whether or not a husband has delegated the right to divorce to his wife. If the right to divorce is granted to the bride at the time of signing, she is able to later file for divorce in a manner similar to her husband.[76] That is, she pronounces *talaq* upon herself, as he would have pronounced *talaq* upon her. In cases where the woman was not granted the right to divorce at the time of *nikkah*, if she chooses to separate from her husband without his consent, she must forego some or all of her financial rights (also referred to as *haq mehr*) to obtain a dissolution of marriage through the courts in a process called *khula*.[77] Due to the stipulation that a woman must be prepared to waive her financial rights and 'buy her way out of the marriage', *khula* has been compared to 'ransom' in some scholarship.[78]

While *khula* does not stipulate a restriction on the grounds of divorce, it is likely to be more successful if there is evidence of cruelty (including physical, financial, or emotional abuse perpetrated by the husband), impotency, adultery, or desertion, or in the event that the husband contracts a second marriage without his first wife's permission.[79] In some cases, if evidence of 'cruelty' or domestic abuse is found, the court may order the husband to pay his wife her financial dues. For example, as cited in *Muhammad Faisal Khan v Sadia*, 'Where in view of [the] Judge, husband by his arrogant, cruel and obnoxious nature or behaviour compelled wife to seek *khula* then she would be entitled to all due benefits along with dissolution of marriage'.[80] These cases, however, are few and far between. It is not uncommon for a man to employ multiple tools to counter allegations of cruelty, by claiming that he is prepared to continue the marital relationship[81] and that the *khula* has been sought independently by his wife with no legitimate reason and 'without any fault of his'.[82] This could enable him to evade the possibility of a financial or maintenance order.

On this legal terrain, when case files of divorce and *khula* are examined, they evidence a large number of cases where the reason for dissolution of marriage specifies acts of domestic violence. These are often cited in legal

[76] MFLO, s 8.

[77] This process is regulated by the Dissolution of Muslim Marriages Act 1939 [PAK], hereafter 'DMMA.'

[78] HA Jawad, *The Rights of Women in Islam: An Authentic Approach* (Palgrave Macmillan 1998) 78, 81.

[79] DMMA, s 2.

[80] *Muhammad Faisal Khan v Sadia* [2013] PLD 12.

[81] Such claims are often accompanied by a Restitution of Conjugal Rights suit. I discuss these suits in Chapter 6, 'Enacting victim-subjects: Anticipative performances'. See generally, SA Cheema, 'Islamisation of Restitution of Conjugal Rights by the Federal Shariat Court of Pakistan: A Critique' (2019) 58(4) Islamic Studies 535.

[82] ibid. See *Muhammad Nazim v Muneer Akhtar* [2015] YLR 1433.

documents as examples of cruelty, maltreatment, torture, or abuse.[83] Similar instances come to the surface in cases relating to custody and guardianship of children.

Custody and guardianship

The custody and guardianship of minors under Pakistani law is regulated by the Guardian and Wards Act of 1890. Section 17 of the Act specifies that the court must consider the welfare of the minor in appointing a guardian:

> In considering what will be for the welfare of the minor, the Court shall have regard to the age, sex and religion of the minor, the character and capacity of the proposed guardian . . .[84]

Additionally, Islamic law principles are typically cited in legal judgments relating to custody disputes, which rely on Islamic law principles in their adjudications. By way of these principles, the father is the natural custodian of children, while a mother is entitled to the *hizanat* or custody of her male child until he is seven years old, and of her female child until she has attained puberty.[85] However, case law from Pakistan clarifies that Islamic law principles on this matter are not absolute, and in accordance with Section 17 of the Guardian and Wards Act, they are subject to determinations regarding the welfare of the child.[86] An assessment of that welfare must therefore take into account the character, conduct. and capacity of the proposed guardian.

The relevance and consideration given to the character of the proposed guardian in child welfare assessments means that accounts of domestic violence often surface in custody cases and are frequently cited as the main reason for custody disputes.[87] For example, in a Guardian and Wards judgment from Karachi, it was stated:

[83] See for example, *Haseeb Ahmad v Wajiha Wakeel* [2018] YLR 20; *Khalid Khan v Noreen Mumtaz* [2019] CLC Note 16; *Shahbaz v Fakhir Bibi* [2021] MLD 1506; *Shamim Akhtar v Arshad Mehmood* [2017] PLD 40; *Talat Farooq v Zeshan Shehzad* [2019] CLC 2046; *Muhammad Sabil Khan v Saima Inshad* [2017] CLC 1184; *Asghar Ahmed Khan v Safeena Parveen* [2019] YLR 2298; *Khudai Noor v District Judge* [2017] YLR 2349; and *Mohammad Raziq v Farhana Bibi* [2018] CLC 93.

[84] Guardian and Wards Act 1890 [PAK], s 17 (2).

[85] See *Raja Muhammad Owais v Nazia Jabeen* [2021] CP SC 240.

[86] ibid.

[87] For custody and guardianship cases where claims of domestic violence feature prominently, see: Guardian and Ward judgment, Family Court, 1093/22 Karachi Central (Apr 2022);

> The applicant [father] became even more violent when the respondent [mother] became pregnant. In his fits of rage he would beat her, pull her hair and even kicked her in the abdomen. On one occasion the applicant tried to throw the respondent down the stairs and the only way she was able to stop the fall was by holding on to the railings. In the sixth month of pregnancy, under severe stress, the respondent started bleeding and feared miscarriage. After the birth of the child [. . .] the applicant remained neglectful towards the needs of the respondent and the minor.'[88]

As such, in investigating the use of character allegations that frame women as 'bad' and/or 'mad' as gendering strategies in the construction of victim-subjects of domestic violence in Pakistan, this book does not limit itself to analysing cases under a specific law. Rather, it brings forth empirical and theoretical insights from the larger legislative landscape of domestic violence, which encompasses both criminal and family law ambits. Doing so not only helps demonstrate how legal understandings of domestic violence are shaped and regulated in Pakistan, but more significantly helps to provide a conceptual roadmap through which to shadow the stories and experiences of women victims as they travel through the legal system, together with any roadblocks they may find along the way.

Chapter overview

By way of four main thematic investigations, the forthcoming discussion explores the construction of victim-subjects of domestic violence through the discursive mediation of gendered allegations, and the legal practices that animate them. In what follows, Chapter 2 develops a conceptual framework to question and examine why and how the subjectivities of women victims of domestic violence are constructed in particular ways, and how these subjectivities are captured and negotiated within the legal system. I navigate subject formation by broadly drawing on feminist poststructuralist accounts relating to the social construction of gendered subjects through power relations, discourses, and social practices, and by

Guardian and Ward application, Family Court, 2313/21 Karachi Central (Jan 2021); Guardian and Ward judgment, Family Court, 50/22 Karachi Central (Apr 2022); and Guardian and Ward judgment, High Court, 419/21 Lahore (Sept 2021).

[88] Judgment, GW 1708/19 and GW 1853/19, Karachi South.

particularly drawing on Smart's theorizing of the use of gendering strategies[89] in institutional and disciplinary settings. I also engage with interdisciplinary South Asian postcolonial thought relating to the social control of women, as well as feminist perspectives on law and psychiatry, to provide conceptual tools through which to explore the subjectification of women through character allegations. This chapter also reflects on the research methods adopted in the book, leveraging Haraway's concept of situated knowledges[90] and Hemming's ideas surrounding the political grammar of feminist storytelling[91] to inform the book's epistemological framework. It additionally maps out the ethical approach taken in the access, management, and use of empirical sources, which includes more than one hundred case files and judgments, and comprehensive qualitative work in the form of seventy-two semi-structured interviews as well as court observations in the cities of Karachi, Lahore and Islamabad over a cumulative six-month period of fieldwork in 2021 and 2022.

Opening the empirical part of the book, Chapter 3 identifies and explores how victims of domestic violence are *silenced* through gendered narratives. This refers to the institutional and societal gendered discourses that employ silence as a mechanism in situations of disagreement. By centring the stories and experiences of Pakistani women, this chapter contributes to literature on the victim-survivor paradox and examines why Pakistani women may be more inclined to identify as 'victims' rather than as 'survivors'. In addition, by highlighting the kinds of allegations that are used to dismiss women's narratives and shape the subjectivity of their experiences in legal and communal settings, I contend that framing women as 'bad' and/or as 'mad' is a silencing technique that works to produce subjectivities that suppress opposition to dominant constructions of gendered normativity. Amidst such silencing techniques, I also draw out what 'justice' means for victims of domestic violence and locate their agency in judicial negotiations. This informs the legal steps that women take in response to the harms they experienced and helps situate them as complainants in the Pakistani legal system.

Chapter 4 makes the transition towards legal processes and explores how victim-subjects are *policed* through gatekeeping strategies. This refers

[89] See C Smart, *Feminism and the Power of Law* (Routledge 1989).

[90] See D Haraway, 'Situated Knowledges: The Science Question in Feminism and the Privilege of Partial Perspective' (1988) 14(3) Feminist Studies 575.

[91] C Hemmings, *Why Stories Matter: The Political Grammar of Feminist Theory* (Duke University Press 2011).

both to how women are policed in society through gendered constructions of propriety and social control, and to the gatekeeping tactics used by law enforcement officers when women approach them to seek legal remedies for domestic violence. This chapter opens with an assessment of the paternalistic attitudes of police personnel, by looking at how they understand and navigate their 'duties' towards the protection and sanctity of the family structure. Particularly, I look at how character tropes are used by police officers to minimize women's experienced harms, and at how compromise is used as a tool to mask the narrative truths of victims as 'public secrets'. I also provide an overview of complaint processes, investigatory procedures, and evidential practices in law enforcement, which offers insight into how and why cases of domestic violence may be found scattered across both criminal and family courts, and attempts to locate those women that 'disappear' from police stations and the legal system during this process.

Chapter 5 then follows cases of domestic violence to the courts, by arguing that victim-subjects are *scripted* through lawyerly practices. This chapter opens with an assessment of pre-drafted suits that are routinely filed in response to women's claims of abuse. These boilerplate 'scripts' often contain allegations relating to her character and mental state. I then examine how lawyers build on these scripts to subjectivize women in courtrooms, by employing restrictive questioning tactics, presenting peculiar forms of 'evidence', and making strategic use of suggestibility. Viewing character allegations as a gendering strategy that is part of a 'script' also unpacks the naturalizing effect of these practices, rendering them as commonplace and therefore left unquestioned within the law. This further assists in investigating how these practices construct the victim-subject of domestic violence in a way that not only subjectivizes her but also secures her within the field of that subjectification, setting her up to be viewed by the judiciary through the lens of the allegations and labels applied to her.

Chapter 6 subsequently examines courtroom practices, contending that victim-subjects are *enacted* through anticipatory performances. By presenting a relational analysis that looks at how the ideas of 'playing to the judge' and 'playing the victim' anticipate judicial reactions and discretions, I argue that legal actors perform to the judge as audience. This chapter subsequently looks at the distorting effects that may occur when litigation is enacted as a performance for spectators through gendered allegations and practices, and the role this plays in how victim-subjects of domestic violence are perceived and ultimately adjudicated. I then go on to examine discursive sites of male power as they are articulated and legitimized in institutional structures through an interaction of language and performance, questioning whether the constructed subjectivities of victim-subjects of domestic violence may then circulate as forms of legal knowledge.

And finally, Chapter 7 draws together the diverse empirical material to provide a concise account of how character allegations are used as a gendering strategy to construct victim-subjects of domestic violence. In doing so, I identify four cross-cutting conclusions that shed light on how such allegations work to mould the subjectivity of women complainants and alter their narratives, and how this relates to secondary victimization outcomes. This chapter also presents a vision for the way forward, by reflecting on how the law can be (re)imagined as a space that recognizes and values women's lived experiences, how the iterative relationship between domestic abuse and mental health can be accommodated for within legal settings, and how, ultimately, legal responses to domestic violence can prioritize the safety of women and clear pathways for justice.

2
Navigating the construction of victim-subjects

Jis ki bandariya, wohi nachaye
[Whosoever's (female) monkey, he will make her dance][1]

Introduction

In 2015 a man petitioned the district court in Karachi for permanent custody of his two children, which was at the time retained by the children's mother, his ex-wife. At previous hearings, the respondent had testified to the mental, physical, and sexual abuse perpetrated by her husband during their marriage. In one case, she said that he pushed her against a wall and fractured her shoulder during an argument, and in another, he 'forced her to have sexual intercourse with other individual and wanted to be present in the same room to see the act'.[2] In response to her testimony, her ex-husband submitted the following claims:

> The petitioner provided cozy life and mirth beyond the imagination of the respondent. The petitioner, being an uxorious [. . .] husband never injured her pride and never provided a chance of complaint of whatsoever nature. He further asserted that from the very inception of marriage association the respondent proved herself to be arrogant, bellicose, virago, jilt, slattern and belligerent. The petitioner found that she was under influence of period medicine. According to him, as the respondent was mentally disordered, she could not retain the custody of the wards . . . He further alleged that the respondent being a psycho patient and under the influence of her mother was unable to tend or look after the

[1] An Urdu proverb: see S Rasul, 'Gender and Power Relationships in the Language of Proverbs: Image of a Woman' (2015) 9(2) FWU Journal of Social Sciences 53.
[2] *SR Abbas v SS Sattar* [2015] YLR 489.

Domestic Violence in Pakistan. Daanika Kamal, Oxford University Press. © Daanika Kamal 2025.
DOI: 10.1093/9780198953470.003.0002

> minors properly . . . the respondent is not qualified to retain custody of the minors as she is a woman of bad character and is leading an immoral life . . . He further contended that the respondent smokes shisha and cigarette and her mother also does so, therefore it would not be in the welfare of the minors to let them live in such atmosphere.[3]

In this extract, there are two main ways through which the respondent is subjectivized. The first is that 'she is a woman of bad character and is leading an immoral life'. This assertion is made alongside claims that she is 'arrogant, bellicose, virago, jilt, slattern, belligerent' and that she 'smokes shisha and cigarette'. The second prominent assertion is that the respondent is 'mentally disordered' and a 'psycho patient'. The allegations of domestic abuse made against the petitioner are largely ignored. Instead, the petitioner attempts to subjectivize the respondent as a 'bad' and 'mad' woman, in attempt to argue that she is unfit to fulfil her maternal duties and retain custody of the wards.

Subjectivity, as it is used and understood in this book, is shaped by feminist post-structuralist accounts that attempt to overcome ontological and textual positions through a more relational conceptualization of how gendered subjects come into being. Here, subject positions are seen as constituted *in* and constituted *by* the social forces that surround them.[4] Subjectivities are accordingly conceptualized as those which 'fit' the ways of seeing, or that have been deemed as relevant or suited to members of a particular (social) institution.[5]

Acknowledging that feminist post-structuralism encompasses a range of perspectives, I particularly draw on Carol Smart's theorizing of gendering strategies, which considers discourses as shaped by power relations and suggests that individuals are subjectivized through the subject positions made available to them in those discourses.[6] Smart explains gendering strategies as the practices, institutional mechanisms, and social processes through which gendered norms, rules, and expectations are constructed, regulated, and enforced, positing that it is through gendering strategies that the 'Woman' subject is brought into being.[7] Subjectification can

[3] ibid.
[4] N Fairclough, *Discourse and Social Change* (Polity Press 1992) 3, 4.
[5] See C Smart, *Feminism and the Power of Law* (Routledge 1989).
[6] ibid.
[7] C Smart, 'The Woman of Legal Discourse' (1992) 1(1) Social and Legal Studies 29, 34. Also see V Munro, 'Legal Feminism and Foucault—A Critique of the Expulsion of

accordingly be explored through the transformations required of the subject by the varying networks of power and social relations in which she lives—interwoven within intersecting networks of language, practices, and performances of masculinities and femininities.[8] A compelling quote from an interviewee helps illustrate:

> *Yahan ke mard log, un ko maan chahiye, un ko biwi chahiye, un ko mehbooba chahiye. Laiken aurat nahi chahiye. Aurat kabhi nahi chahiye.* [The men here, they want a mother, they want a wife, they want a lover. But they don't want a woman. They never want a woman.][9]

As such, a key relevant aspect of feminist post-structuralism is the assumption that reality is constructed (rather than reflected) by temporarily fixing meanings that are relative to discourses. This helps shape bodies, minds, and emotions to (re)produce varying forms of subjectivities and relations of power.[10] Gendering strategies operate in similar ways, where understandings of what it means to be a woman, or what is means to be a 'good' woman or a 'sane' woman, are developed and constructed through different institutional and social practices that 'constitute discursive fields to produce meanings, subject positions and subjectivity'. [11] This theorizing suggests that the term 'subject' refers both to the process of becoming a subject of a (linguistic) occasion, and to the process of becoming subordinated, or subjected to, a power or system. And it is through the performative iterations of gendered language, gestures, and roles that she, as a subject, is simultaneously produced and subjugated.[12]

Exploring gendering strategies in the creation of victim-subjects of domestic violence in Pakistan is accordingly a useful concept through which to locate how certain women may get positioned as not only different, but

Law' (2002) 28 (4) Journal of Law and Society 546; and C Weedon and A Hallak, 'Feminist Poststructuralism: Discourse, Subjectivity, the Body and Power' in J Angouri and J Baxter (eds), *The Routledge Handbook of Language, Gender and Sexuality* (Routledge 2021) 437.

[8] See B Davies, 'Subjectification: The Relevance of Butler's Analysis for Education' (2006) 27(4) British Journal of Sociology of Education 425.

[9] Interview with victim support personnel, Lahore, 15 June 2022.

[10] See J Butler, *Gender Trouble: Feminism and the Subversion of Identity* (Routledge 1990); and M Foucault, *The History of Sexuality* (Vol 1, Penguin 1981).

[11] C Weedon and A Hallak (n 7).

[12] J Butler, *Bodies That Matter: On the Discursive Limits of 'Sex'* (Routledge 1993) 124.

also 'troubled'[13] and potentially marginalized. In tracing the role that rhetoric and discourse play across vernaculars, and the means through which constructed meanings and subjectivities come to appear as 'natural', these accounts help identify the institutions and disciplines which foster that naturalization.[14] It considers the gendered subject of discourse to not only study *how* we make meaning, but also to consider *who* makes meaning, in an attempt to investigate discursive sites of male power as they are articulated and legitimized in institutional structures and forms of knowledge.[15] Indeed, representations of domestic violence too are constitutive of gender and characteristic to the performance of masculinity, in a way that it is simultaneously gendered and gendering.[16]

In what follows, I explore the use of gendering strategies in institutional and disciplinary spaces to examine why the respondent in the case extract above was subjectivized in particular ways, and how these subjectivities are captured and negotiated within the Pakistani legal system. In doing so, I acknowledge that the varying gendering strategies used in institutional and disciplinary subject-making may also overlap or shape one another, as per the social practices that help inform their construction and the discourses through which interpretations and meanings are continuously negotiated.[17] Hafez posits that subject-making should be understood as 'deeply embedded in wider, complex, and imbricated social and historical processes'. [18] The focus is on the multiplicity, and at times the simultaneity, of discourses. Bearing this in mind, I occasionally purposefully blur the boundaries between different narrative frames in attempt to participate within them as a form of storytelling.[19]

[13] M Wetherell, 'Positioning and Interpretative Repertoires: Conversation Analysis and Poststructuralism in Dialogue' (1998) 9(3) Discourse and Society 387.

[14] S Crowley, *Toward a Civil Discourse: Rhetoric and Fundamentalism* (University of Pittsburgh Press 2006) 63.

[15] L Hutcheon, 'Postmodernism, Poststructuralism, and Feminism' (1985) 6(3) Canadian Woman Studies 36.

[16] M Hume, 'Questioning Violence: Meanings, Myths and Realities' (2009) 28 Bulletin of Latin American Research 22.

[17] J Potter and M Wetherell, *Discourse and Social Psychology* (SAGE 1986).

[18] S Hafez, *An Islam of Her Own: Reconsidering Religion and Secularism in Women's Islamic Movements* (New York University Press 2011) 5.

[19] I will be expanding upon this idea in the next section, 'Why stories matter: Reflections on research methods'. See generally, C Hemmings, 'Telling Feminist Stories' (2005) 6(2) Feminist Theory 115.

Gendering strategies in discursive spaces

In recent years, there have been a myriad of media outlets reporting that Pakistani women have been killed by their husbands for seeking higher education,[20] for refusing to quit her job,[21] for leaving the house without his permission,[22] for serving cold food,[23] for not serving food fast enough,[24] for wearing new clothes in the absence of her husband,[25] and for texting.[26] These reports are indicative of domestic abuse typically being premised on the social control of women, relating to ideals of respectability, character and 'honour' (more aptly captured by the Urdu word '*izzat*').[27] As Shah describes, honour is a male value derived and viewed against a woman's body.[28] Particularly in intimate and domestic settings, violence perpetrated against women stems from a man's desire to exert control over a woman's behaviour, a man's (perceived) loss of control over a woman's behaviour, and community or family involvement in augmenting the shame associated with that loss of control.[29]

Social control is often regarded as the societal processes and methods that make individuals conform to certain sets of gendered norms, expectations,

20 'In Pakistan, Passion for Higher Studies Costs Woman Her Life' *The Express Tribune* (16 September 2019) <https://tribune.com.pk/story/2057291/1-passion-higher-studies-costs-woman-life> accessed 15 March 2021.

21 'Pakistani Journalist Shot Dead by Husband for Not Quitting Job' *The Daily Times* (27 November 2019) <https://dailytimes.com.pk/508366/pakistani-journalist-shot-dead-by-husband-for-not-quitting-job/> accessed 20 March 2021.

22 'Mistrustful Man Kills Wife for Leaving House Sans Permission' *The Express Tribune* (05 December 2021) <https://tribune.com.pk/story/2332545/mistrustful-man-kills-wife-for-leaving-house-sans-permission> accessed 06 December 2021.

23 'Man Murders Wife over Cold Dinner in Pakistan' *Khaleej Times* (30 November 2017) <https://www.khaleejtimes.com/international/pakistan/man-murders-wife-over-cold-dinner-in-pakistan> accessed 21 March 2021.

24 *Abdul Aziz Bhatti v The State* [2019] YLR Note 49; S Hanif, 'Husband Axes Wife to Death in Badin for 'Taking Too Long' *Dawn News* (23 June 2016) <https://www.dawn.com/news/1266741> accessed on 1 April 2021; 'Layyah Woman Killed by In-Laws over Delay in Cooking' *Dawn News* (10 July 2024) <https://www.dawn.com/news/1844881> accessed 2 September 2024.

25 S Bhanbhro, M Wassan, M Shah, A Talpur and A Wassan, 'Karo Kari: The Murder of Honour in Sindh Pakistan, an Ethnographic Study' (2013) 3(7) International Journal of Asian Social Science 1467.

26 'Woman Killed for Texting' *Dawn News (*27 June 2018) <https://www.dawn.com/news/1423071/woman-killed-for-texting> accessed 22 March 2021.

27 AK Gill and A Brah, 'Interrogating Cultural Narratives about "Honour"-Based Violence' (2014) 21(1) European Journal of Women's Studies 72.

28 N Shah, 'Honour Killings: Code of Dishonour' (1998) The Weekly Review, Dawn.

29 NV Baker, PR Gregware and MA Cassidy, 'Family Killing Fields' (1999) 5(2) Violence against Women 164.

and subjectivities through which moral and social order is made possible.[30] Honkatukia and Keskin speak of two dimensions where the social control of women is particularly enacted. The first is 'formal institutional control', which relates to legislation and dominant discourses in public discussions, and the second is 'normative control in close relationships', referring to the explicit rules and sanctions enforced by authoritative familial persons such as husbands and fathers.[31] These dimensions are not separate, but rather understood as an interweaving 'continua'. [32] While the examples provided above fall under the 'normative' dimension of Honkatukia and Keskin's framework, the social control of women in Pakistan is arguably also deeply entrenched in the 'formal institutional' dimension, where gendering strategies are used to serve the State's religio-nationalist discourse. As Stark poses, 'rather than ask who uses violence', investigations relating to the gender and violence nexus should 'identify how violence functions in relationships to preserve and extend gender inequalities'.[33]

The 'bad' subject

Against the backdrop of postcolonialism, Pakistan has witnessed competing legal and normative orderings since independence in 1947. The State's attempts to establish a unified identity through religio-nationalist ideals found itself in a hybrid legal system, where Islamic law, English (secular) legal principles, and customary law produced an 'amoebic, boundary-less set of regulatory norms'.[34] The secular statutory law governed the public sphere and matters relating to the State (such as administration and financial regulations), while Islamic law governed the private sphere (including marriage, divorce, and guardianship). The contentions amongst these orderings are visible not only in constitutional and legal developments, but also in the construction of normative citizen-subjects to manage difference,

[30] See M Innes, *Understanding Social Control. Deviance, Crime and Social Order* (Open University Press 2003); and S Cohen, *Visions of Social Control* (Polity Press 1985).

[31] P Honkatuki and S Keskinen, 'The Social Control of Young Women's Clothing and Bodies: A Perspective of Differences on Racialization and Sexualization' (2018) 18(1) Ethnicities 142.

[32] ibid 147.

[33] E Stark, 'Do Violent Acts Equal Abuse? Resolving the Gender Parity/Asymmetrical Dilemma' (2010) 62 Sex Roles 210.

[34] SS Ali, 'Testing the Limits of Family Law Reform in Pakistan: A Critical Analysis of the Muslim Family Laws Ordinance 1961' (2002) International Survey of Family Law 317.

where the nation-state's unity is questioned and threatened through multiple racially segmented and marginalized populations.[35]

As the dominant discourse, Islam served a functional purpose in facilitating a national identity, promulgating that Pakistan represents a new Muslim homeland in the Indian sub-continent—albeit with little understanding of whether this translates to a democracy or a theocracy;[36] that is, a country 'of Muslims' or 'for Muslims'.[37] Such codification of religion, borne from nationalist imaginaries, is significant not least in its incorporations of language, practices, and performances of piety into normative ideals of citizen-subjects, but also because those ideals are invariably gendered. As Ali states, 'all laws affecting the status of Muslim women have been historically relegated to Muslim personal law'. [38] Islam was selectively mobilized as 'patriarchal opportunism',[39] an ideological apparatus used to both regulate and subjugate women to serve the nationalist project, with State institutions and judicial structures functioning as a 'matrix of subject formation'.[40]

The use of gendering strategies in the management of gender and sexuality was arguably most visible during Zia ul Haq's regime in the 1980s, popularly referred to as the political campaign of *Islamization*.[41] As Khan and Kirmani posit, this campaign was particularly detrimental to women by making their bodies 'symbols of the Islamic nation' through a series of legislative measures based on the principle of '*chadar aur chaar diwari* [behind a veil and within the four walls of the home]'.[42] Mumtaz and Shaheed similarly find that Zia's regime 'appeared to be giving everyone the license to pass judgement on the "morality" of people in public spaces, the prime indicator of which seemed to be women's apparel and presence'.[43] These

[35] S Rouse, *Shifting Body Politics: Gender, Nation, State in Pakistan* (Women Unlimited 2004).

[36] R Saeed, 'Law and Coloniality of Empire: Colonial Encounter and Normative Orderings in the Indian Sub-Continent' (2016–17) 19 Yearbook of Islamic and Middle Eastern Law 103.

[37] S Rouse, 'The Outsider(s) Within: Sovereignty and Citizenship in Pakistan' in P Jeffery and A Basu (eds), *Resisting the Sacred and the Secular: Women's Activism and Politicised Religion in South Asia* (Kali for Women 1999) 54.

[38] Ali (n 34).

[39] S Toor, 'Gender, Sexuality, and Islam under the Shadow of Empire' (2011) 3(9) The Scholar and Feminist Online 22.

[40] J Butler, 'Is Judaism Zionism?' in E Mendieta and J Vanantwerpen (eds), *The Power of Religion in the Public Sphere* (Columbia University Press 2011) 72.

[41] D Collins, 'Islamization of Pakistani Law: A Historical Perspective' (1987) 24(3) Stanford Journal of International Law 567.

[42] A Khan and N Kirmani, 'Moving beyond the Binary: Gender-Based Activism in Pakistan' (2018) 30 Feminist Dissent 156.

[43] K Mumtaz and F Shaheed, *Women in Pakistan: Two Steps Forward, One Step Back?* (Zed Books 1987) 72.

efforts reflect a contentious interaction of the public–private dichotomy, where the former is used to protect the sanctity of the latter.[44] The Hudood Ordinances of 1979, for example, regulated the sexual behaviour of women by defining what constituted 'legal' acts of sex, making illicit sexual activity a crime against the State.[45] These laws did not distinctly distinguish between consensual intercourse and rape, instituting a requirement to produce four male witnesses to prove the latter. This meant that women who were unable to fulfil this condition when reporting sexual assault were instead prosecuted for engaging in immoral pre- or extra-marital sexual activity.[46]

The transformative effects that colonial rule had on norms of gender and sexuality through State institutions 'maintain[ed] and reinforce[d] the privilege of men over women',[47] by constructing the male identity in terms of 'rights' and the female identity in terms of 'duties'.[48] In instances where the Pakistani State extends rights to women, such as the right to vote, it is construed as part of a woman's duty to consolidate the nation-state.[49] As noted by Yuval-Davis, women are implicated in both biologically and culturally reproducing the nation.[50] Ideas of the nation are maintained through women's bodies, not only as biological instruments to reproduce citizens but also as repositories of culture, tasked with its dissemination. McClintock similarly considers nations to be 'symbolically figured as domestic genealogies', positing that the family is key in ensuring the 'organic continuity' of the State.[51] She argues that the family furnishes nationalist discourses by mitigating the threat posed by social difference in claim of a unified identity by not only organizing men and women into material arrangements, such as familial forms, but further legitimizing and

[44] The complex relationship between the public and private realm has been well documented in South Asian feminist scholarship. See for example, S Roy (ed) *New South Asian Feminisms: Paradoxes and Possibilities* (Palgrave Macmillan 2012).

[45] Offence of Zina (Enforcement of Hudood) Ordinance 1979 [PAK].

[46] See Toor (n 39). Also relevant here is Alexander's hybrid term 'heteropatriarchy', which refers to the 'twin processes of heterosexualisation and patriarchy' that structure the State's regulation of women's bodies. See MJ Alexander, 'Erotic Economy as a Politics of Decolonization' in MJ Alexander and CT Mohanty (eds), *Feminist Genealogies, Colonial Legacies, Democratic Futures* (Routledge 1997) 65.

[47] Rouse (n 35) 7 [parenthesis added].

[48] R Saigol, *Symbolic Violence: Curriculum, Pedagogy, and Society* (Society for Advancement of Education 2000).

[49] A Jalal, 'The Convenience of Subservience' in D Kandiyoti (ed) *Women, Islam, and the State* (Temple University Press 1991) 77.

[50] N Yuval-Davis, *Gender and Nation* (Sage Publications 1997).

[51] A McClintock, 'Family Feuds: Gender, Nationalism and the Family' (1993) 44 Feminist Review 63, 66.

naturalizing familial hierarchies, such as that of husband and wife. From a feminist perspective, egalitarian principles are 'displaced and overlaid by a (predominantly) political interest in hierarchical orderings of marriage'.[52] The husband's position as 'provider' places him as superior to his wife, justified on the preservation of the family.[53] The husband then is also tasked with controlling the 'bad' dissenting wife for the purpose of preservation, with domestic violence being a means for the same. A common case cited in Pakistani literature is that of *Abdul Kadir v Salima*, where the court summarized the nature of gendered roles and rules of marital relationships by positing that the *nikkah* [marriage] contract 'imposes submission [of the wife] to him [the husband] when summoned to the couch and confers on him the power of correction when she is disobedient or rebellious'.[54] The construction of a national identity correspondingly constructs the subjectivity of the ideal, 'good' Pakistani woman as one who complies with these gendered duties. Entangled in respectability politics, the social control of women is considered central to the nationalist project. As Rouse states, women who dissent are seen as 'bad' and 'other'—not only a threat to the sanctity of the family but also a threat to the nation.[55]

Weare maintains that the distinction between 'good' and 'bad' women is not new, but an age-old patriarchal gendering strategy.[56] It is when women's behaviours, ways of dressing, or relationships with men are seen to dissent by exceeding the 'limit', or not adhering to the 'standard', that they are labelled as 'bad' women.[57] The difference between women who are 'good' or 'bad' accordingly lies in the ways in which their lifestyle and behaviour accords with appropriate feminine behaviour as prescribed by gender discourse. And if societal beliefs about family relations dictate that men have not only the right but also the obligation to punish and discipline 'bad' women, then the acts used to do so 'can be seen—and even lauded—as necessary to maintain

[52] P Werbner and N Yuval-Davis, 'Introduction: Women and the New Discourse of Citizenship' in P Werbner and N Yuval-Davis (eds), *Women, Citizenship and Difference* (Zed Books 1999) 6.

[53] K Millett, *Sexual Politics* (Virago Press 1971) 35.

[54] *Abdul Kadir v Salima* [1886] ILR 8 ALL 149 [parenthesis added].

[55] Rouse (n 35) 101.

[56] S Weare, '"The Mad", "the Bad", "the Victim": Gendered Constructions of Women who Kill within the Criminal Justice System' (2013) 2 *Laws* 337.

[57] AS Adikaram, '"Good Women" and "Bad Women": How Socialisation of Gendered Behavioural Norms Influences Sri Lankan Working Women's Interpretation of Sexual Harassment at Workplaces' (2014) 1(1) South Asian Journal of Human Resources Management 61.

order at home and in society at large'.[58] As Zia posits, 'the onus of transgression falls on the woman and not the man, since *he* is in fact often seen as the victim of her sexuality' and womanhood.[59] Comparably, by locating the subject positions which challenge the normativities at stake in everyday contexts of lived experience, Wetherell posits that it is through verbal practices, as individuals are made to either justify or be held accountable for certain acts and transgressions, that subjectivities become 'troubled', 'inappropriate', or destabilized; and where they are challenged and must be managed.[60] In addition to the examples above, where domestic violence was used as a means of control to manage dissenting subjects in the private sphere, the autonomy of women in the public sphere can also be perceived as a contentious mode of dissent by State institutions. For instance, Pakistan's current women's movement, *Aurat March*, organizes an annual rally to claim public spaces, mobilizing thousands of women. Since 2018, the March has been condemned by representatives of the State for reasons relating to propriety, and provincial resolutions have been passed to condemn it as 'shameful' and '*fahashi*'[61] [vulgar or obscene]. The movement has had petitions and court-endorsed complaints registered against its organizers,[62] has faced legal accusations of blasphemy,[63] has been baton-charged by police officers,[64] and has also been physically attacked.[65] These instances too are exemplar of using gendering strategies to manage those subject positions that challenge State-endorsed normativities of gender and sexuality.

[58] L Hajjar, 'Religion, State Power and Domestic Violence in Muslim Societies: A Framework for Comparative Analysis' (2004) 29(1) Law and Social Inquiry 1, 3.

[59] A Zia, *Sex Crime in the Islamic Context: Rape, Class and Gender in Pakistan* (ASR Publications 1994) 15 [emphasis added]. Also see, A Jamal, 'Piety, Transgression and the Feminist Debate on Muslim Women: Resituating the Victim-Subject of Honour-Related Violence from a Transnational Lens' (2015) 41(1) Journal of Women in Culture and Society 59.

[60] Wetherell (n 13) 387.

[61] A Hayat and A Akbar, 'KP Assembly Unanimously Passes Resolution against Aurat March, terming is "shameful" *Dawn News* (20 March 2019) <https://www.dawn.com/news/1470834> accessed 2 April 2021.

[62] Sirajuddin, 'Peshawar Court Orders Registration of FIR against Aurat March Islamabad organisers' *Dawn News* (26 March 2021) <https://www.dawn.com/news/amp/1614730> accessed 4 April 2021.

[63] M Anis, 'Govt Orders Probe into Objectionable Activities of Aurat March' *The News International* (15 March 2021) <https://www.thenews.com.pk/print/804425-govt-orders-probe-into-objectionable-activities-of-aurat-march> accessed 4 April 2021.

[64] I Ahmad, 'Islamabad Police Baton Charge Aurat March Participants' *The Nation* (9 March 2023) <https://www.nation.com.pk/09-Mar-2023/islamabad-police-baton-charge-aurat-march-participants> accessed 15 March 2023.

[65] N Danish and F Rabbani, 'Men Pelt Stones at Aurat March Islamabad Participants' *Samaa TV* (8 March 2020) <https://www.samaa.tv/news/pakistan/2020/03/men-pelt-stones-at-aurat-march-islamabad-participants/> accessed 5 April 2021.

Another relevant example of the kinds of gendering strategies used to manage dissenting subjects comes from Dhanda's chapter 'Psychologising Dissent'. She describes psychologizing as a technique through which reality is constructed in subjective terms alone, ignoring the social, economic, and political conditions external to the individual.[66] Psychologizing a subject converts dissent from 'a protest against a subsisting external reality' to a 'reaction originating from the dissenter's troubled mind', thereby shifting the problem to being not one of the institution or society, but of the individual.[67] Dhanda argues that psychologizing could be used as a mechanism to make the real delusional, or the conscious sub-conscious—that is, 'the situs of the experience may be changed',[68] altering the nature of external reality. A key example that she provides to illustrate this process is that of Freud's encounter with a female patient, who told him about her experiences of childhood sexual abuse by her father. Freud later explained the patient's account of abuse not as rooted in actual, lived experience, but a fabricated, wishful fantasy, interpreted as the patient's subconscious desire for her father.[69] In contemporary times, Dhanda provides examples of how the psychologizing process is used by army authorities in India that employ (involuntary) psychiatric detention as a means of 'disciplining' those that are 'recalcitrant', and workplaces dismissing women's claims of sexist behaviour as 'hypersensitive, nervous and overwrought'.[70] Against this backdrop, and acknowledging the plurality and complexity of gendered subjectivities, framing women as 'mad' or mentally unsound through the use of 'psy' labels is particularly interesting to examine in South Asian settings, where the 'psy' disciplines have a history of being used for the social control of citizens, and primarily for dissenting, 'bad' women.[71]

[66] A Dhanda, 'Psychologising Dissent: Psychiatric Labelling and Social Control' in A Dhanda and A Parashar (eds) *Engendering Law: Essays in Honour of Lotika Sarkar* (Eastern Book Company 2007) 321.

[67] ibid. There is a link here to the Marxist idea of 'camera obscura', which speaks of the distorted image of reality in ideological formations. See M Barett, *The Politics of Truth: From Marx to Foucault* (Polity Press 1992).

[68] Dhanda (n 66) 322.

[69] ibid citing L Dennerstein, J Astbury and C Morse, *Psychosocial and Mental Health Aspects of Women's Health* (WHO Geneva, 1993). Also see D Epstein and L Goodman, 'Discounting Women: Doubting Domestic Violence Survivors' Credibility and Dismissing Their Experiences' (2019) 167(1) University of Pennsylvania Law Review 406, 433.

[70] Dhanda (n 66) 332.

[71] As discussed in Chapter 1, 'psy' labels refer to labels that relate to, or are adjacent to the disciplines of psychiatry, psychology, and pop-psychology (also collectively referred to as the 'psy' disciplines in this book).

The 'mad' subject

In Colonial India, psychiatry was introduced towards the late nineteenth century through the establishment of mental asylums, weaving accompanying legislation into the political and social fabric of the subcontinent. Western medicine was used to 'elbow out' indigenous medicinal systems and assist the colonizers in consolidating their hegemony.[72] Scholars have suggested that psychiatry was mobilized to justify colonization in the name of its 'civilizing mission', [73] with mental asylums functioning to manage those 'whose transgressions risk compromising the social order'.[74] It was similarly argued that the 'ingenious benevolence' of the asylum imposed a 'religious and moral milieu . . . in such a way that madness was *controlled*, not cured'.[75] In some ways, colonial psychiatric asylums also 'obviated the law as a self-contained juridical institution',[76] by encapsulating ideological formations through discursive regularities. Such regularities, which Hall explains as 'objects of knowledge and their own subjects', operate through a system that constitutes its own method of deciding what is 'true' and 'excluding what is false within their own regime of truth'.[77]

These developments brought what Mills refers to as the 'mad' subject into being.[78] Arguably, they also brought in gendering strategies in the creation of that 'mad' subject.[79] For example, an assessment of the Ranchi mental asylum in Colonial India consistently found twice as many women and girls being admitted in comparison to men.[80] While reasons for this were not commented on at the time, it has since been argued that the social control of women, interwoven with respectability politics and (in)tolerance towards female behaviour, was a factor at play.[81] The gendered trend of patients in

[72] S Poornima, *Medicine in Colonial Andhra: A Study in the Production of Medical Knowledge Systems, 1880–1930* (University of Hyderabad, CAMH Archive 1995) 36.
[73] HK Bhabha, *The Location of Culture* (Routledge 1994) 124.
[74] M Foucault, *Madness and Civilization: A History of Insanity in the Age of Reason* (trans. Richard Howard, Random House 1965) 269.
[75] ibid 242 [emphasis added]. Also see R Porter, *Madness* (Oxford University Press 2003) 12.
[76] A Alden, *Disorder in the Court: Morality, Myth and the Insanity Defence* (University of Alabama Press 2018) 20.
[77] S Hall, *The Toad in the Garden: Thatcherism among the Theorists. Marxism and the Interpretation of Culture* (University of Illinois Press 1988) 51.
[78] C Mills, *Decolonizing Global Mental Health: The Psychiatrization of the Majority World* (Routledge 2014).
[79] See LP Varma, 'History of Psychiatry in India and Pakistan' (1953) 4(1) Indian Journal of Psychiatry 26.
[80] W Ernst, *Colonialism and Transnational Psychiatry: The Development of an Indian Mental Hospital in British India 1925–1940* (Anthem Press 2013) 43.
[81] ibid.

psychiatric care continues in present-day Pakistan, with multiple studies reporting high women-to-men ratios.[82] One study conducted over a period of four years in Karachi found that two-thirds of psychiatric patients were women, 70 per cent of whom were victims of domestic violence.[83] In another, 80 per cent of women patients were said to be 'suicidal', citing conflict with their husbands and in-laws as the 'source' of illness.[84]

Some feminists account for this overrepresentation of women by arguing that the 'psy' disciplines play a gendered role in creating pathological behaviour,[85] in order to socially construct the subject position as a 'mad woman' to be controlled.[86] Through the use of gendering strategies, 'binary conceptualisations of mental illness, such as illogicality and emotionality' are typically assigned to women.[87] For example, Ussher writes that in nineteenth-century Europe, the number of women being diagnosed with the mental illness of 'hysteria' was so common that it was said to be 'a woman's natural state'.[88] More recently, psychiatric illnesses that are classified as 'women's diseases' (such as anorexia, depression, borderline personality disorder, and anxiety disorder)[89] have been criticized for suggesting that what is considered 'madness', regardless of whether it appears in women or in men, is 'either the acting out of the devalued female role or the total or partial rejection of one's sex role stereotype'.[90]

South Asian postcolonial theorists posit that one of the key facets of colonial discourse was the role of 'fixity' in constructing identities of 'otherness'. In this context, fixity refers to the ways of knowing which come to be fixed as the truth; 'the truth that the subject *has* but does not *know*'.[91] This is reminiscent of the 'stickiness' of 'psy' labels as posited by Rosenhan,[92] which implies that all further evidence is interpreted in relation to that label. In

[82] See for example U Niaz, 'Women's Mental Health in Pakistan' (2004) 3(1) World Psychiatry 60.
[83] U Niaz, 'Contemporary Issues of Pakistani Women: A Psychosocial Perspective' (1997) 6 Journal of Pakistan Association of Women's Studies 29.
[84] U Niaz, 'Human Rights Abuse in Family' (1994) 3 Journal of Pakistan Association of Women's Studies 33.
[85] WR Gove and JF Tudor, 'Adult Sex Roles and Mental Illness' (1972) 78(4) American Journal of Sociology 812.
[86] J Ussher, *The Madness of Women: Myth and Experience* (Taylor and Francis Group 2005).
[87] N Potter, *Mapping the Edges and the In-between: A Critical Analysis of Borderline Personality Disorder* (Oxford University Press 2009) 167.
[88] Ussher (n 86) 9.
[89] ibid 10.
[90] P Chesler, *Women and Madness* (Doubleday 1972) 56.
[91] Bhabha (n 73) 141.
[92] DL Rosenhan, 'On Being Sane in Insane Places' (1973) 179(4070) Science 250.

doing so, 'psy' labels not only produce particular subjects, but go one step further to also secure them within the field of that subjectification. This is consistent with Dhanda's theorizing of 'psychologizing dissent', where she argues that facets from the 'psy' disciplines may be adopted and enacted in other discursive spaces—such as within the law—to construct subjects.[93] In recounting instances of legal cases in India, she demonstrates the significant role that legal actors play in activating provisions relating to the 'psy' disciplines when dealing with women 'dissenting from dominant perceptions of behaviour'.[94] Here, psychologizing is largely seen as an interpretative method, where situations are viewed through a psychological lens as legal actors take on the role of psychiatrists in their determinations of the unsoundness of mind of legal subjects. To elaborate further, understandings associated with 'psy' labels such as 'psycho' or 'hysterical' are commonly related to unreliability and a lack of credibility.[95] As such, in cases where a 'psy' label is employed, it is plausible for domestic abuse perpetrators to claim that the said label undermines the victim's credibility and ability to perceive or recount events accurately.[96]

Literature has posited that a great amount of weight is given to information relating to mental health in determinations of credibility within the law, even in the absence of medical reports or expert testimony.[97] As illustrated in the case extract from *Abbas v Sattar*, it is unlikely for courts to fully examine whether the litigant's mental state, as implied by a label, is probative of the issue at hand.[98] Rather, the court tends to rely on assumptions about what such character allegations signify and how it implicates fact-finding. This is problematic, because legal scholarship from Pakistan not only demonstrates significant ambiguity in judicial understandings and knowledges relating to the 'psy' disciplines but also sheds light on instances where legal actors have asserted judicial authority in establishing the parameters of what is considered a mental disorder, thereby blurring the boundaries between the disciplines of law and psychiatry. Numerous scholars have commented on a Supreme Court judgment from 2016 which

[93] Dhanda (n 66) 323.
[94] ibid.
[95] See for example, K Wahlbeck and E Aromaa, 'Research on Stigma related to Mental Disorders in Finland: A Systemic Literature Review' (2011) 42(1) Psychiatria Fennica 87.
[96] D Smith, 'The Disordered and Discredited Plaintiff: Psychiatric Evidence in Civil Litigation' (2009) 31(3) Cardoza Law Review 749.
[97] ibid.
[98] *Abbas v Sattar* (n 2).

is reflective of this expansive authority.[99] In this case, a woman had filed a petition to defer the death sentence of her husband, who had been convicted of murder and put on death row over a decade prior. She provided medical evidence citing that he was a schizophrenia patient and requested that the death sentence be held, in line with international human rights law, until he was able to seek treatment and write his will. In response, the Supreme Court stated that mental illnesses such as schizophrenia cannot subjugate the death penalty. In an eleven-page judgment, the bench held that 'schizophrenia is not a permanent mental disorder, but rather an imbalance which can increase or decrease depending on the level of stress and hence didn't offer sufficient grounds to plead insanity as he cannot be deemed a lunatic'.[100] It went on to note that schizophrenia is a 'recoverable disease' and therefore did not fall within the legal definition of 'mental disorder'.[101] While later appeal processes remedied this decision, announcing what has been hailed as a 'landmark' judgment which bars the execution of mentally ill defendants in Pakistan,[102] the language and arguments used by judicial actors reflect the ambiguities that shape legal constructions of 'madness'.

A second example from 2017 helps illustrate. In *Sakina Bibi v Sessions Judge*, the judge did not bring in a medical professional to establish whether or not the litigant was mentally disordered, but rather sought to determine this himself. The court held that 'from a careful perusal of all answers given by . . . in reply to questions put to him by the learned Sessions Judge during the inquiry it is evident that he said nothing to hold him an abnormal or mentally disordered person'. However, the judgment subsequently went on to say that 'he is a little bit imbalanced and mentally handicapped', and in the next paragraph said '. . . whom he loves despite his mental condition'. [103] The contradictory statements highlight the ambiguities in legal understandings of mental illnesses and reflect how the merging of the law and 'psy' disciplines may invoke a lapse in the rules used to establish a psychiatric or psychological diagnosis when the judiciary is

[99] See for example, RI Habib, S Liaquat, MA Aslam and N Akhtar, 'Schizophrenia—a Mental Disorder or Not? An Analytical Study of the Judgment of the Supreme Court of Pakistan in Safia Bano Case' (2019) 39(3) Pakistan Journal of Social Sciences 795.

[100] *Safia Bano v Home Department Government of Punjab* [2016] SC 10816.

[101] ibid. Also see Habib and others (n 99) 796.

[102] J Jamshed, J Jan, AA Muhammad and K Baig, 'Mental Illness and Criminal Justice System of Pakistan: Analysis of the Landmark Judgement in Safia Bano case' (2023) 11(1) Pakistan Journal of Humanities and Social Sciences 102.

[103] *Sakina Bibi v Sessions Judge Sargodha* [2017] YLR Note 346.

granted (or assumes) the authority to ascertain whether or not a legal subject is mentally ill.[104]

As such, while the 'psy' disciplines have medical standards and procedures to establish matters relating to mental health, these terms may be suspended in judicial settings, with the use of 'psy' labels serving a more subjective (rather than diagnostic) purpose. As seen in the case example at the beginning of this chapter, 'psy' labels were brought in to detract from the respondent's claims of domestic abuse, and to instead build on claims that she was unfit to fulfil her maternal duties. These claims were presented without any medical evidence that may be able to corroborate allegations that she was a 'psycho patient' and 'mentally disordered'.[105] And in the absence of medical diagnoses, these 'psy' labels were used in a descriptive manner—through the naturalization of knowledges and practices implicit to them—to subjectivize the litigant. Examining the subjectification relating to 'mad' women as a gendering strategy consequently assists in exploring how these practices are being adopted and circulated in legal settings, and what kinds of social processes they capture while doing so.

The legal subject

Smart posits that in setting itself above other disciplines, law claims to have the method to establish the objective 'truth' of events by disqualifying other kinds of knowledges, and by translating everyday experiences into legal relevance before they are able to pass through the legal system.[106] To achieve this, law shapes certain kinds of subjects by selecting the features of an individual's life which are relevant for the purpose of conceptualizing and interpreting them as such. One such prominent feature, she argues, is gender. This is because the features or characteristics particularly relevant in establishing the legal subject are in terms of a specific set of capacities that are culturally associated with the masculine: the cognitive capacity relating to reason, the volitional capacity to behave appropriately, and the moral capacity to differentiate between what's right and wrong.[107]

[104] See S Zaccour, 'Crazy Women and Hysterical Mothers: The Gendered Use of Mental-Health Labels in Custody Disputes' (2018) 31(1) Canadian Journal of Family Law 57.

[105] See *Abbas v Sattar* (n 2). The nature of medication specified was not related to psychiatry, but rather 'period medicine'. I discuss this idea in Chapter 5.

[106] Smart (n 5); Smart (n 7).

[107] Alden (n 76) 47.

Smart's analysis of 'law as gendered' accordingly focuses on strategies adopted by legal institutions to 'fix' gender to systems of meaning. Here, law is studied for its insistence in creating (and consequently applying) gender differences, and its inability to operate without a gendered subject. It therefore perpetuates a binary construction of men as competent/rational, and women as incompetent/irrational.[108] Allen further stipulates that legal discourse brings sexual and gender-based divisions not only into what the law can reasonably do, in terms of particular procedures, but more importantly also into what it is able to reasonably argue.[109] This creates a link to the use of gendered character allegations that circulate through courtrooms, because 'legal discourse simply cannot conceive of a subject in whom gender is not a determining attribute'.[110] 'Law as gendered' similarly aims to assess how gendering strategies work within law, and how law works to produce the gendered legal subject.

A core component of legal subjectivity is legal capacity, explained as 'the ability or fitness to acquire rights and exercise them, and to accept duties and perform them'.[111] An implicit (and at times explicit) tenant of most legal systems is that the rule of law applies to those who have the capacity to 'comprehend its terms and abide by its prescriptions'.[112] The ideal legal subject accordingly has full development of reason and discretion—traits often associated with the masculine. For example, a Pakistani scholar of Islamic law stipulates that women's legal capacity is 'imperfect' due to external attributes related to her gender, which in turn impedes her recognition as a complete and legally valid subject.[113] While Nyazee attributes the 'full' legal capacity of male legal subjects to qualities such as 'reason, discrimination and obligation', he shifts his focus to social norms relating to masculinity and femininity when explaining the imperfect legal capacity of women. In matters relating to evidence, for example, he argues that the differential treatment given to women's testimony in Pakistani legal systems is due to their (perceived) emotionality and the impact that their testimony may have on the accused.[114] It is pertinent to note that the criterion which

[108] Smart (n 7) 33.
[109] H Allen, *Justice Unbalanced* (Open University Press 1987).
[110] ibid 30.
[111] I Nyazee, *Outlines of Islamic Jurisprudence* (3rd edn, Advanced Legal Studies Institute 2005) 40.
[112] DN Robinson, *Wild Beasts and Idle Humours* (Harvard University Press 1996) 20.
[113] Nyazee (n 111) 39.
[114] ibid 46. Nyazee writes, 'Evidence . . . is a duty and not a right. Women have been spared the burden of this duty. The purpose is to waive the penalty of *hadd*, which is usually an extreme punishment, and to show mercy to the accused in an indirect way.'

determines the imperfect legal capacity of women is the effect that her evidence will have on another person, thereby curtailing her legal capacity to protect the liability of the (complete) legal subject against whom she may testify.[115] And in becoming a legal subject, a woman's 'femaleness' acts as a qualifier, shaping her legal capacity and consequently her credibility.

Under Pakistan's Law of Evidence, a woman's testimony continues to be worth half that of a mans in certain financial and civil matters.[116] This procedural requirement is considered necessary due to the 'female psyche', a justification that feminist scholars have frequently criticized for shaping the female legal subject as inherently defective, finding it to be a nuanced form of gendered social control.[117] The experience of the law for women is thus 'one of abstraction, [requiring] the erasure of [women's] subjectivity in order to become the necessary kind of legal subject'.[118] There is a circular argument here, in the production of the legal subject as what the law says, versus the determination of that legal subject as the law requires her to be.

Changes in the legal status of women are mirrored in doctrinal shifts relating to credibility in law which 'developed to reflect particular interests and understandings of the social world in which we live'.[119] Wigmore posits that any trait importing itself as a defective power of observation, recollection, or communication is admissible as evidence in matters of credibility, provided that it is defective as judged by the 'average standard of mentality'.[120] As discussed above, considerations relating to women's psyche and consequently their legal capacity are one example of how certain 'traits' relating to gendered norms of masculinity and femininity are deemed relevant when assessing the credibility of a legal subject. Further, cases of domestic violence are emblematic of credibility in law, where the (typically)

[115] Also see F Seedat, *Sex and the Legal Subject: Women and Legal Capacity in Ḥanafī Law* (PhD dissertation, McGill University 2013).

[116] Article 17, Law of Evidence (Qanoon-e-Shahadat Order) 1984 [PAK].

[117] See for example R Saigol, 'His Rights/Her Duties: Citizen and Mother in the Civics Discourse' (2003) 10(3) Indian Journal of Gender Studies 379; N Hamadeh 'Islamic Family Legislation: The Authoritarian Discourse of Silence' in M Yamani (ed) *Feminism and Islam: Legal and literary perspectives* (Ithaca Press 1996) 331, 337. On the long-standing association between femininity and irrationality, see CE Cooper and PL Sweet, '"Daddy Issues" and Diagnoses: Gendered Weaponisation of Mental Health in Intimate Relationships' (2024) Violence Against Women 2 <https://doi.org/10.1177/10778012241277894> accessed 2 October 2024.

[118] R Hunter, 'Law's (Masculine) Violence: Reshaping Jurisprudence' (2006) 17(1) Law and Critique 40 [parenthesis added].

[119] EA Sheehy, 'Evidence Law and "Credibility Testing" of Women: A Comment on the E Case' (2002) 2(2) Queensland University of Technology Law and Justice Journal 157.

[120] JH Wigmore, *A Treatise on the Anglo-American System of Evidence in Trials at Common Law* (3rd ed. Little Brown and Company 1940).

female victim and male perpetrator are offering two opposing versions of events.[121] In the justice system, the personal and at times invisible nature of domestic violence predominantly relies on the victim self-reporting and the legitimacy of her testimony.[122] As it is the victim's testimony against that of her spouse,[123] for example, there is a high reliance on what Epstein and Goodman call 'personal trustworthiness'.[124] The credibility of a woman's testimony is therefore assessed against her behaviours and actions and their socially ascribed meanings, evidence provided by her own body, and, pertinently, 'against her unconscious'.[125] All of which are impacted by allegations relating to her character and her mental state. Additionally,

> [b]ecause the defendant and victim had an intimate relationship with each other, the defendant, and therefore the defence attorney, has substantially more knowledge about the victim compared to cases in which the defendant and victim are not intimately acquainted. Thus, the defence has a great deal more 'ammunition' available to discredit the victim.[126]

While this extract is from a piece discussing character evidence in domestic violence felony trials, such 'ammunition' could potentially also include information, prior events, or instances that are interpreted as supporting the gendered allegations applied to the victim within the courtroom. Given that the general approach undertaken by the defence is to present a more plausible version of events, combined with undermining the credibility of the plaintiff,[127] defendants may use gendering strategies by way of claims and assertions relating to the woman's character or mental state because they can serve as a 'powerful means to discredit a person' in legal proceedings related to gender-based violence.[128] This may be enshrined within the law, too, as Article 151 of Pakistan's Law of Evidence Order of 1984, 'impeaching

[121] Epstein and Goodman (n 69) 399.
[122] S Ramon, 'Intersectionalities: Intimate partner Domestic Violence and Mental Health within the European Context' (2015) 4(2) A Global Journal of Social Work Analysis, Research, Polity, and Practice 76.
[123] C Hartley, 'He Said, She Said: The Defense Attack of Credibility in Domestic Violence Felony Trials' (2001) 7(5) Violence Against Women 510.
[124] Epstein and Goodman (n 69).
[125] Sheehy (n 119) 158.
[126] Hartley (n 123).
[127] Smith (n 96).
[128] ibid.

credit of witness', had an explicit section relating to sexual offences which said: 'when a man is prosecuted for rape or an attempt to ravish, it may be shown that the prosecutrix was of generally immoral character.'[129]

In line with the discussion above, it appears that allegations relating to the 'bad' character of women complainants are considered relevant to the law's gendered approach in determining their credibility and consequently in determining legal 'truths'. Similarly, Walklate notes that when gendered discourses in psychiatry and law interact, the resultant effect is that it is often women who are denied a sense of agency and credibility.[130] And while the respective power of different discourses may vary, at times in coalition and at other times in conflict, gendering strategies can work to construct particular kinds of victim-subjects in cases of domestic violence because the 'traditional mode of power responds rapidly to such appeals by men who are attempting to re-establish patriarchal authority in the family'.[131] As such, in *Feminism and the Power of Law*, Smart engages with the law as a discursive site on which to expose and challenge gendered constructions of women's experience,[132] considering whether it should be approached not only as a space where meanings about gender are contested, but also as a platform to advocate for legal reforms that curtail gendered narratives. Examples include feminist efforts to rally against the laws of provocation in England which facilitated men's claims to moral justifications for murdering unfaithful 'bad' wives. Here, a key argument related to the dispositioning of domestic violence as a private matter which shielded it from public intervention.[133] Similarly, the rise of national women's movements, coupled with international human rights discourses, has led to a series of legislative developments relevant to women's rights and protections in Pakistan, shifting acts of gender-based violence from the private sphere to the public. As discussed in Chapter 1, in recent years these include instituting laws against domestic violence, acid crimes, and honour crimes—albeit not without

[129] Article 151(4), Law of Evidence (Qanun-e-Shahadat Order) 1984 [PAK]. While this clause was omitted through the Criminal Law Amendment (Offences Relating to Rape) Act of 2016, evidence of the 'bad' character of victims continues to be used in litigative practices. See Chapter 5 for examples from cases such as Judgement, Sessions Court [2017] OSC 124, as cited in FY Bokhari, 'Accountability for Rape: A Case Study of Lodhran' (2018) Centre for Human Rights, University College Lahore 1, 41.

[130] S Walklate. *Gender, Crime and Criminal Justice* (2nd edn, Willan Publishing 2004) 180.

[131] Smart (n 5) 19.

[132] Smart (n 5).

[133] L Woods, 'Litigation on Behalf of Battered Women' (1979) 5(1) Women's Rights Law Reporter 7, 12.

reservation. Prior to devolution, Pakistan's federal domestic violence bill lapsed in the Senate in 2009 due to opposition that deemed it to be 'discriminatory' and 'violating the sanctity of the home', alongside concerns that such legislation would increase divorce rates.[134]

As per the government's own words, the State 'follows a progressive and well-defined agenda for gender equality and women empowerment in the country'.[135] However, Pakistan continues to rank second to last globally for the same metric.[136] While the government may endorse the rhetoric of women rights, or rather 'may desire to be seen to subscribe [to it] by the international community',[137] there is noticeable incongruity between the existence of formal laws and the practical enforcement of them. The non-implementation of laws may be attributed to the State's struggle in appearing modern and progressive while simultaneously attempting to maintain ideals of tradition and authenticity as per its nationalist project—thereby providing men with legal and/or social impunity.[138] As observed by Mullally,

> the pursuit of gender equality has frequently been sacrificed to religious–cultural claims defining and limiting women's status. Yielding to such claims has served the interests of nation-building while at the same time guarding against any serious threat to the modernizing agendas of Pakistan's political elite. Lost within such compromises is the recognition of women as bearers of rights, with equal rights to participate in the definition of religious–cultural norms.[139]

This raises a question: given that the sanctity of the family is emphasized as 'inviolable' in Pakistan's Constitution,[140] how does this interact with the

[134] R Buckwalter-Poza, 'Troubled History of Domestic Violence Legislation in Pakistan' *Huffpost* (10 July 2010) <https://www.huffpost.com/entry/troubled-history-of-domes_b_753400> accessed 2 February 2021.

[135] Committee on the Elimination of Discrimination against Women, 'Fifth Periodic Report submitted by Pakistan' (2018) CEDAW/C/PAK/5 2.

[136] World Economic Forum, 'Global Gender Gap Report 2024' (2024) <https://www.weforum.org/publications/global-gender-gap-report-2024/> accessed 26 September 2024.

[137] SS Ali, 'CEDAW? What's that? "Domesticating" "International" Women's Human Rights in Muslim Jurisdictions: Reflections on Pakistan's Engagement with CEDAW' in *Modern Challenges to Islamic Law* (Cambridge University Press 2016) 188 [parenthesis added].

[138] See Hajjar (n 57).

[139] S Mullally, 'As Nearly as May Be: Debating Women's Human Rights in Pakistan' (2005) 14 Social and Legal Studies 341.

[140] Article 14, Constitution of the Islamic Republic of Pakistan 1973 [PAK].

prospect and sight of women leaving their (feminine) 'duties' to seek (masculine) 'rights', when they attempt to access legal remedies and protection from familial forms of violence? In other words, when subject positions are challenged and seen as dissenting, can character allegations be used as a gendering strategy to manage and control women complainants of domestic violence in legal settings?

While 'law as gendered' aims to deconstruct law to assess how gender works within the discipline, and how law works to *produce* gender,[141] this concept can be expanded to examine how subjectivities from other discursive spaces, such as those relating to 'bad' and 'mad' women, are situated and nurtured within the law. Doing so builds on understandings of gendering strategies within the law and questions how those processes engage with gendering strategies in other institutional and disciplinary spaces to bring constructed subjectivities into being. As mentioned earlier, law sets itself above other discourses by claiming to have the method to establish 'truth', and in doing so, it disqualifies experiences and knowledges which are deemed as not having legal relevance. However, in an attempt to extend its legitimacy, law also incorporates ideas from other discourses. Smart explains this through an example of when the medical profession construed homosexuality as a 'perversion' in need of treatment, and the law concurrently extended its powers over homosexual activity.[142] By adopting facets from other discourses and disciplines, law is therefore able to exercise 'new contrivances of power in the form of surveillance and modes of discipline'.[143] As such, in engagement with feminist legal scholarship that highlights how legal systems have hidden, invisible (and often adverse) impacts on women's lives,[144] I develop the ideas discussed above not only to look at the effect of using gendered character allegations as a technique of control in legal settings, but I also pick up on Dhanda's account of 'psychologizing dissent' to assess whether the use of 'psy' labels are testament to law 'embracing' objects from other discourses in order to shape the subjectivity of women litigants in particular ways.[145] Examining these claims alongside one another, while also evaluating whether the latter can indeed build on the former, assists in investigating the use and effect of character allegations

[141] Smart (n 7) 34 [emphasis added].
[142] Smart (n 5) 17.
[143] ibid.
[144] For example, see M Davies and V Munro, 'Editors' Note' in M Davies and V Munro (eds), *The Ashgate Research Companion to Feminist Legal Theory* (1st edn, Routledge 2013) 1.
[145] Dhanda (n 66).

as gendering strategies in the construction of victim-subjects of domestic violence in Pakistani courtrooms.

Recalling that subjectivity can be explored through the transformations required of the subject by the varying and intersecting networks of power and social relations in which she lives, the key feature of this concept—that character allegations are a kind of gendering strategy—is that it draws on the multiplicity and simultaneity of gendering strategies in institutional and disciplinary spaces to explore why and how women complainants of domestic violence are subjectivized in particular ways. Specifically, it allows for an examination into how character allegations work to control women that are perceived as 'dissenting' through practices and institutional mechanisms that discredit and marginalize their harms and experiences, in an attempt to make them conform to certain sets of gendered norms and expectations. And to effectively identify and disentangle the ways in gendering strategies can construct the subjectivities of women victims of domestic violence, as well as the particularities of the subjects that it brings into being, it is essential to adopt a methodological approach that speaks to this theoretical framing.

Why stories matter: Reflections on research methods

Feminist epistemological frameworks complement the use of feminist post-structuralist approaches to question and deconstruct the gendered power dynamics that shape knowledge production, and that challenge the privileging of some voices over others. In reflecting on the different ways in which knowledges are produced and located, and in speaking to the contextual drawing of narratives from lived experiences, there are two ideas within feminist epistemology that steer the methodological approach to this project. The first is Haraway's concept of situated knowledges, and the second is Hemmings' ideas surrounding the political grammar of storytelling.

Feminist epistemologies challenge positivist theories of research by finding that no knowledge production can be fully objective,[146] such that scientific knowledge is not found but rather, it is made. And while positivist objectivity stems from knowledge claims that have been deduced through

[146] M Stoetzler and N Yuval-Davis, 'Standpoint Theory, Situated Knowledge and the Situated Imagination' (2002) 3(3) Feminist Theory 315.

scientific methods (and can therefore be scientifically verified), feminist objectivity recognizes knowledge to be a product of a certain context.[147] For example, Haraway's approach to 'situated knowledges' takes into account both the agency of the knowledge producer and that of the object of study.[148] In her view, feminist theorists are sometimes trapped between feeling drawn towards a constructivist view of knowledge, truth, and objectivity, on the one hand, and towards empiricist positions relating to claims of scientific knowledge, on the other.[149] Haraway posits that neither of these options are unproblematic. Constructivism bows towards relativism, which is 'a way of being nowhere while claiming to be everywhere',[150] and empiricism bows towards universality, which can be framed as a way of being everywhere while dismissing the need to be anywhere. She argues that both approaches are unable to recognize that knowledge is always located, and its perspective is therefore necessarily partial. Situated knowledges accordingly acknowledge that social positions shape and limit what a person can and does know. Lived experience, knowledge, and awareness are all shaped by one's personal positionings. And adopting Haraway's approach to partiality and situatedness thus assists in referring to knowledges as self-reflexive—concerning the material, historical and social conditions under which they came into being. Situated knowledges is about communities, and the 'way to find a larger vision is to be somewhere in particular'.[151] As alluded to earlier in this chapter, doing so allows one to participate within the multiplicity and simultaneity of discourses as a form of storytelling.

Accordingly, the second approach that informs my methodological choices stems from Hemmings' book *Why Stories Matter*.[152] Hemmings uses storytelling in relation to feminist theory to distinguish between which stories are told, and how those stories are told. Particularly, her interest lies in the 'technologies of the presumed', which she describes as elements of feminist history that are accepted as 'true'.[153] She does this by

[147] U Narayan, 'The Project of Feminist Epistemology: Perspectives of a Non-Western Feminist' in CR McCann and SK Kim (eds), *Feminist Theory Reader: Local and Global Perspectives* (Routledge 2003) 308.
[148] D Haraway, 'Situated Knowledges: The Science Question in Feminism and the Privilege of Partial Perspective' (1988) 14(3) Feminist Studies 575.
[149] ibid.
[150] ibid 584.
[151] ibid 590.
[152] C Hemmings, *Why Stories Matter: The Political Grammar of Feminist Theory* (Duke University Press 2011).
[153] ibid 19.

purposefully blurring the ontological positions that form the core of (most) historical narratives of feminist theory, and instead focusing on how these stories are framed and what is remembered and forgotten as a result of that framing.[154] There is a stark link here to the centrality of storytelling in the justice system.[155] It is through storytelling, and the ways in which facts are organized into different kinds of framings and 'meaningful patterns',[156] that judges assess the reliability and plausibility of those facts. As observed by Amsterdam and Bruner:

> The law is awash in storytelling. Clients tell stories to lawyers who must figure out what to make of what they hear. As clients and lawyers talk, the client's story gets recast into plights and prospects, plots and pilgrimages into possible worlds . . . The lawyers retell their clients' stories in the forms of pleas and arguments to judges and testimony to juries... Next, judges and jurors retell the stories to themselves or to each other, in the form of instructions, deliberations, a verdict, a set of findings or an opinion . . . This endless telling and retelling, casting and recasting is essential to the conduct of the law.[157]

For the victim of domestic violence too, accessing justice or safety requires her to present a story of her experience, as the 'need for narrative form is so strong that we don't really believe something is true unless we can see it as a story'.[158]

While Hemmings' methodological approach to storytelling focuses on citation practices, I am more interested in how her ideas inform the use of character allegations and gendering strategies as they relate to the rhetorical power of language in the construction of narratives. This research therefore draws on Hemmings' work to not only tell different stories, but also tell stories differently. In that, it tells different stories—sometimes in the spoken words of victims of domestic violence, sometimes in the written words of judgments—and goes on to try to understand the patterns that may emerge, and the presumptions that may be implicit in those framings, to tell stories differently. Acknowledging that these concepts and practices are situated and thereby shaped (and limited) by their social origins,

[154] ibid 226. Hemmings speaks of this tactic as making space for 'unpredictability'.
[155] AG Amsterdam and J Bruner, *Minding the Law* (Harvard University Press 2002) 110.
[156] Epstein and Goodman (n 69).
[157] Amsterdam and Bruner (n 155).
[158] HP Abbott, *The Cambridge Introduction to Narrative* (2nd edn, Cambridge University Press 2018) 44.

positions, and conditions, this epistemological approach disincentivizes the use of bold statements that employ terms such as 'always', as I pause to reassess the conditions under which that statement is, or may have been, 'true'.

Sources of knowledge

As discussed in Chapter 1, all four provinces in Pakistan have passed laws relating to domestic violence in their respective constituencies over the past decade. These laws specify, first and foremost, that they seek to protect women in domestic relationships.[159] However, implementation has been slow in some provinces and stagnant in others, meaning that domestic violence is found along a spectrum of legal cases, with some instances more concealed than others in their categorization. For instance, when examining applications for *khula* [divorce] at a legal aid centre in Karachi, Zia found that most women sought dissolution of marriage due to 'cruelty', 'maltreatment', or 'torture'.[160] She observes that the lack of proper identification systems in Pakistani courts leads to inaccurate classifications, and ultimately results in a loss of data which could be used to understand the prevalence of domestic violence more accurately. Preliminary research conducted for this project revealed similar ideas, where accounts of domestic violence were reflected across a varied range, such as in cases of guardianship on one end and cases of murder on the other. These cases were not classified separately as 'domestic violence', nor were they additionally petitioned under the relevant domestic violence laws. And while I acknowledge Zia's concerns regarding the absence of clear identification systems leading to a loss of data, I am also interested in how these legal categorizations tell a story in themselves, by situating women victims of domestic violence differently and making some more visible than others.

It is for these reasons that I did not limit research to cases filed under domestic violence laws, but also examined other criminal and civil cases that highlight an element of familial violence. This includes cases that fall under

[159] For example, the 'Preamble' of the Baluchistan Domestic Violence (Protection and Prevention) Act 2014 [PAK] specifies, 'it is expedient to institutionalize measures which prevent and protect *women and children* from domestic violence'. However, this scope is expanded in the definition of 'aggrieved person' which includes 'any woman, child, man or any vulnerable person who is or has been in a domestic relationship with the accused'. [Emphasis added].
[160] M Zia, 'Understanding Domestic Violence within the Legal Framework of Pakistan' (2018) Legal Aid Society 18.

criminal legislation, such as murder, honour crimes, acid crimes, rape and sexual assault, and more broadly those under the 'hurt offences' of the penal code, where the victim and the accused are (or were) in a domestic relationship. It also includes cases that fall under family and civil litigation, such as *khula* and guardianship, where divorce or child custody is sought by women due to incidents of domestic violence. The study adopts a mixed methods approach, which supplements case law analysis with qualitative empirical work to add 'rigor, breadth, complexity, richness, and depth'[161] to the research. Accordingly, the three knowledge sources used are case files and judgments, semi-structured qualitative interviews, and ethnographic court observations which were collected and/or conducted through a cumulative six months of fieldwork between 2021 and 2022 in Pakistan.

Accommodating for legislative developments in this area, relevant cases were primarily retrieved over a period of five years, dating between 2016 and 2021. In some instances, ongoing cases that commenced between 2014 and 2015, as well as cases that were filed during fieldwork in 2022, have also been included. Case judgments in Pakistan are typically reported in law journals as well as through official court websites.[162] As such, I first commenced my search for case law through online legal databases,[163] as well as through local judicial case management systems. However, I soon realized the limitations of both legal data systems. For example, the online legal databases would occasionally default to blocking access from outside Pakistan, without warning or schedule, and so I was at times unable to search for cases for a period of many weeks while based in London. In addition, I encountered numerous challenges relating to searching for cases by key terms. As mentioned earlier, the spectrum on which domestic violence cases presented themselves in the courts meant that I was searching for cases that were of both civil and criminal nature. They accordingly appeared under varying sections of the law, and therefore, various courts. Considering this, I tried to retrieve relevant cases by using key search terms, including but not limited to 'violence', 'abuse', 'husband', and 'wife'. However, this posed an additional problem, as I quickly started to come across family law cases where there was an element of domestic violence evident, but this

[161] NK Denzin, 'Triangulation 2.0' (2012) 6 Journal of Mixed Methods Research 80, 82.

[162] Pakistan Legal Decisions (PLD) is the main publisher for judgments, housing multiple legal journals, including Pakistan Criminal Law Journal (PCrLJ), Civil Law Cases (CLC), Monthly Law Digest (MLD) and Yearly Law Reports (YLR).

[163] Examples include 'Pakistan Law Site' <https://www.pakistanlawsite.com/> and 'East Law' <https://eastlaw.pk/>

was not specified as such in the text of the judgment. For example, one reported judgment of a custody case stated that the accused had a 'temper' and 'pushed her [his wife] against the wall with the result her shoulder was got fractured [sic]', without any reference to the terms 'domestic violence' or 'domestic abuse'.[164] A similar challenge related to the use of language in judgments that were translated from Urdu into English before being reported. In a criminal appeal order for a murder case, for instance, the word *izzat* (commonly interpreted as 'honour') was translated as 'escutcheon'.[165]

In addition to law journals, I sought judgments through the official Supreme Court and Provincial Court websites. Most of these websites do not provide an option to do a 'keyword' search, instead typically requiring specific information, such as the case number, court name, date, and the presiding judge's name. At this stage, I did not have such details for the cases that I was seeking, and therefore started with the limited case management systems that allowed the selection of broad categories (with murder, 'hurt offences', and dissolution of marriage being the three main areas of interest and possible relevance). The resulting cases were then skimmed through, downloading cases that were relevant (that is, they related to domestic relationships and/or had an element of domestic violence present) and disregarding those that were not. The judgments were then further read to identify those that made any reference to the possible use of gendering strategies, such as allegations which referred to the character and/or the mental state of the parties involved in the case.

The limitations and challenges that came forth during the search for cases via online means prompted me to find other avenues. While case files and judgments were available through the courts directly and in person, those too would require me to have some basic details of the case. And so, I shifted my efforts towards identifying relevant cases elsewhere, by primarily tapping into the expertise and networks of my interviewees during fieldwork. During this process, judgments and case files were retrieved directly from the courts through case citations provided by lawyers who were actively part of that case, and by seeking permission from the judges of the respective courts. A summary of legal documents consulted for analysis during the research period is presented in Table 2.1 below, which includes those case files and judgments collected through online legal databases as well as those sought from the courts directly.

[164] *Syed Raza Abbas v Sana Saeed Sattar* [2015] YLR 489.
[165] *Muhammad Ismail v the State* [2017] SCMR 713.

Table 2.1 Summary of consulted case files and judgments by category

Nature of case	Type (as classified by law)	Number of cases
Criminal	Murder[166]	37
	Domestic violence[167] and 'hurt offences'[168]	16
Family	Dissolution of marriage[169]	31
	Guardianship[170]	10
Other	Police reports	9
Total		**103**

Preliminary analysis of case files and judgments proved them to be a rich source of knowledge, particularly as they provided interpretive insights into the reasoning of judges, the different shapes and forms of domestic abuse, and the varying arguments, rationales and justifications, provided by legal actors—some with evidence and some without. However, judgments at times faltered in the level of detail provided. In determining which parts of the proceedings are relevant enough to be included in the judgment, some information may be disregarded or obscured, thereby playing a part in how knowledges are situated and how litigants are subjectivized through those choices. This also links back to Hemmings' ideas relating to storytelling; how stories are told, how they are framed, and what may be lost because of that framing. Case documents are therefore interesting to study in their construction of narratives, particularly alongside different narratives of proceedings provided by those present in the courtroom.

An example of the narrative construction of judgments (and concurrently a limitation of relying solely on judgments for research)[171] is

166 This includes attempted murder cases and 'honour' killing cases where the victim and perpetrator were related by marriage or kinship.

167 One of these cases led to the death of the victim and was being prosecuted as a suspected murder. A domestic violence petition was filed separately by the family.

168 As discussed in Chapter 1, 'hurt offences' is an umbrella term used to refer to Sections 332–337 of the PPC. This number includes cases of acid crimes, as well as cases of rape and sexual assault.

169 Including *khula* (divorce), recovery of belongings, and maintenance cases.

170 Primarily cases relating to child custody.

171 D Watkins and M Burton (eds), *Research Methods in Law* (Routledge 2013) 15.

demonstrated by a memo[172] shared with me relating to a case heard under the Sindh Domestic Violence Act. In 2019, the complainant accused her husband of perpetrating acts of abuse and violence against her. As per the medical report presented in court, she had been strangulated, had multiple abrasions over her face and neck, and presented signs of coerced sexual activity leading to genital bruising and infection.[173] Her husband was convicted by the lower courts, and filed an appeal soon after. During the appeal process, the advocate for the victim sent a memo to a women lawyers' network in Pakistan regarding the arguments made by the appellant's lawyer, an excerpt of which is reproduced in Vignette 2.1.

Vignette 2.1 Memo from Respondent's Counsel, December 2019, Karachi

. . . He clearly had not reviewed the lower court record thoroughly at all, and his entire case relied on maligning the survivor and asserting that domestic violence cannot be considered a crime in an 'eastern' society and 'Islamic' country. He insisted that sexual abuse cannot be possible within a marriage—in fact, no woman can ever be forced to have sex (essentially, he denied that rape is a crime). According to him, any violence by the accused was provoked because the survivor was denying him sex. He also said that Hadith permits a man to beat a disobedient wife. At this point, the judge, who remained silent throughout the arguments, asked whether Hadith would permit a man to kill a disobedient wife. To this the lawyer kindly conceded that killing the wife would be extreme, but the husband can beat her. This was the crux of the argument on appeal and the lawyer did not point out any errors in the lower court's assessment of evidence actually on the record or application of the law as it is in reality (as opposed to his opinion of what the law should be).

In my response, I naturally pointed to the fact that domestic violence has been declared a crime by our legislature and the law must be followed. Although I had shared the Sindh DV Act with the judge previously, he did

[172] Such memos are comparable to the concept of live blogs of legal trials, which has been gaining momentum in the digital world: L Flower and MS Ahlefeldt, 'The Criminal Trial as a Live Event: Exploring How and Why Live Blogs Change the Professional Practices of Judges, Defence Lawyers and Prosecutors' (2021) 43(8) Media, Culture and Society 1480.

[173] Criminal Petition, Magistrate 457/17 (Feb 2019) Karachi West.

> not have the law in his file or chambers and seemed unfamiliar with the key provisions. I tried to walk him through the relevant provisions, but he lost interest pretty quickly and said enough of his time has already been wasted![174]

It appears that during the appeal process, the appellant's lawyer did not deny the allegations of abuse, nor dispute the evidence provided to the lower court which led to a conviction. Rather, he focused on the argument that domestic abuse should not be considered a criminal offence to begin with, because religion allows a man to beat his 'disobedient wife' if she is denying him sex. These observations from the courtroom are in contrast to the judgment for the criminal appeal announced a month later, which simply stated that 'the learned counsel for the appellant did not pointed out any material ground in the impugned judgement so as to warrant interference [sic]', making no mention of the nature of the arguments used by the appellant's lawyer.[175] This example is indicative of judgments not always providing a full account of arguments made in court, potentially obscuring some of the character allegations, gendering narratives, and knowledges circulating in the courtroom. Considering this, I turned to semi-structured interviews as a second knowledge source, as a means to tap into the experiences and recollections of those that are and were part of the court process. In producing and situating different knowledges, interviews help to 'see between'[176] and allow for an examination into how the law engages with storytelling.[177]

While case files and judgments were collected from across Pakistan, interviews were primarily conducted in the three cities of Karachi, Lahore, and Islamabad[178] with the following groups of people: lawyers (including victim's counsel, defence counsel, and State Prosecutors); judges; police personnel (including first responders and investigating officers); and victims of

[174] Reproduced with permission. Interview with lawyer, Karachi, 6 January 2022.
[175] Criminal Revision Application No. 10/2019 (Jan 2020) Karachi West.
[176] SL Turley, 'To See Between: Interviewing as Legal Research Tool' (2010) 7(1) Journal of the Association of Legal Writing Directors 283.
[177] Scholars have discussed the 'heightened sensitivity to the importance and pervasiveness of storytelling in the law'. See RK Sherwin, 'The Narrative Construction of Legal Reality' (2009) 6 Journal of the Association of Legal Writing Directors 88, 93.
[178] These cities were chosen primarily due to concerns regarding accessibility, geographical viability, and safe mobility and lodging options when conducting fieldwork as a sole woman researcher, while also providing the benefit of sourcing knowledges from different provinces.

domestic violence (complainants). As opportunities arose, interviews were also conducted with managers of domestic violence shelters, legal aid personnel, psycho-social support workers, and medico-legal officers. These individuals are categorized more broadly under 'victim support personnel'. For the first three categories, interviews were conducted to understand the processes through which cases of domestic violence progress from law enforcement agencies or legal aid centres to the courts, and to gain insight into the character allegations and gendering strategies used in litigating cases of domestic violence. This consequently helps relay the practices and viewpoints of defendants. For the next two categories, interviews were conducted to gather testimonies of court proceedings from the perspective of complainants, and to hear directly from women about their experiences.[179] These interviews particularly helped highlight courtroom dynamics which may not be included or explicit in legal documents.

For access to interviewees, my existing network in Pakistan was mobilized for identification and initial contact. This included legal aid centres and women's rights organizations that I had previously worked with, and women lawyers' networks that I continue to engage with. I interviewed lawyers and legal aid personnel first, and therefore only got contacts of women complainants through them. At this stage, I inquired whether they would be comfortable speaking with me, the nature of the conversation they would be comfortable with, and whether there are any potential risks of harms (such as risks of reprisals) that should be taken into consideration. Using this procedure therefore allowed me to conduct my own risk assessment prior to each interview with a vulnerable person, and I refrained from approaching women victims who may have been put at risk through their participation. Bearing in mind that routes of access may affect the data collected,[180] I was acutely aware of my personal location as a 'native',[181] educated woman in being able to have and navigate my social and professional networks to secure this access.

All interviews were conducted in a semi-structured format to allow flexibility in how the conversation is steered. This facilitated interviewees in

[179] See R Shulamit and SE Chase, 'Interviewing Women' in J Holstein and JF Gubrium (eds) *Inside Interviewing—New Lenses, New Concerns* (1st edn, Sage Publications 2003) 222.

[180] T Miller and L Bell, 'Consenting to What? Issues of Access, Gatekeeping and "Informed" Consent' in T Miller, M Birch, M Mauthner and J Jessop (eds), *Ethics in Qualitative Research* (Sage Publications 2005) 53.

[181] For a discussion on how the 'native' tag may impact researchers, see K Narayan, 'How Native is a "Native" Anthropologist?' (1993) 95(3) American Anthropologist 671.

determining the substantive content of the interview while retaining sufficient structure to allow for analysis and comparison across the research materials.[182] As much as possible, and bearing in mind that the Covid-19 pandemic at times limited the option to do so, interviews were held in person. Conducting interviews face-to-face not only helps in building rapport with interviewees, but has the additional benefit of observing the non-verbal cues, inflections, facial expressions, and body language of participants.[183] In addition, for vulnerable participants particularly, this mode of interviewing grants them 'greater control over the information they disclose'[184] and, accordingly, the stories that they choose to communicate and the manner through which they share them.

Interviews are summarized by category in Table 2.2 below. Of the seventy-two interviews completed, sixty-four were held in person and eight were conducted through audio or video platforms. Of the sixty-four held in person, eighteen were conducted in Islamabad (ICT), eighteen in Lahore (Punjab), and twenty-eight in Karachi (Sindh). Of the eight online interviews, four were conducted with respondents in other cities in the provinces of Sindh and Punjab, and four were conducted with respondents in the provinces of Balochistan and Khyber Pakhtunkhwa. All interviews were based on the schedules approved by the Queen Mary Ethics Committee

Table 2.2 Summary of interviewees by category

Interview group	Number of interviewees
Lawyers	36
Judges	2
Police personnel	5
Victims	18
Victim support personnel	11
Total	72

182 S Sarantakos, *Social Research* (4th edn, Palgrave Macmillan 2013).
183 A Irvine, P Drew and R Sainsbury, '"Am I not answering your questions properly?" Clarification, Adequacy and Responsiveness in Semi-Structured Telephone and Face-to-Face Interviews' (2013) 13(1) Qualitative Research 87.
184 S Wolf, 'Talking to Migrants: Invisibility, Vulnerability, and Protection' (2021) 26(1) Geopolitics 207.

and commenced only after the participant information sheet had been explained in detail and consent forms had been signed.[185]

For the most part, the lawyers I conversed with were forthcoming about their participation and curious to learn more about my research. Their support extended to offers of sharing case files that might be of interest, offers to shadow them in the courts, and offers to connect me with other lawyers, judges, and previous clients who may be willing to be interviewed. This is also known as the 'snowballing' technique, where one research participant recommends other potential participants or avenues for research.[186] Less often, lawyers were discouraging when I told them I would like to speak with judges as well, with one lawyer stating that doing so would be 'fruitless' because lawyers are better informed than judges.[187]

When interviewing (male) lawyers, there were two occasions when I found myself actively choosing not to interact with a certain line of questioning, instead thanking them for their contributions and reasserting the value of their time. The first instance was shortly after concluding an interview when the lawyer asked, 'how does your husband feel about the focus of your research topic?' When I responded to say that I was not married, the follow-up question inquired if, due to my 'inexperience', I felt confident in my ability to understand the reasons why some men may have to 'resort to violence' in marital life.[188] On another occasion, a lawyer proposed that my next research project should look at how the 'Aurat March aunties[189] are violating men', and recommended that I should consider changing my research topic because '*aurton ko waise bhi aaj kal hadd se zyada haq mil rahe hain* [these days, women's rights are already exceeding the (normal) limit]'.[190] When interviewing victims, on the other hand, I found myself freely interacting with their questions regarding women's rights, as well as questions about my marital status, my experience being previously married, and my own encounter with the Pakistani legal system at the time of divorce.

[185] Ethical approval was granted on 8/12/2021 for a period of three years (Reference Number QMERC20.558).

[186] For more on the 'snowballing' technique, see N Semmens, 'Methodological Approaches to Criminological Research' in P Davies, P Francis and V Jupp (eds) *Doing Criminological Research* (2nd edn, Sage Publications 2011) 72.

[187] Interview with lawyer, Islamabad, 9 June 2022 [e].

[188] Interview with lawyer, Karachi, 5 January 2022 [b].

[189] Referring to the supporters of Pakistan's current women's movement, Aurat March. See, for example, D Kamal 'Networked Struggles: Placards at Pakistan's Aurat March' (2022) 30 Feminist Legal Studies 219.

[190] Interview with lawyer, Karachi, 5 January 2022 [c].

Vignette 2.2 Fieldwork diary, 12 January 2022, Karachi

The entrance to the shelter was barricaded. It had a tall, black steel gate with spikes firmly placed along every edge. I looked for a bell to ring but couldn't find one. And so, I called out. An eye appeared through a tiny hole on the other side of gate, asking who I was. I introduced myself, mentioning that I had a meeting scheduled with the manager of the shelter. I was then asked to go through a scanner and wait in a room at the other side of the pavement while he informs the office of my arrival...

The manager led me towards the administrative section of the shelter through the main courtyard. I saw one woman reading under the protection of a towering tree, and another soaking in sunlight amidst the cool winter breeze while her young son played with a toy car by her feet. The corridor I walked through had one side opening into a courtyard, allowing streams of light to come through the branches of red and pink bougainvillea hanging above us, while the other side had a series of room with doors half ajar. As we walked, I passed by an art room, a fitness room, and a music room. I peeked in to briefly observe some women chatting and giggling, and others lounging on the floor cushions with a stack of stitching supplies next to them . . .

I requested to interview residents in a room where they were more comfortable, rather than the official meeting room in the administrative section of the shelter where I had been seated. I was mindful of the sensitive and difficult conversation we were about to have, and hoped to be in an environment where that dialogue felt safe, rather than interrogative. We decided to do some interviews in the courtyard, and others in the art room. I was provided with a chair, but decided to take my sandals off and sit cross-legged on one of the large, colourful woven rugs, as I had seen residents do earlier. 10 minutes later, a middle-aged woman came and took a seat next to me – her face mask concealing the hint of a smile that her eyes revealed. Through the creases of the loose *dupatta* covering her head, I noticed burn scars along the back of her ear, neck and upper chest.

In line with the epistemological approach to this project, I felt it important to interview victims and hear from them directly. Being mindful that victims of violence are prone to having their experiences (re)interpreted for legal or support purposes (and mindful that this is a risk I too may run during the course of research), I hoped that my conversations with victims would help reflect on the possible modes of these interpretations, and consequently on how their stories are understood and further relayed. Additionally, while elite interviews with lawyers for example may bring out certain knowledges, these knowledges relate to and build on the experiences of victims. Speaking to victims directly therefore helps to further situate those knowledges. As reflected in Vignette 2.2, my approach towards interviewing victims of violence accordingly shifted slightly from that which I undertook during elite interviews. Here, my approach centred on consent, empathy, and active support.[191] I reiterated the interviewee's choices in directing the course of our conversation, as well as in deciding which questions they would be comfortable responding to and how many details they would like to share. This was therefore one step further than the regular consent process I had adopted in elite interviews. At times, I paused the interview to offer comfort when participants were visibly upset,[192] and retained sources of support when needed. For instance, while visiting a domestic violence shelter, the in-house psychologist mentioned that one of the residents who wanted to speak with me had 'heightened sensitivities'. In that case, the psychologist was requested to remain in the room with us during the interview, with the consent of the participant, to ensure that she had access to necessary support while recounting traumatic experiences.

In my role as a researcher, I had the difficult task of creating a safe environment and forming a relationship with the respondent in the short amount of time allocated to interviews.[193] I therefore tried to steer away from questions relating to the nature of the violence that women had experienced, and focused more on their interactions with police officials and legal actors. However, the women I interviewed openly shared their experiences, their emotions, and their resolve. At times, victims also spoke of their experience recounting incidents of abuse to family members, friends, and others in the community, outlining both the feelings of support and alienation they felt in doing so. On numerous occasions, they paused to ask if I believed them, to which I responded affirmatively. Additionally, victim support personnel

[191] R Campbell, AE Adams, SM Wasco, C Ahrens and T Sefl, '"What has it been like for you to talk with me today?" The Impact of Participating in Interview Research on Rape Survivors' (2010) 16(1) Violence Against Women 60.

[192] See K Dyregrov, A Dyregrov and M Raundalen, '"Refugee Families" Experience of Research Participation' (2000) 13(3) Journal of Traumatic Stress 413.

[193] A Liebling, 'Doing Research in Prison: Breaking the Silence?' (1999) 3 Theoretical Criminology 147.

were able to relay accounts of cases on which they had previously worked, as well as the sentiments and experiences of women with whom they worked. These narratives particularly shed light on how complainants navigated the legal process before and after court hearings, both practically and emotionally, which are accounts that were largely missing from those shared by police officers, lawyers, and judges.

Finally, the third knowledge source selected for this project relates to ethnographic observational research in court settings, which is a method frequently adopted by researchers studying sensitive topics (such as sexual offences).[194] Court observations provide an opportunity to gain insight into the culture of the courts,[195] and assist in understanding the 'set of everyday interactions and decisions' between different legal actors.[196] This enables one to examine the norms and practices that are embedded within the legal system as commonplace or implicit, which may not come to form through interviews. My interest in court observations was also sparked by the encouragement of State Prosecutors during early interviews, who highlighted that my research would benefit from 'shadowing' them in the courts. The main reasoning presented was that court observations would help make sense of '*unkahi baatein* [what is left unsaid]', and to ensure that my research does not purely rely on the '*bharosa* [credibility]' of my interviewees.[197] In addition, several ongoing cases relating to domestic violence were brought to my attention. These cases were of particular interest because they provided an opportunity to investigate courtroom proceedings in 'real time'.[198]

From a feasibility point of view, accompanying both State Prosecutors and family lawyers to the courts was incredibly helpful in securing access to court proceedings, although I had been informed that courts are generally open to the public and hearings are rarely *in camera* (that is, either

[194] For example, see O Smith, 'Researching English Sexual Violence Trials Using Court Observation Methods' in *SAGE Research Methods Cases* (SAGE 2020); and M Burman, L Jamieson and J Nicholson, *Impacts of Aspects of the Law of Evidence in Sexual Offence Trials: An Evaluation Study* (Edinburgh: Scottish Government 2007).

[195] The idea of 'court culture' has been discussed in J Baldwin, 'Research on the Criminal Courts' in R King and E Wincup (eds) *Doing Research on Crime and Justice* (Oxford University Press 2007) 375.

[196] D Berti and D Bordia, 'Introduction' in D Berti and D Bordia (eds), *Regimes of Legality: Ethnography of Criminal Cases in South Asia* (1st edn, Oxford University Press 2015) 1.

[197] Interview with lawyer, Karachi, 15 January 2022. I found this reasoning very interesting given that a key aspect of my research examines how the credibility of women complainants is perceived and understood in court settings.

[198] L Back and N Puwar, 'A Manifesto for Live Methods: Provocations and Capacities' (2012) 60(1) Sociological Review 6.

at the discretion of the presiding judge, or at the request of the litigants). Initially, when I had mentioned the possibility of court observations to lawyers who practice in the district court, I was told that I could just 'slip in', as no one would notice. When I asked for clarification about what this meant, the response was that judges in lower courts are typically going through a turnover of 40–50 cases a day, due to which their courts and chambers are always full of people. Possibly detecting my unease, they also proposed that I could accompany them to proceedings, and offered to introduce me to judges so that I could seek official permission to observe their courts.

While challenging due to planned court closures for a few weeks of holiday over the summer months, and further unplanned closures due to the Omicron variant of Covid-19, extensive monsoon rains, and urban flooding, I spent a total of eleven days in court observations, seven of which were at the district court in Karachi, with two days each at the city court and district court of Lahore and Islamabad respectively.

In addition to notes taken during court observations, I continued to maintain a fieldwork diary to record my thoughts, observations, and questions as they occurred. As fieldwork is situated 'between autobiography and anthropology',[199] the research diary provides a platform through which the interaction of the subjective and objective aspects of the work are brought into a productive relationship.[200] Reflexivity continues to help bring forth the partial situatedness of knowledge created, and the use of ethnographic vignettes in this book, in addition to larger extracts from interviews, helps locate the production of different knowledges to allow for a contextual drawing of narratives.[201] My fieldwork diary was not limited to journaling through text but also used visual means, as I photographed my travels through various cities, including the locations where I conducted interviews and the rooms in which I waited, sometimes for long hours. Looking at these images continuously brings me back to how I was feeling in those moments—at times excited, sometimes anxious; at times distressed, sometimes tense—enabling me to explore the 'politics of discomfort' as an interpretive resource in the search for patterns and stories.[202]

[199] K Hastrup, 'Writing Ethnography—State of the Art' in J Okely and H Callaway (eds), *Anthropology and Autobiography* (Routledge 1992) 116.

[200] RG Burgess, 'Keeping a Research Diary' (1981) 11(1) Cambridge Journal of Education 77.

[201] Haraway (n 148).

[202] See Chadwick R, 'On the Politics of Discomfort' (2021) 22(4) Feminist Theory 556; Also see S Holz and A Bano, 'Navigating Respectability in Patriarchal Contexts: Ethical Dilemmas of Women Researchers in Pakistan' (2022) 53 International Quarterly for Asian Studies 553.

Further, in centring on domestic violence, the nature of this research dealt with the disclosure of sensitive, personal information, and working with vulnerable individuals who may have either experienced violence themselves or been closely associated with it. This required an ethically sound approach not only in the collection of research materials, as discussed above, but also in the processing of those materials. As such, to safeguard the identities of interviewees (and primarily of victims), I chose to uniformly anonymize all interviews across the board. This included the removal of direct identifiers, including interviewees' names, job titles, and place of work. Instead, I categorized their occupations more broadly under 'lawyer' or 'legal aid personnel' and listed the city where the interview was held. For interviews with victims, I additionally removed indirect identifiers that may have been mentioned during the interview, such as the name of the specific village where she lived, or the name of the shelter she was residing in. Instead, I made a note of the larger city which corresponded to these details. Similarly, while reported judgments were left unchanged, I removed all identifiers from case files that were secured through the courts as an added risk mitigation, citing them based on the nature of the case, case number, name of the court, location, and date.[203] The process of anonymization ensured that, despite having sought permission, any unforeseen risks associated with unauthorized disclosure of information or unauthorized identification of individuals were minimized.

Additionally, interviews were transcribed by hand. The main reason for not using transcription software is that most interviewees switched freely between English and Urdu.[204] I, too, regularly switched to the language which I gauged the interviewee as being more comfortable with. Due to the sensitive nature of the research, it was important to maintain a certain level of comfort with participants throughout, while also acknowledging that they would be able to capture their thoughts and emotions more accurately if they were conversing in the language that felt most linguistically natural. This accordingly meant that it would be difficult to effectively make use of automatic language detection and transcription systems. Transcribing the interviews by hand, despite the many hours spent on this process, provided

[203] These refer to the handful of judgments and case files that were retrieved directly from the courts. The case citations were identified by lawyers who were actively part of that case; copies of cases were provided by the court after seeking permission from the respective judges.

[204] Similar challenges relating to transcription services for audio interviews have been highlighted in L MacLean, M Meyer and A Estable, 'Improving Accuracy of Transcripts in Qualitative Research' (2004) 14(1) Qualitative Health Research 113, 115.

the benefit of identifying emerging themes for analysis at early stages of fieldwork which could be elaborated during later interviews. One of the main challenges (and limitations) of this process, however, was translating the transcripts into English to uniformize the research sources. The majority of transcripts were translated as literally as possible, but in some cases I struggled to translate sentences in such a manner that they maintained the essence and emotion with which they were spoken.[205] In these cases, I chose to use the best fitting translation, but also retained the statements in their original language, simply transcribing them into the roman alphabet. In line with the methodological approach to this project, adding this step helped to maintain narratives as they were relayed to me, while positioning them alongside any risk of my own (re)interpretation of those framings.

When processing the three knowledge sources, themes were identified and coded as they surfaced.[206] Judgments and case files were particularly read through both iterative approaches and interpretive approaches. While the former assists in identifying themes and patterns in the use of language and legal reasoning to construct narratives (which can then be mapped on to interview transcripts and notes from court observations), the latter looks beyond the reasoning provided in the text to assess what may be implied or left unsaid. In other words, it is 'reading *through* or *beyond* the data',[207] and allows for a progressive, thematic refining through which to explore how character allegations are used as gendering strategies to construct victim-subjects of domestic violence in the Pakistani legal system. Adopting a mixed methods approach for this project accordingly brings forth the silences and at times incompatibilities that emerge when knowledges produced by a variety of sources are assessed together. And in using feminist epistemological approaches, it also speaks to how knowledges are situated and negotiated within discursive spaces.[208] The findings, themes, and ideas presented in the following chapters are accordingly informed by the multiplicity of research sources analysed, in an effort to tell different stories and tell stories differently.

[205] See B Temple and A Young, 'Qualitative Research and Translation Dilemmas' (2004) 4 Qualitative Research 161, 171.

[206] MG Miles and AM Huberman, *Qualitative Data Analysis* (2nd edn, SAGE 1994).

[207] J Mason, *Qualitative Researching* (2nd edn, SAGE 2002) 149 [emphasis in the original].

[208] A Nightingale, 'A Feminist in the Forest: Situated Knowledges and Mixing Methods in Natural Resource Management' (2003) 2(1) ACME International E-Journal for Critical Geographies 79.

3
Silencing victim-subjects: Gendered narratives

Kadi kukri di bang wee rawa hoi ay?
[Has the clucking of a hen ever been meaningful?][1]

Introduction

Victims of domestic violence have 'lived a life of silence'.[2] Police officers refuse to talk to them if they are not accompanied by a male relative, lawyers speak on their behalf and ask them to remain quiet if they try to interject, and judges are unlikely to address them directly during court hearings.[3] Epstein and Goodman suggest that any time a woman must go through a gatekeeper to access resources, safety, or justice, 'she has to tell some sort of a story about her domestic violence experience'.[4] And the way she presents her narrative must assist listeners and observers in organizing facts into 'meaningful patterns', because 'the need for narrative form is so strong that we don't really believe something is true unless we can see it as a story'.[5] The plausibility of her story is therefore central to whether or not she will be deemed as credible and reliable, both in law and in society. When Pakistani women are confined to silence and not permitted to speak, their experiences and narratives are often presented by others in ways that could

[1] A Punjabi proverb. See LA Khan, MA Khan and A Hussain, 'The Good Woman Is the Silent One: A Feminist Critique of Proverbial Stance on Gendered Talk' (2021) 12(1) Pakistan Journal of Applied Social Sciences 57, 66.
[2] Interview with victim, Karachi, 12 January 2022 [a].
[3] Interview with police, Karachi, 2 August 2022 [c]; Interview with lawyer, Lahore, 17 June 2022 [a]. I discuss these instances in more detail in Chapters 4–6.
[4] D Epstein and L Goodman, 'Discounting Women: Doubting Domestic Violence Survivors' Credibility and Dismissing Their Experiences' (2019) 167(1) University of Pennsylvania Law Review 406.
[5] HP Abbott, *The Cambridge Introduction to Narrative* (Cambridge University Press 2008) 3.

Domestic Violence in Pakistan. Daanika Kamal, Oxford University Press. © Daanika Kamal 2025.
DOI: 10.1093/9780198953470.003.0003

implicate how they are subjectivized and consequently perceived as victims of domestic violence. Silencing could then be seen as a kind of gendering strategy, as 'it is always the males that are all talking . . . when does she get to tell her story?'[6]

Vignette 3.1 Lubna's story, Karachi

I was eighteen years old when my parents forcibly got me married to him. He must have been over thirty years old at the time. I had no understanding of anything, and everyone forced me to have a child immediately. And then, my husband divorced me because I was not able to give him *waaris* [legal heirs]. He wanted two sons. My firstborn was a son, so that was okay, but then I got pregnant again and it was a daughter.

They tried to force a miscarriage when I was pregnant with my second child. When they found out I was carrying a girl, my mother-in-law told me to come to the top floor of the house to clean clothes and kitchen utensils. I told her I was in pain climbing up so high and doing this work—I was already in my fifth month of pregnancy. But she made me fill a bucket with water and clothes, and then she told me to carry that bucket up to the roof. You know how our village houses are—we do not have walls on all sides of the stairs—and she tried to trip me two times by pulling my *dupatta*, but I didn't fall. Thanks to Allah, I got all the way up to the roof. When I finished washing all the clothes and emptied out the bucket, I started going back downstairs. And then my mother-in-law pushed me from behind, and I fell to the ground floor.

They kept my first child very well, because he was a boy. But when they found out the second one was a daughter, they pushed me down from a top floor. By some miracle, I survived, and the baby also survived. My first child, my son, he was only one year old at the time. He was sitting in the courtyard and he saw me fall. I went straight to my doctor when this happened. She was a very supportive doctor, and gave me all the medicines and injections for free. She also told me not to worry, that if my husband refused to give money for the baby's delivery then she would do that for free as well. Thank God my baby girl was born healthy. But my husband still divorced me after her birth.

[6] Interview with lawyer, Lahore, 17 June 2022 [a].

> Then he launched a case against me to take away my children through the arbitration council in the *Jamat Khaana*. They [in-laws] kept both my children and sent me to my parents' village and told me that they would come back and get me in a few days. But they didn't come back and instead they filed a case at the council and told them all sorts of things. That I had a tendency to have affairs; that I was crazy, aggressive, had no sense of anything, and that I needed psycho treatment. When I went to the council, no one even let me speak. They only heard him. It was as if they had turned a deaf ear to me, like I was invisible. They let my husband keep my children and he divorced me. And I was made to just simply accept it.[7]

In Vignette 3.1 above, a victim of domestic violence recounted the abusive acts to which she was subjected by her in-laws. She outlined how she was not given many opportunities to speak during the arbitration hearing, and even when she was able to voice her experiences and defend against the allegations that her husband made against her—that she was a 'bad' woman with a 'tendency to have affairs' and a 'mad' woman in need of 'psycho treatment'—she felt she was invisible because 'they only heard him'. Here, in addition to seeing the kinds of allegations that were used to construct the victim-subject in particular ways, the victim's narration allows us to unpack the process of victimization that results from these gendering strategies and silencing techniques. The abuse appears to have been initially perpetrated due to the victim's 'inability' to give her husband two legal heirs (or two sons), where her body was censured for not performing the 'respectable' duties expected of it. In turn, when her husband filed for divorce and launched a case to 'take away' her children, the allegations that resulted brought forth further claims about her body and her mind as a means to silence her and perhaps justify the legal case in question.

Thiesmeyer argues that silencing works to produce subjectivities that suppress opposition to dominant constructions.[8] Similarly, victim support personnel I interviewed talked about how women are silenced and further victimized when they leave their homes in search for protection from domestic abuse, or to seek their rights:

[7] Name has been changed for anonymity. Interview with victim, Karachi, 12 January 2022 [c].

[8] L Thiesmeyer, 'Introduction' in L Thiesmeyer (ed), *Discourses and Silencing: Representation and the Language of Displacement* (John Benjamins 2003).

> I have been working with victims of domestic violence for over twenty years and what I know is that domestic violence has a hundred different shades. The thing is, when a woman tries to leave her home to seek her rights, when a woman goes to the police, or to court, or to shelter homes, or to legal aid centres, she is silenced. The husband is a man of this society and he knows what he needs to say to overcome all. He will say that this woman has a bad character, that *zehni tor peh theek nahi hai* [mentally, she is not okay], that she is having an affair and wants to marry elsewhere. And honestly, it is likely that the majority of the society will believe him. Here, the woman who speaks loudly, or who speaks of her rights, we do not like her. People in our society will say, 'see how she talks, she probably runs her mouth with her husband too, no wonder he has to hit her, or no wonder he has to control her'. You know, that is why these women that come to me, that I work with, they often say that 'I am not a survivor, I am a victim'. Because even after they leave, they are still victimized.[9]

This chapter centres the stories and narratives of victims in an effort to counter the silencing of women that often occurs through institutional and societal means.[10] In doing so, it first looks at the victim–survivor paradox in order to better understand why Pakistani women may be more inclined to identify themselves as victims of domestic violence, rather than as survivors. A key exploration here relates to the recognition and acknowledgement of the harms that the label 'victim' represents to them, amidst the gendered technologies of power that work to silence and dismiss those harms. Subsequently, I reflect on how labels may shape the subjectivity of women's experiences, and how the application of character allegations and 'psy' labels work to construct them as particular kinds of victim-subjects. Working within the politics of respectability, I contend that these labels function through (and within) a similar rhetoric, where shifts in perceiving the victim as unfavourably loud and 'active', instead of as favourably quiet and 'passive', may correspond to the use of such gendering strategies to silence women. Among such techniques, I also explore how victims of domestic violence negotiate their agential relationship with the law. This

[9] Interview with victim support personnel, Lahore, 15 June 2022.

[10] For a discussion on how the voices of oppressed and colonized groups are often silenced and distorted by dominant discourses, see GC Spivak, 'Can the Subaltern Speak' in C Nelson and L Grossberg (eds), *Marxism and the Interpretation of Culture* (Macmillan Education 1988) 271.

accordingly informs the legal steps that women take in response to the harms and violence they experience, and helps situate them as complainants in the Pakistani legal system.

'I am not a survivor, I am a victim': How labels shape subjects

In many ways, victimhood and victimization relating to gender-based violence are dependent upon the way in which individuals, and women in particular, are perceived as weak, vulnerable, or deserving of care.[11] The 'hierarchy' upon which victims are positioned, and the notion of what makes for an 'ideal' victim, are similarly based on comparable perceptions.[12] Walklate suggests that the term 'victim' is predominantly associated with the passivity and perhaps powerlessness that often accompanies the feminine sex role stereotype.[13] As such, 'the more one exemplifies such qualities, the more one *is* a victim'.[14] This has often been discussed as a cornerstone idea in feminist scholarship which questions whether the term 'victim' should be framed in an alternative manner. For example, using the term 'survivor' instead arguably provides a buffer from associations of victimhood and projects a more agency-centric approach.[15] In doing so, there is a shift from viewing women as passive victims to seeing them as active survivors, as well as a shift from framing the oppression of women in terms of victimhood to instead highlight their resistance and agency.[16]

Such variations in verb forms suggest that the use of labels can invoke different perceptions of women who have experienced violence.[17] As Papendick and Bohner posit, using the label 'victim' evokes associations relating to the individual having 'a weak physical constitution, who passively suffers from severe long-term consequences of the experienced

[11] See N Christie, 'The Ideal Victim' in EA Fattah (ed), *From Crime Policy to Victim Policy* (Palgrave Macmillan 1986) 17.
[12] ibid.
[13] S Walklate, *Imagining the Victim of Crime* (Open University Press 2006) 27.
[14] J Kennedy, 'The Citizen Victim: Reconciling the Public and Private in Criminal Sentencing' (2019) 13 Criminal Law and Philosophy 91.
[15] Walkate (n 13) 27, 41.
[16] See L Kelly, S Burton and L Regan, 'Beyond Victim or Survivor: Sexual Violence, Identity and Feminist Theory and Practice' in L Adkins and V Merchant (eds), *Sexualising the Social* (Palgrave Macmillan 1996) 77.
[17] See for example, A Setia, M Marks and S An, 'Double Standards in Perceived Traits of Women Labelled Victims versus Survivors' (2020) 24(5) Sexuality and Culture 1562.

violence'.[18] On the other hand, the label 'survivor' is associated with the perception of 'activity, strength, optimism, and positive coping with a potentially life-threatening experience'.[19] Some women may therefore choose to distance themselves from the unfavourable associations that may accompany the term 'victim', opting to refer to themselves as survivors instead.[20] However, the complexity of the term 'survivor' could contribute to a gendered double standard when it comes to women victims of physical and sexual violence,[21] where adjectives associated with the 'survivor' label—such as dominant, confident, brave, and strong—are seen as largely positive characteristics for men, but perceived as negative when held by women. Such labels could also influence the perceived severity of the abuse and violence, where the term 'victim' may be seen as designating more serious harms than 'survivor',[22] with the former thereby also facilitating more compassion and empathy.[23] These ideas contribute to Thompson's finding that the switch from 'victim' to 'survivor' may not be readily adopted. Rather, the victim–survivor paradox is a dilemma that women frequently face,[24] where wanting to make observers take the event of violence seriously as a *victim* may conflict with the need to cope with its effects as a *survivor*.

As such, empirical work addressing the use of these two labels indicates that some women may refer to themselves as both victims and survivors of their experiences.[25] Others, however, explicitly call themselves victims as a means of acknowledging the harm they experienced, and to express that they have indeed suffered and are deserving of sympathy, redemption, and justice.[26] During fieldwork, the latter idea came to the surface in numerous interviews. Pakistani women generally dissociated from the term 'survivor', choosing to refer to themselves predominantly as victims. For them, the

[18] M Papendick and G Bohner, 'Passive Victim—Strong Survivor? Perceived Meanings of Labels Applied to Women Who Were Raped' (2017) 12(5) PLoS ONE 2.
[19] ibid.
[20] M Thompson, 'Life after Rape: A Chance to Speak' (2000) 15 Sexual and Relationship Therapy 329.
[21] Setia and others (n 17).
[22] Papendick and Bohner (n 18).
[23] JM Hockett and DA Saucier, 'A Systematic Literature Review of "Rape Victims" versus "Rape Survivors": Implications for Theory, Research and Practice' (2015) 25 Aggression and Violent Behaviour 1.
[24] Thompson (n 20).
[25] I Skjelsbaek, 'Victim and Survivor: Narrated Social Identities of Women Who Experienced Rape during the War in Bosnia-Herzegovina' (2006) 16 Feminism and Psychology 373.
[26] A Leisenring, 'Confronting "Victim" Discourses: The Identity Work of Battered Women' (2006) 29 Symbolic Interaction 307.

label did not carry a negative connotation, but rather was a means to ensure that their experiences were recognized. In many ways, it also signified that the effects of those experiences continue to play a large role in their identity, long after the violence itself may have ceased. As one woman said:

> *Aap ko patah hain na, jo log bolte hain—keh aurat per ki jooti hoti hai, ek ko utar, doosri mil jayegi. Aisi soch hai, is liye tasshadud hai. Aur phir agar woh zinda bhaag gayi toh phir kehte hain key yeh toh bach gayi. Aise tasshud se kabhi koi bachta hai? Tasshud mere undar hai. Tab bhi mazloom thi, abhi bhi hoon* [You know [the saying] right, that people say—that a woman is like a shoe, take one off and you'll find another. That is how people think, that is why there is [domestic] violence. If she manages to escape it alive then they'll say that she survived. Does one ever survive such violence? The violence is inside me. If I was a victim then, I am a victim now too].[27]

My choice in this book to refer to women who experienced domestic violence as 'victims' and not as 'survivors' is therefore a choice grounded in accordance with how the women that I interviewed chose to refer to themselves. While there may be something to be said about how Pakistani women are perhaps internalizing the label, it appeared through fieldwork and interviews that this choice was primarily seen as a recognition of their harms and ordeals. In many ways, opting to adopt the 'victim' label could be said to reflect their agency amidst the victimization process. When their stories and narratives are frequently silenced, and when their claims to justice and retribution are routinely dismissed by family, friends, law enforcement agents, and the courts, the recognition of their harms, as provided by that label, was paramount.

For similar reasons, while conversing with lawyers, judges, victim support personnel, and police officials, women complainants were predominantly referred to as victims by interviewees.[28] During my conversation with a medico-legal officer, this choice was quite firmly communicated in response to my question about 'survivors' of domestic violence: 'The victims—I will not call them survivors, I will call them victims. Keep in mind that many of them are killed, many of them do not survive.'[29] Perhaps

[27] Interview with victim, Karachi, 12 January 2022 [a].
[28] The term 'victim' is also used in legal cases relating to gender-based violence. See *Muhammad Khan v the State* [2020] PCrLJ Note 10 Sindh; *Saeed Ahmed Khan v the State* [2018] MLD 371 Sindh; *Adnan Zar v Khadeeja Khanum* [2020] MLD 1147 Islamabad.
[29] Interview with medico-legal officer, Karachi, 14 August 2022.

this also informs the reasons why Pakistani women may associate themselves more with the 'victim' label than the 'survivor' one, for the latter is often used to tell women that they should be *grateful* for that survival. Put differently, this term may be used rather dismissively to tell women to be thankful that the violence they experienced wasn't worse. For example, one woman whose husband attacked her with acid recalled, 'When I told [my family about the attack], they just said, *yeh toh hota rehta hai, aise nahi keh tumhe maar dala, bach gayi na* [these sorts of things happen, it's not like he killed you, you survived, right?]'.[30] Nario-Redman and Branscombe argue that imagining hypothetical situations that could have had worse outcomes for the victim—such as her death or additional injury—enables the perceived severity of the actual event(s) to be reduced.[31] That reduction in perceived severity can in turn act as a gendering strategy which minimizes the harms that were inflicted on her, ultimately reducing the blameworthiness of the perpetrator. Such reinterpretations of the event, through terms such as survivor and more significantly through adjacent expressions of survival, may therefore be seen as belittling the abusive and violent experiences of these women.

Vignette 3.2 Zeba's story, Lahore

I told so many people about my abuse—that I was being abused by my father, my uncle, my brother who is a bit younger than me, they all used to physically torture me due to marriage issues. They wanted me to get married, I did not. I wanted to finish my education. My friends would always say 'yes, what happened was bad', but that was the extent of it. Sometimes they would even say that 'yes it was bad, but be grateful that it was not worse'. No one tried to help me or offer me a place to stay or anything else. Everyone in my family and extended family knew, too. I would go to them one by one and ask for help, but their mindset was that this is normal. *Keh haath uthana aur zubaan gandi karma normal hai* [that raising your hand and dirtying your tongue is normal]. I knew what was happening was wrong, but why is everyone saying that it is normal? It is not normal. All

[30] Interview with victim, Islamabad, 7 June 2022 [b] [parenthesis added].

[31] MR Nario-Redmond and NR Branscombe, 'It Could Have Been Better or It Might Have Been Worse: Implications for Blame Assignment in Rape Cases' (1996) 18(3) Basic and Applied Psychology 349.

because of questions and decisions about my marriage. Then with some help from a woman at my university, I managed to escape and found a shelter.

. . . The problem is, I signed the *nikkah* [marital] forms a few months previously. My uncle just put the form in front of me and told me to sign it. I was not sure what I was signing, there was so much pressure at the time. Then I found out. And even after I signed it my father would continue to hurt me because he said I was not sincere and would not fulfil my marital duties. He would tell me that even if I don't want to, I have to fulfil those duties. So my family is now saying that the *nikkah* is done, and the man—I do not think of him as my husband, I have no marital relations with him, I have never even been to his house—but just to get that one signature finished it is taking me so long. Because my family approached the courts and the judge saying that I am staying here [at the shelter] illegally and someone has brainwashed me. The man has also filed a separate case that I have deserted him and he wants his wife back. Even though he is getting married to someone else. He is moving on, but they are all still after me. The judge has not given the decision on the habeas case yet and even with the *khula* case they are using delay tactics. They have been keeping me hanging and I am very anxious about this.

And even after all this, I did not go to the police—I was not confident enough. Even though I have audio recordings and videos and pictures of the abuse. But my family has reach in the police, so I never felt safe. What is the point of filing criminal charges—do you think they would ever get jail time? No, they wouldn't. I even asked someone about domestic violence, I asked them if I could do a criminal complaint, and I was told that there would be no jail. Even if I register a complaint, they [police] would just call my family and tell them not to do it and they'll say okay—and then *mera hi gala parka jaye ga* [it will be my neck on the line]. *Sab bolte hain ke buss shukar karo bach gayi. Laikin aise kya bachna? Kis ka shukar karoon? Hum aise bachte nahi hain, hum mutasireen hain* [everyone says I should just be thankful that I survived, but what is this kind of survival? What should I be thankful for? We do not survive like this, we are victims].[32]

[32] Name has been changed for anonymity. Interview with victim, Lahore, 14 June 2022 [a] [parenthesis added].

In Vignette 3.2 above, a woman outlines the process of victimization to which she was subjected. First, she was deemed as a disobedient, 'bad' woman in need of control through abusive acts when she refused to agree to her family's wishes relating to her marriage, and was subsequently coerced into signing the marital contract. Second, when she managed to flee to a domestic violence shelter, her family and 'husband' respectively claimed that she was 'brainwashed' (thereby insinuating that she was incapable of independently deciding to reside at the shelter) and that she had 'deserted' her marital duties (thereby implicating her character). Despite this, she was told by some in her social circle that what happened to her was 'normal', while others told her she should be grateful that she survived.

The different connotations associated with the labels 'victim' and 'survivor' may accordingly influence the perceived subjectivities of women complainants, including but not limited to their character, mentality, and credibility.[33] For example, Bohner assessed how the language used in cases of sexual assault linked to victim-blaming responses, finding that attributions of responsibility can be influenced by the use of passive voice.[34] As such, despite the risk of being viewed as weak and vulnerable, women are often told to assume a role of passivity as victims.[35] This links to the quote from a member of victim support personnel reproduced earlier: 'the woman who speaks loudly, or who speaks of her rights, we do not like her.'[36] This is because one of the central attributes of the victim is innocence, and the 'real' victim is passive; she does not play any part in her victimization.[37]

Based on a similar assumption, the justice system has often been criticized for pushing victims towards the role of passive bystander in their own violence and experiences.[38] Victims may be asked to provide a retelling of the event in question and to provide relevant information about the injuries or harms they have suffered. However, it is the courts that interpret and consequently assign meaning to that testimony. Passive victims are

[33] Setia and others (n 17); J Van Dijk, 'Free the Victim: A Critique of the Western Conception of Victimhood' (2009) 16(1) International Review of Victimology 1.

[34] G Bohner, 'Writing about Rape: Use of the Passive Voice and Other Distancing Text Features as an Expression of Perceived Responsibility of the Victim' (2001) 40(4) British Journal of Social Psychology 515.

[35] Thompson (n 20).

[36] Interview with victim support personnel, Lahore, 15 June 2022.

[37] JL Dunn, '"Victims" and "Survivors:" Emerging Vocabularies of Motive for "Battered Women Who Stay"' (2005) 75(1) Sociological Inquiry 3.

[38] M Andersson, C Mellgren and AK Ivert, 'How Victims Conceptualise Their Experiences of Hate Crime' (2018) DoC Malmo University 4.

therefore quieter, speak only of what is asked about, and are told to remain silent unless instructed otherwise. Karmen argues that this is in an effort to move away from victim-blaming responses, where the 'ideal' victim is largely seen and treated not as a subject, but as an object.[39] He posits that when victims are seen as objects, they are perceived as having no responsibility or contribution towards the incident.[40] On the other hand, 'active' victims are seen as subjects that either provoked the offender, or bear some blame for the incident due to their own indiscretions. Assigning the role of subject to victims, or bringing their subjectivities into question through the use of gendered character allegations, could then be a strategy used to associate them with guilt.

In the narratives above, women recounting their stories touched upon some of the ways in which they were silenced and subjectivized. For example, Lubna* was said to be having affairs, and called crazy, aggressive, and in need of 'psycho treatment' during her arbitration hearing. And Zeba* was said to be 'brainwashed' and at the shelter illegally, having deserted her duties both as a daughter and as a wife.[41] When silenced from telling their own stories, the experiences of victims of domestic violence are told by others: by family members, police officers, lawyers, and, most pertinently, their own perpetrators. In doing so, these narratives often bring in gendering strategies through allegations and claims about the woman's character (that she is engaging in illicit relations, or abandoning her 'duties') and by insinuating her untoward mental state (by claiming that she is 'brainwashed' or in need of 'psycho treatment').

Such gendered narratives reframe the experiences of victims in a manner which casts doubt upon their credibility and reliability. This is in line with Karmen's suggestion that subjectivizing victims may be a means to associate them with blame or guilt, or conversely to disassociate blame and guilt from the alleged perpetrator. Silencing through the use of gendered narratives can then be seen as a way to construct the victim-subject. More often than not, the retelling of narratives by others is premised on the politics of honour and respectability, and ultimately on the social control of women. This notion is encapsulated succinctly by a scene from a Pakistani movie, as recalled by an interviewee here:

[39] A Karmen, *Crime Victims: An Introduction to Victimology* (Wadsworth Belmont 2010) 140.

[40] ibid; Also see T Lacerda, 'Victim: What Is Hidden behind This Work?' (2016) 10 International Journal of Transitional Justice 179.

[41] Names have been changed for anonymity.

> There is this old movie we used to make fun of—there is this scene, where the main character's sister was out and about, and she was picked up and taken by some man. So, the character went and got her dupatta back and tells his mother, '*Ma, mein apni behen ki izzat bacha ke le aaya hoon*' [mother, I have saved my sister's honour and brought it back]. This is the thing, about what happens when women go outside the home and how we attach a woman's honour to her scarf or her veil. It is a symbol.[42]

In Pakistan, women are seen as the custodians of respectability, with conforming to gendered, dominant norms and rules of social propriety often seen as 'the external manifestation' of her moral character.[43] As explored in Chapter 2, the politics of respectability are intrinsic to perceptions of dissent and practices relating to social control of women.[44] Drawing on the discussion above, when a woman dissents from what is deemed 'respectable' by protesting 'against a subsisting external reality',[45] allegations that cast aspersions on her character or mentality are a form of social control that frames her protest as originating from her dubious disposition and troubled mind. For example, Lakkimsetti talks about the case of Sri Reddy, an actress from the Telugu Film Industry who 'protested semi-naked' in Hyderabad in 2018.[46] Reddy's protest was in response to sexist practices in the industry, including instances where aspiring actresses were made to offer sexual services in exchange for roles. Media outlets broadcasting the protest 'tried to discipline her body by attempting to cover it up while they livestreamed [it]', and members of the industry she was calling out deemed her actions to be 'debauchery' and 'insulting to everyone'.[47] More pertinently, she was called 'mentally unstable and even deranged, or else why would she have resorted to such self-destructive and outrageous action?'[48]

Smart's work on gendering strategies and Dhanda's work on 'psychologizing dissent', as introduced in Chapter 2, provide some insight into how

[42] Interview with victim support personnel, Lahore, 15 June 2022.

[43] S Holz and A Bano, 'Navigating Respectability in Patriarchal Contexts: Ethical Dilemmas of Women Researchers in Pakistan' (2022) 53(4) International Quarterly for Asian Studies 562.

[44] A Dhanda, 'Psychologising Dissent: Psychiatric Labelling and Social Control' in A Dhanda and A Parashar (eds), *Engendering Law: Essays in Honour of Lotika Sarkar* (Eastern Book Company 2007) 321.

[45] ibid 321, 322.

[46] C Lakkimsetti, 'Stripping Away at Respectability: #MeToo India and the Politics of Dignity' (2021) 33(3) Feminist Formations 303.

[47] ibid 308.

[48] ibid.

and why Reddy was subjectivized in this way. For the most part, it was the tropes of respectability and Reddy's refusal to abide by patriarchal norms that led to gendered narratives and responses which were used to frame her as a 'bad' and/or 'mad' woman by the predominantly male masses. Character allegations that work as gendering strategies through the use of 'psy' labels, for example, insinuate that the victim 'does not know her own mind', and therefore 'her experience has to be reinterpreted' by those in authority or by laypersons.[49] It is through this retelling of her narratives—in a manner that is dismissive of her experience by iterating that it was a product of her 'debauchery' and unsound mind—that she is subjectivized. Activists too, felt that this instance was yet another indication of the 'conspiracy of silence' which keeps women from sharing their experiences of violence.[50]

The use of allegations and labels based on character tropes to silence women is evident through the cases of women I interviewed and discussed above, as well as numerous others. One lawyer I spoke to recalled a case of a woman who had been raped and coerced into marrying her perpetrator. She had filed for a *khula* to annul the marriage on those very grounds:

> Recently there was a case where a girl was raped, and her signature had been forcibly put on a blank piece of paper, and they used that for the *nikkahnama* [marriage contract]. Then what happened—they managed to hide it. The man said that she is crazy for saying this, that she's not in her right mind—that mentally she must have some problem. He said, 'So what if I did sex, I am her husband, it is my right'. But the courts don't see under what conditions she was made the wife. They first raped her, traumatized her, they took her pictures and videos in a naked position and then took her forcibly to another house and made her sign the piece of paper. But what came in the judge's mind was that she was married, and this is her husband. She even said that I do not accept this *nikkah,* but the judge instead told me to talk to my client and convince her to compromise, because the marriage had already been done. I challenged this in the high courts. What kind of life is this for the girl?[51]

Here, it was the victim's 'dissent'—in using legal remedies to escape a coercive and violent marriage—that was seen as 'institutional indiscipline' and

[49] Dhanda (n 44) 323.
[50] A Tambe, 'Reckoning with the Silences of #MeToo' (2018) 44(1) Feminist Studies 197.
[51] Interview with lawyer, Karachi, 19 July 2022.

a 'departure from role stereotypes',[52] requiring a measure of social control through allegations that were used to silence her. The accused first draws on respectability politics by framing the sexual violence inflicted on the woman as justified ('. . . so what if I did sex, I am her husband, it is my right'). Such inflection of dominant societal norms was positioned against the re-telling of the woman's experiences, subjectivizing her through the application of 'psy' labels ('she is crazy . . . she's not in her right mind . . . mentally she must have some problem'). Further, against the backdrop of her 'immoral' character, evidenced by pictures and videos of her 'in a naked position', the resulting effect was that the court felt it pertinent to encourage the victim to compromise for the sake of societal norms because the 'marriage had already been done'. In other words, she was asked to retreat from being an 'active' victim to a 'passive' one, with character allegations being used as a gendering strategy to discredit and silence her.

Vignette 3.3 Momina's story, Karachi

My parents educated me and I became a doctor. It was during my work as a doctor that I met him and got married to him without my parents' permission . . . A few years later, the marriage turned abusive because my husband wanted to have a second wife, and I refused. I was pregnant with his second child at the time. I continued to refuse to give him permission and he continued to beat me. He never gave me any spending money, nor did he even give me clothes or shoes to wear. The woman he wanted to marry was his uncle's daughter, his cousin. When I refused to give him permission, he knew that they wouldn't agree to the second marriage because in Islamic law he cannot bring a second wife without my permission. So, he decided to leave me in the village where I worked, and went and told his family members that I had died during childbirth. His uncle came to my workplace to check whether or not I was still alive. Only after the uncle saw me and refused my husband's proposal for his daughter, then my husband returned home . . . He did not have a job, and the house was running on my salary. I was taking care of my children with that money. But he kept threatening me by saying he would harm the children if I do not give him all my earnings. One day he forced me to go to the bank and tricked me into

[52] Dhanda (n 44) 337.

signing off my savings to him. I kept tolerating all this because I had two young children.

And then, one time, when he returned from a visit to his family, he was very angry and he put petrol over me and lit a match and burnt my body. I have grafting all over my chest. My children were witnesses to this. *Main itna tarap rahi thee* [I was convulsing in pain] and I was looking around the courtyard for something to help and spotted a *ralli* [quilt] so I put it on myself to try and put out the fire. It wasn't until the next morning at 10am that he took me to the closest city for medical treatment . . . I couldn't tell anyone all this was happening. I couldn't even tell my family because my husband would tell me that he would kill me if I tried talking to anyone. I only told my brother a few weeks later, that my husband had burnt me. My brother told me to go to the police, but I couldn't bring myself to lodge a criminal complaint against my husband. Where would I go? My parents would not keep me. I had married him against their wishes.

When people saw the burn marks on me, *us ne bola ke maine apna aap par petrol phenk kar apne jism ko jala dia kyun ke mera koi zehni masla hai* [he told them that I had doused myself in petrol and burnt myself because I have some mental problem] . . . He used to frequently say to my children, 'come on, let's take her to the mental hospital'. He used to say that all the time. When he would go to [the city], he would tell my children on the way, 'Let's drop her off at the mental hospital'. I would tell him, 'I am not "psycho", *mein maar peet khati hoon* [I am a victim of violence]' . . . twenty-one years I lived like this.

Eventually I did file a police complaint a few months ago, because my husband stole all my legal papers. I told police that my identity documents, medical documents, passport, property papers were all stolen by him. I even told them that my husband was abusive. But when they went to ask my husband, he told my children to tell the police that he had never hit me and that I was lying because of a mental problem. This is what I have heard—that my children gave testimony against me.[53]

As per the victim's narrative in Vignette 3.3, the domestic abuse first started as a means of control, when her refusal to give her husband permission to take on a second wife was seen as insubordination. Despite the severe

[53] Name has been changed for anonymity. Interview with victim, Karachi, 12 January 2022 [d] [parenthesis added].

harms perpetrated, including but not limited to burning her, her husband continued to dismiss those harms by stating that she had a 'mental problem'. Upon choosing not to passively agree to his wishes and instead to actively resist them, Momina* was threatened with further violence and framed as being mentally unsound. These strategies were used to silence her, and to coerce her into subsequently retracting her claims and rights. As she herself said, she is not 'psycho', she is a victim of violence.

This testament—of how women resist being subjectivized by character allegations and 'psy' labels as victims of violence—was also touched upon by another victim that I interviewed. Sidra* recalled that when she was about ten years old, her stepfather started physically abusing her. He would hang her upside down and hit her with shoes, pipes, and cable wires.[54] In one instance, she said,

> . . . he would take my clothes off and make me stand outside in the scorching heat. When he took my clothes off, he first slapped me and was threatening to hit me with a rod. Then he made me stand under the sun. I was only wearing a small knicker [panty], and I was there for over thirty minutes. My Nani [grandmother] saw me from outside and came running. She took me and put some clothes on me and put toothpaste all over my face and feet where I had started to get burns . . . When she told my mother, my mother said that it was my fault because I must have not been behaving . . . My destiny is such, that first I was beaten by my [step]father, and then I was beaten by my husband.[55]

As an adult, Sidra* was married off to a man twice her age, who started physically and sexually abusing her when she asked to wait for a few years before having a child. 'I was nineteen; I was a child myself', she said. As a result of the abuse, she got pregnant. Her husband and her in-laws would make her 'sleep in the middle of them in the bed'. Without specifying, she added, 'you can only imagine how I had a child'. When she confided in her mother about the abuse, her mother told her that she 'had always had some mental issue, had always been *paagal* [insane]' and required treatment. To this, Sidra* responded,

[54] Name has been changed for anonymity. Interview with victim, Karachi, 12 January 2022 [b].

[55] ibid [parenthesis added].

> *Maine kaha agar mujhe ilaaj ki zaroorat hai, agar mein paagal hoon, toh aap sab ki wajah se bani hoon. Bachey shuru mein paagal nahi hote. Bacha whiteboard hota hai, jo usko upar lekhein gi bacha waise hi banega. Maine kaha bacha khali glass hota hai, aap us me ganda paani bharein gi to woh glass ganda ho jaye ga* [I told her if I needed treatment, if I am crazy, I have become so because of you all. Children are not crazy at the beginning. Children are like whiteboards, whatever you write on them, that it was they will become. I told her, children are like empty glasses, if you put dirty water in it, the glass will become dirty].[56]

Sidra* too actively resisted the labels applied to her. Here, it appears that when she was abused by her stepfather as a child, it was excused or perhaps justified by others through an assumption that she 'must not have been behaving'. When she was abused by her husband as an adult, she was subjectivized and dismissed by others who alleged that she had 'always had some mental issue'. In both instances, she was silenced through gendered allegations that enabled a retelling of her experiences by others in a manner which associated her with blame or guilt, and/or that dissociated blame or guilt from her perpetrator.

Thiesmeyer's silencing theory of language describes the various ways in which oppressed individuals are silenced from speaking about their experiences of violence.[57] By using Foucault's work on the technologies of power, she argues that silencing works through the strategic manipulation of sociocultural contexts through language, as well as the subjectivities or 'docile bodies'[58] that are produced as a result. Character allegations can similarly be employed to silence women victims of gender-based violence as a means of social control, as 'silencing results from an act of language where language is used in order to enable some kinds of expression and disable others'.[59] Perhaps it is for this reason that victims are preferred to be silent and 'passive' in societal and institutional settings, where withholding their agency suppresses opposition to dominant discourses of respectability. On the other hand, victims who are loud and therefore 'active' are perceived as dissenting, and accordingly need to be managed and silenced from telling their stories. Using character allegations and 'psy' labels as a gendering

[56] ibid.

[57] Thiesmeyer (n 8).

[58] ibid; for an account of 'technologies of power', see M Foucault, *Discipline and Punish: The Birth of the Prison* (A Sheridan tr, 2nd edn, Random House 1977) 135.

[59] Thiesmeyer (n 8) 11.

strategy to dismiss women's claims is one way of doing this, as these labels are employed through language to shape constructions of social reality,[60] positing that victims' narratives are a product of their immorality or unsound mind.[61] And in doing so, the power that language may afford them is withdrawn,[62] while simultaneously providing space for others to use language as a means to shape and narrate the experiences of victims differently.

The prevalent use of character allegations as a gendering strategy to silence victims is therefore also likely to inform the victim's relationship with legal avenues for protection, redress, and justice. In my conversations with women with lived experience of domestic violence, there were a range of ways through which this relationship was negotiated. Amid the silencing techniques discussed above, Pakistani women strategically challenged and resisted their experiences, using the law in various ways as a tool through which to navigate their agency.

'What is justice, really?' Locating agency in negotiations

In line with the discussions above, the legal conceptualization of domestic violence has been regarded as dichotomous, where women are either passive and helpless victims, or agents who live without oppression. Mahoney suggests that this approach leads to law viewing agency as primarily associated with an actor that is autonomous and active, thereby disassociating it from passive victims.[63] Lewis and others argue against this conceptualization, stating:

> What these notions of an abstract person acting with 'agency' neglect, is the lived experience of both victimisation and resistance. Relying on dichotomous frameworks, the law and, indeed, much social scientific thought, is unable to conceive of a victim who also acts with agency.

[60] See PJ Adams, 'Interventions with Men Who Are Violent to Their Partners: Strategies for Early Engagement' (2012) 38 Journal of Marital and Family Therapy 458.

[61] ibid.

[62] AJ Towns and PJ Adams, '"I didn't know whether I was right or wrong or just bewildered": Ambiguity, Responsibility and Silencing Women's Talk of Men's Domestic Violence' (2016) 22(4) Violence Against Women 496, 500.

[63] M Mahoney, 'Victimisation of Oppression? Women's Lives, Violence and Agency' in MA Fineman and R Mykitiuk (eds), *The Public Nature of Private Violence* (Routledge 1994) 59.

> That is, a survivor who resists the abuse, and makes attempts to end her victimisation (either by leaving the relationship or by stopping the violence) but nonetheless, is constrained in the courses of action she can take because of ongoing oppression imposed by a violent partner (violence and/or threats of violence) or by wider socio-economic conditions (childcare responsibilities, job market restrictions, etc).[64]

When research relating to domestic violence focuses largely on outcomes—such as by statistically assessing the number of police reports filed, or by determining the percentage of convictions or favourable responses in courts—the law is seen as 'a monolithic entity imposed upon passive recipients'.[65] In this framing, the accounts and voices of women victims are often lost. Rather, one should assess how women might use the law, 'purposefully and actively, as part of a strategic process of challenge and resistance'.[66] To do so, it is important to question what 'justice' is, or what it may mean for victims of domestic violence in Pakistan.

> No matter whether the woman wants civil or criminal litigation to seek justice [for domestic violence], there are a few things that she would look at. First of all, is like some magic force that can show their abuser that there can be some intervention. Something that says, 'if you do this, I will teach you a lesson'. Then, there is blockage or protection. How they can keep themselves or their children safe, like putting some distance between them and their abuser. And then, of course, is understanding where the law and policy can actually help her. Like how to file a case, how to go to the courts, if he will be punished . . .[67]

Similar to the explanation provided by a member of victim supportpersonnel above, women whom I interviewed spoke of the different ways in which they negotiated their relationship with the law and the legal avenues available to them. In the context of what 'justice' means to them, the three main ideas that women spoke of are broadly categorized as: (1) recognition of harms; (2) protection from harms; and (3) penalization or

[64] R Lewis, RP Dobash, RE Dobash and K Cavanagh, 'Protection, Prevention, Rehabilitation or Justice? Women's Use of the Law to Challenge Domestic Violence' (2000) 7(1) International Review of Victimology 179, 184.
[65] ibid.
[66] ibid; Interview with lawyer, Karachi, 11 August 2022 [a].
[67] Interview with victim support personnel, Lahore, 13 June 2022 [parenthesis added].

prosecution for those harms. An assessment of this is relevant not only because it helps better understand how and why cases relating to domestic violence are found scattered across varying courts and domains of the law, but also because it highlights the agency often denied to women who make different choices when negotiating their wants and needs among prevailing gendered, silencing techniques. It is to avoid the risk of assuming those wants and needs that I foreground the voices of victims in effort to locate and acknowledge their agency in navigating justice mechanisms. This assessment also informs the legal steps that women victims may take in response to the harms they experience, and accordingly helps situate them as complainants in the Pakistani legal system.

'Justice' as recognition of harms

When visiting the district courts in Karachi, I spoke to Reema*, who was waiting for a meeting with her lawyer. She shared that she was pregnant, and that her husband had deserted her and taken on a second wife without informing her. She was in court hoping to send a legal notice to her husband for withdrawing the provision of maintenance costs for her and her child. She said, 'Even when he repeatedly beat me, I never wanted him to go to jail. Even now I do not. I am pregnant with his child, what would I tell my child, that I sent the father to jail? No, never.'[68] Reema* explained that she had asked her husband to return home and support her financially on numerous occasions, but he had not. She had no intention to file a criminal case against him for incidents of domestic violence. Rather, she was hoping that a legal notice for maintenance would act as a threat and convince him to bear expenses relating to her pregnancy. 'I am still his wife, and the court still sees me as his wife', she added.[69]

In my conversation with her, it appeared that Reema* was hoping to use the law for recognition: recognition of her harms, recognition that she was still the man's wife and bearing his child, and recognition that she had certain legal rights that were unfulfilled. Similarly, one lawyer explained that using the law in this way gives women victims of domestic violence 'negotiating power':

68 Name has been changed for anonymity. Interview with victim, Karachi, 4 July 2022.
69 ibid.

> The thing is, we always assess the law by how many cases were taken forward, how many convictions there were, and I think we sometimes miss the agency that women have through the law. I know a lot of women who use the law by saying, 'If you do this, I will take you to court', or 'if you don't stop doing this, I will call the police', and that gives them a bit of negotiation power versus where they don't have those laws. They want to use the law as a threat against husbands, as a way to recognize that what is happening is wrong and it needs to stop. So, they use law as a tool as opposed to actually taking them to court.[70]

This is one example of how women may use the law strategically and 'actively' as a form of resistance.[71] Another lawyer who provides legal aid services for victims of gender-based violence shared a similar sentiment:

> Sometimes, they just want a notice to be sent by the court so that once the husband sees it, he recognizes what he has done and stops doing it, because he knows that she will take a big step if he doesn't. And basically, he enters into a sort of compromise—that if you don't go to the police or the court then I will stop doing this. Here, it is the woman just sending a notice so that he owns up to what he is doing to her, but she does not go ahead with a case.[72]

By navigating their relationship with the law in such ways, women are able to negotiate with their husband or families. What justice looks like for them is not necessarily seeing their perpetrators behind bars, but rather working within their socio-economic conditions, and within the prevalent gendering strategies and sociocultural discourses that inform what the woman may consider to be her duty towards her family, her marriage, or her children. However, using the law in this way also enables her harms to be acknowledged and recognized within those settings, and provides her with some negotiating power to (hopefully) end the ongoing experience of abuse or violence. Similar to what Lewis and others posited, she is a victim who also acts with agency, in that she resists the abuse by using the law to gain bargaining power, while also working within the constraints of possible courses of action by choosing not to go through with formal legal

[70] Interview with lawyer, Karachi, 11 August 2022 [a].
[71] Lewis and others (n 64).
[72] Interview with lawyer, Karachi, 11 August 2022 [b].

remedies. Here, it is the *threat of* rather than the *attempt at* filing criminal or civil cases which assists them in reconciling. The victim's choice in using the law in this manner is as reflective of agency as it is for those who use the law for protection, or those that seek some form of penalization or prosecution for their harms.

'Justice' as protection from harms

Kandiyoti defines patriarchal bargain as the various ways through which 'women strategize within a set of concrete constraints'.[73] This refers to the 'overly monolithic conception of male dominance' through patriarchal structures and respectability politics that need to be deconstructed in order to understand and assess the workings of historical and cultural arrangements between genders.[74] Even working within those constraints or restrictions, one can 'situate agency', wherein something that may seem like a submission could in fact be hiding more subtle strategies of resistance.[75] For some Pakistani women, the way they view and access justice within the constraints of patriarchal norms and institutions may not be to punish the men that have harmed them, but rather to protect themselves. This largely shifts the focus from criminal engagements to civil ones. Yet, what might be seen as a 'patriarchal submission' in avoiding criminal proceedings could in fact be a strategy of resistance which centres the agency of the victim. This may come in the form of women approaching the police for protection (but not for criminal complaints) or by then approaching the civil courts for *khula* [divorce] or custody proceedings. As one lawyer said, this is a way to put some distance between them and their perpetrators, without becoming the 'aggressor' themselves:

> Very often, by the time the women ask for a *khula* [divorce] it's because they are just desperate to get away from the man. They do not necessarily want to pursue a case of domestic violence because they just want to put a distance between them and their husbands. It is protection focused. It comes down to the question of what is

[73] D Kandiyoti, 'Bargaining with Patriarchy' (1988) 2(3) Gender and Society 274.

[74] F Peter, 'Gender and the Foundations of Social Choice: The Role of Situated Agency' (2003) 9(2) Feminist Economics 13, 27.

[75] ibid.

> justice for them? . . . They just want to get away and to not become the aggressor.[76]

An interview with a victim of domestic abuse presents a similar notion, where filing a criminal case was seen as a less appealing option for 'justice' than filing for a *khula*. The patriarchal bargain here was to seek protection over legal rights, particularly given the prevalence of gendering strategies and silencing techniques through, for example, the use of character allegations in legal spaces:

> He was already married. He told me he did not get along with the first wife and that he will divorce her before our marriage. But turns out he has not. When I found out, I confronted him, I was so upset. And when I would question him, he would beat me over and over . . . Now it has been six to seven months since he deserted me. He still has not contacted me, only his lawyer has. I was sent a notice to appear in court, and it said that I should get a medical examination done only then will they speak with me—saying that I'm mentally ill so I need to get some treatment. This was all done just to pressurize me and shame me so that I filed for *khula*. Eventually it worked, they created such circumstance that even I said fine, just leave everything. Even my workplace found out about it because they sent a copy of the notice with these allegations to my job also, that I am mentally disturbed and that I am a 'psycho'. I didn't want to take *khula* because I would have to forfeit my *haq mahr* [financial rights]. They had put a high amount because they didn't give me anything at the time of wedding. But they are forcing me to take *khula* so that they don't have to give me my right.
>
> The court notice for the hearing that they sent to me, nothing is happening. I keep coming and they don't show up, so it's one date over another date, one after the other, I am exhausted. My lawyer told me I could file a domestic violence case, but what good will it do? He already put these allegations on me; it impacted my job also. I asked myself, *mere liye insaaf asal mein hai kya?* [for me, what is justice, really?]. For me, right now, it is to be rid of him. *Buss jaan chorwani hai* [just be rid of him]. That way I can at least protect myself. So, I decided to file a *khula* case so I can give my statement in front of the judge and just get on with my life.[77]

[76] Interview with lawyer, Karachi, 11 August 2022 [a].
[77] Interview with victim, Karachi, 4 August 2022.

In the extract above, a key consideration in the victim's choice to opt for civil remedies over criminal ones related to her husband sending her a court notice, copying her employer, which alleged that she was 'mentally disturbed' and a 'psycho'. As such, in order to 'protect' herself, the best option for her was to simply 'be rid of him' by filing for *khula*, even though that meant forfeiting her financial and legal rights. Similarly, Lewis and others suggest that when women make choices about the extent of intervention that they deem appropriate, such as seeking protection orders or in this case filing for *khula* or divorce, the choice to do so instead of seeking prosecution or sanction is reflective of their agency in relation to their own wants and needs.[78] This is because a major feature of a woman's process in negotiating her options is the 'consequent sense of responsibility for invoking legal intervention in her own and her partner's life'.[79] In the extract above, this is illustrative when the victim asks 'what good will [filing a domestic violence case] do? He already put these allegations on me.'[80] In other words, depending on how she views 'justice', she will have to shoulder the burden of those processes in the same patriarchal institutions she is bargaining with—and she may not be ready to do so.

'Justice' as prosecution for harms

The third way in which victims navigate the law when it comes to domestic violence is by seeking penalization or prosecution for their harms, by going to the police and/or to the courts with an intent to pursue a criminal case. In some ways, this encapsulates both recognition of her harms and protection from those harms, but it goes on to also include reparations for those harms. As reflected during interviews:

> . . . I was near a shrine when the incident happened, when my sister's husband threw acid on me because he wanted to marry me and I kept rejecting him. After he attacked me, I went straight to the police to file a criminal case.[81]

[78] Lewis and others (n 64) 194.
[79] ibid.
[80] Interview with victim, Karachi, 4 August 2022 [parenthesis added].
[81] Interview with victim, Islamabad, 7 June 2022 [d].

> . . . I was divorced from my husband when he did it. I was staying separately and sleeping at my own home. He tied me with rope and raped me . . . I was already divorced, and I thought I was safe. But me and my children will not be safe unless he is in jail so I went to police to issue an FIR complaint.[82]

Particularly when instances of violence are severe, most women 'do not hesitate' when choosing to file a criminal case.[83] As one victim was quoted as saying in a study conducted by the Legal Aid Society in Karachi, 'he needed to be punished—not just through one beating but through a proper court process'.[84] A member of victim support personnel whom I interviewed shared this sentiment, although he clarified that

> most women that I work with want to take criminal action, but in reality they are let down. I would do all the formalities for them, the medico-legal exam, going with them to the police station, but you will find that 80 to 90 per cent of cases relating to physical violence and domestic violence end up in closure at the police stage. In 2022, when a lot of legislation and administrative measures have been taken, even now if I compare to the 1990s to see which hurdles have been taken care of for women, I would say sorry, none.[85]

When women attempt to take legal action, such as by filing a complaint for gender-based violence with the police (or even seeking civil remedies on the basis of that violence), they are seen as implicating the politics of respectability. Here too, gendering strategies and allegations relating to a woman's character or mentality come into play as a means to silence her, reframe her narratives, and ultimately construct her as an unfavourable victim-subject. A powerful quote by an interviewee resonates: 'if she stays quiet, then she can make sure that she is the only one with control over her story.'[86]

In approaching the idea of justice differently, the 'situatedness' of strategic negotiations of agency is in many ways also linked to the politics of

[82] Interview with victim, Islamabad, 7 June 2022 [b].
[83] M Zia, 'Understanding Domestic Violence within the Legal Framework of Pakistan' [2018] Legal Aid Society 26.
[84] ibid 26, 27.
[85] Interview with victim support personnel, Lahore, 13 June 2022.
[86] Interview with victim support personnel, Lahore, 15 June 2022.

silence discussed throughout this chapter,[87] in that these negotiations are often positioned against the repercussions of what may happen if those silences are broken. In taking the initial step of 'going public' by invoking the law, either through law enforcement agents or through the courts, women are then 'condemned'—at police stations, in the courts, and even in wider society—when they 'attempt to assert their agency in using the law rather than remaining passive recipients of the law.'[88]

Conclusion

A common question posed during my interviews with women victims of domestic violence was whether I thought that their asks—from family, from friends, from institutional actors, and from society—were 'too much'. Women often questioned whether they had 'overstepped' in asking their husbands or families for certain rights or liberties, or even in simply asking for comfort. They wondered whether those asks, those 'transgressions' from the politics of respectability, or from the duties and expectations of being a woman in Pakistan, were unreasonable.

Vignette 3.4 Hira's story, Islamabad

I was married to my husband for five years, and I have two daughters from that marriage. He died when my daughters were two and four years old. When he passed, my family wanted to bring me home to my parents, but my mother-in-law said that she wants me to stay and get married to my husband's brother. His brother was already married and he had children also, so that means I would be the second wife. I think they wanted me to marry him so that they could ensure all the property I inherited from my husband remained in the family. I initially denied but they kept pressurizing me. The first wife was also not very happy about this arrangement but due to pressure, we did the *nikkah*. Even after that, he would stay with his first wife, and I would stay with my mother-in-law. We fought for three months after the wedding, every day.

[87] R Masika and S Bailur, 'Negotiating Women's Agency through ICTs: A Comparative Study of Uganda and India' (2015) 19(1) Gender, Technology and Development 43, 63.
[88] Lewis and others (n 64) 198.

The day it happened, I was asleep alone in my bed. My one daughter was sleeping with her aunt and the other was sleeping with her grandmother, so I was alone. And I was feeling very anxious, so I asked my new husband to come and sleep in my room. I kept requesting and he kept saying no. He would tell me to stay quiet, that I've lost my mind. His first wife also told me to stay in my limits. He even said that if I didn't shut up then he would seal my mouth shut. That night I was awake till midnight *kyunke mera dil bohot ghabra raha tha* [because my heart was feeling anxious], and when I slept, acid was thrown on me.

I remember I screamed so much. My clothes all got burnt and fell off. My bed also got burnt. I kept asking for something cold to be thrown on me but there was no water, nothing. No one would take me to the hospital either. In the morning, the neighbours came and took me to the small hospital nearby. Everyone kept saying, '*keh yeh toh khatam ho chuki hai, iske liye hum kuch nahi kar sakte* [that she has finished, there is nothing we can do]'. Then I was taken to the bigger hospital. You know, even the car people would refuse to transport me—they kept saying that there was too much smell coming from me and they can't take me in their car. But I am also a human and humans are the ones who burnt me. They had to wrap me up completely just to take me to the city. Even there, I heard people say, 'why did you bring a dead body here'.

At that point, every time I got conscious, I would think to myself, please just give me an injection of poison because I do not want to live. What was my fault? That my husband died? That I compromised and agreed to get married to his brother? I did everything they wanted me to, everything that was expected of me, so then why did they do this? Just because I asked my new husband for a bit of comfort? Was that too much to ask? Did I overstep?[89]

The questions that Hira* posed in Vignette 3.4 stayed with me, as they felt relevant not only to women's experiences with family members, but also to their interactions with police, lawyers, and the courts when navigating the justice system. Is recognition as a victim too much to ask? Is seeking protection from violence too much to ask? Is pursuing reparations for the harms inflicted too much to ask? And ultimately, is a path to justice and acknowledgement of their legal rights too much to ask?

[89] Name has been changed for anonymity. Interview with victim, Islamabad, 8 June 2022 [c].

Literature suggests that it is common for perpetrators of domestic violence to ensure a victim's silence through strategies that include threats to harm her and her children, threats that she will be disbelieved through character assassinations, and in some cases, threats that she will be deemed as mentally ill.[90] To counter the institutional and societal silencing of victims of domestic violence in Pakistan, this chapter foregrounded the stories and narratives of women. It outlined important contributions to the victim–survivor paradox, while examining how labels can shape subjects and subjectivity. The chapter connects these ideas to gendered strategies and character allegations, analysing how perceptions relating to silent, 'passive' victims and loud, 'active' victims are encapsulated among the politics of respectability. I argued that this may similarly inform the silencing techniques used to manage 'dissenting' women, constructing them as particular kinds of victim-subjects that are unfavourable and not to be heard. Among these silencing techniques, I explored how Pakistani women negotiate their relationship with the law by considering what 'justice' means for them, thereby also situating them as complainants within the legal system.

In subsequent chapters, the construction of victim-subjects of domestic violence is explored through a progressive mapping of women's interactions with the police, lawyers and legal actors, and ultimately the courts. This analysis demonstrates how character allegations and gendering strategies can mould women's stories and narratives at each stage of the legal system. As one victim said: 'it is so hard for women in the courts. The only thing I learned through this process was that no matter how terrible the men are, they will always say that the woman is wrong.'[91]

[90] L Laing, 'Secondary Victimisation: Domestic Violence Survivors Navigating Family Law Systems' (2017) 23(11) Violence Against Women 1314, 1322.

[91] Interview with victim, Islamabad, 8 June 2022 [a].

4
Policing victim-subjects: Gatekeeping approaches

> *Doli kaddan mapey, ty manji kaddan sohrey*
> [A woman should leave her parents' home at marriage, and her in-laws' after death][1]

Introduction

Honkatukia and Keskin's analysis of the 'formal institutional' dimension as an arena for the social control of women includes law enforcement as a site where that control could be leveraged and navigated.[2] As discussed in Chapter 2, institutions such as the police may adopt a functional purpose in facilitating the sanctity of the private sphere as a means to serve the State's gendered, nationalist discourse.[3] As such, when women are seen as 'dissenting' by approaching police stations as victims of domestic violence, members of groups which enact 'formal institutional' control must uphold their duty to maintain the family structure. As one police officer noted during an interview, '*hum ghar begharna nahi chahte, hum ghar bachana chahte hain* [we do not want to break the family home, we want to save it]'.[4] The idea that police personnel have a duty to protect the family structure—as opposed to protecting women as victims of violence—was repeated on numerous occasions during fieldwork and is illustrated in Vignette 4.1. This presents a link to feminist critiques of policing which draw a distinction

[1] A Punjabi proverb. See M Shahbaz, *Saday Akhaan [Our Proverbs]* (Aziz Book Depot 2004) 324.
[2] P Honkatukia and S Keskinen, 'The Social Control of Young Women's Clothing and Bodies: A Perspective of Differences on Racialization and Sexualization' (2018) 18(1) Ethnicities 142.
[3] See A McClintock, 'Family Feuds: Gender, Nationalism and the Family' (1993) 44 Feminist Review 61, 63.
[4] Interview with police, Karachi, 2 August 2022 [a].

Domestic Violence in Pakistan. Daanika Kamal, Oxford University Press. © Daanika Kamal 2025.
DOI: 10.1093/9780198953470.003.0004

between the benevolent paternalism of police officials who are 'rescuing' victims and the ways in which State violence may operate to protect gendered normativities, thereby harming victims through those same policing structures.[5]

Vignette 4.1 Fieldwork diary, 2 August 2022, Karachi

I spent the first half of the day at the police administrative offices adjoining the main police station in district Central. I was now at the Women and Child Unit located ten minutes away by car. There was a cat following us from the moment we stepped out of the vehicle—an orange and white-striped tabby who looked as though she had recently given birth. Halfway up the stairs, when I pointed the cat out to the police officer I was accompanying, she smiled and said that the station was for all women and children, (female) cats and kittens included.

I was given a tour of the Unit, which included offices for initial reporting of complaints, rooms for investigating officers, a desk for evidence sampling, and a lock-up for women accused of committing crimes. On the first floor, I was shown a room with light blue walls, dark blue carpeting, and pink Disney curtains. There was a small single bed placed in the middle of the room, a wardrobe full of toys propped against one wall, and some activity games scattered across the floor. This room doubled up as a day care for women police officers who bring their children to work and a safe space for the children of women awaiting trial in the lock-up.

When I peeked into the lock-up, there was a girl sitting in the corner with her face buried in her knees. The police officer accompanying me mentioned that the girl, whose age was disputed, had run away and gotten married to a twenty-year-old boy from her neighbourhood whom she liked, in order to escape the domestic abuse she experienced at home. As per the girl's testimony, she was eighteen years old and had been refusing a marriage proposal set up by her parents, due to which her father and brother had beaten her repeatedly, and she was worried that if she remained at home then they would forcibly get her married off to a man almost three times her age. On the other hand, her family claimed that she was a fourteen-year-old minor and not mentally sound, and that the boy

[5] See for example, AY Davis, G Dent, ER Meiners and BE Richie (eds) *Abolition. Feminism. Now* (Haymarket Books 2022).

she was found with had exploited these vulnerabilities and kidnapped her. The girl refused to go back to her parents' house and her parents refused to let her stay with her husband, unwilling to accept the marriage as valid. As such, the police thought it was best to hold her in the station's lock-up while her case was pending in the courts.

A second police officer who had joined us while we were loitering added that this Unit gets a lot of similar cases. In her opinion, it was the influence of all the *chamak dhamak* [glitter, sparkle] that young girls see in Bollywood films that encourages them to run away and 'contract love marriages', after which 'their poor parents come all destitute and looking for them'. She added that these girls do not know what is best for them and so 'we [the police] have to help them find their way'. It was suggested that the police have a duty to protect, and the best protection for a girl is her family. In response, I questioned whether women can be unsafe within their own homes too, as the girl in lock-up had testified to being a victim of domestic abuse. The police officer shrugged and said, '*Aap is ki baaton mein na ayein, is ke waldein khud kehte hain ke yeh nafsiyati tor peh sahi nahi hai. Isko hifazat ki zaroorat hai, pyaar shaar ki nahi. Kabhi kabhi inko khud se hi bachana parta hai* [Don't get influenced by what she says; her own parents say that she is not mentally sound. She needs protection, not this love stuff. Sometimes we need to save her from herself]'.[6]

Some scholars have argued that the current police structure of Pakistan, having been derived from the criminal justice system developed by the British in Colonial India, follows a similar ideology to the one inherited in 1861.[7] The law enforcement institution was initially designed to 'create an instrument in the hands of the colonial-government for keeping the natives on a tight leash, not a politically neutral outfit for fair and just enforcement of law'.[8] While numerous attempts have been made to transform the institution into a more 'public-friendly' agency,[9] such as through the recent introduction of women and children-specific police units in some districts,

[6] Fieldwork diary, 2 August 2022, Karachi.

[7] See for example Fasihuddin, 'Police and Policing in Pakistan' (2010) 2(3) Pakistan Journal of Criminology 131.

[8] MS Suddle, 'Reforming Pakistan Police: An Overview' (2003) United Nations Asia 94.

[9] QK Mahmood, I Ahmad and MH Bhutta, 'Vigilantism and the Police: Assessing the Perception of Pakistani Women about the Gender-Related Ineffectiveness of the Police and the Preference for Vigilante Acts in Lahore' (2013) 5(1) Pakistan Journal of Criminology 43.

there remains a large trust deficit in the *thaana* [police station] and its accompanying *thaana* culture, particularly for women. For most, this distrust is sparked by the controlling and gatekeeping approaches often employed by police officers in cases of gender-based violence and domestic abuse:

> The general public considers the current police system in Pakistan to be grossly inefficient, unskilled, and corrupt. The police here tend to be predominantly male, underpaid, understaffed, and undertrained. Domestic violence, including the honour killing of girls and women, is often ignored by police officers and treated as a matter to be resolved within the family or community. Even when women are seriously injured by husbands or families, the police discourage from registering complaints.[10]

Despite the existence of provincial domestic violence legislations, as outlined in Chapter 1, these are rarely used by police officials to file cases. On the few occasions where cases are registered, the 'hurt offences' under Pakistan's Penal Code continue to be predominantly adopted in complaints relating to physical violence against women in domestic settings.[11] In doing so, when victims approach the police, they are often told to either sort out the matter privately and internally (that is, within the family), or told that their cases cannot be filed because the high threshold of 'hurt offences' is difficult to meet:

> The first issue that victims of domestic violence face is that the police usually do not file a complaint. They say that this is a family matter, sort it out internally. Until some bone has broken or there is blood flowing from their heads, they won't register a case. Even though these 'lesser' injuries still fall under the penal code sections and the domestic violence law, the police do not lodge these complaints because they consider it a family issue. They tell her, 'This is not the way, go speak to your parents or your husband and in-laws and reconcile'. They will not look at

[10] M Rashid, 'Giving Men Choices: A Rozan Project with the Police Force in Pakistan' in A Grieg (ed) *Partners in Change: Working with Men to End Gender-Based Violence* (INSTRAW 2002) 68.

[11] As discussed in Chapter 1, 'Hurt offences' is an umbrella term referring to Section 332 – Section 337 of the Pakistan Penal Code 1860 (PPC). As defined in s332 of the PPC: 'whoever causes pain, harm, disease, infianity or injury to any person or impairs, disables [disfigures, defaces] or dismembers any organ of the body or part thereof of any person without causing his death, is said to cause hurt'. Accordingly, s 333 to s 337 of the PPC regulate different 'kinds' of hurt offences, as per nature and gravity of harm.

> the issue as a dispute, let alone a crime. Because in our culture if a man is beating or physically torturing his wife, that is not considered to fall under violence.[12]

This chapter accordingly explores the gatekeeping approaches adopted by the police when handling domestic violence complaints from women. Based on an assessment of how police officials perceive their 'duty' to uphold the State-endorsed sanctity of the family structure, I outline some of the ways in which paternalistic attitudes in policing construct the subjectivities of victim-subjects; for example, through character allegations that minimize the harm suffered by women, and the use of compromise as a tool to mask victims' narratives as 'public secrets'. This chapter also provides an overview of police complaint procedures, investigation methods, and evidential practices which helps chart out whether and how women's cases progress from *thaanas* to either the family courts or the criminal courts. In doing so, I also attempt to locate the women who 'disappear' during this process, demonstrating that it is not only the harmful practices employed by police officers that subjectivize victims based on gendered discourses, but also the broader institutional gender biases that marginalize their stories and consequently limit their access to justice.

'We need to save her from herself:' Paternalistic attitudes in policing

Women have historically been regarded as weak and in need of protection, either by a paternalistic State or a male guardian.[13] In instances where that protection is displaced, one may assist the other to help transition it back to where it 'rightfully' belongs. Kapur writes, 'in the colonial relationship, gender essentialism was also conflated with cultural or civilisational backwardness, where the treatment of women was used in part as a justification for colonial intervention and civilising mission'.[14] As we witness South Asian gender essentialism today, Kapur finds that in the name of protecting women's rights, law enforcement policies are invariably based on

[12] Phone interview with lawyer, 1 July 2022, Peshawar.
[13] R Kapur, 'Human Rights in the 21st Century: Take a Walk on the Dark Side' (2006) 28 Sydney Law Review 665.
[14] ibid 678.

assumptions that perceive women as infantile and incapable of making their own decisions.[15] The paternalistic and protectionist approach adopted by police officers towards victims of domestic violence, for example, can then be justified by how they understand their 'duty' towards the State's management of gender and sexuality. And in doing so, they use intervention strategies which reinforce gendered discourse, ideals, and subjectivities.

Paternalistic approaches in policing rest on the trope that women require guidance and protection, even from themselves, and are therefore 'not accorded autonomy of self-governance or self-direction'.[16] The idea that 'we [the police] need to save her [the victim] from herself'[17] similarly demonstrates the paternalistic notions through which victims' narratives are perceived and marginalized in police settings. Similarly, one lawyer recalled a recent experience when trying to register a domestic violence case in Lahore.

Vignette 4.2 Extract from interview with lawyer, June 2022, Lahore

Just last week I was at the police station—so, let me give you some background of this case. My client, her husband, is violent towards her. It is a twenty-five-year marriage. Her father-in-law, so the children's grandfather, had been sexually molesting two of my client's daughters from the age of four. They are now over eighteen years old . . . Like, he would make them lie down on top of him and they could feel a hard-on, and he would make them open their legs. They said the only reason penetration didn't happen is because they were wearing underwear. The girls hadn't spoken to anyone about this till recently. They told their mother, and she told her husband, their father.

. . . The father was first in denial and then he started saying, *'toh kya hua itni bari baat nahi hai rape toh nahi kiya na* [so what, it's not that big a deal it is not like he raped them]'. . . The final conclusion he arrived at was that a faith healer told him that someone has done *kaala jaadu* [black magic] on the girls which affected their mentality and that is why they were falsely thinking that the grandfather had been molesting them. The daughters are

[15] ibid 769.
[16] S Dev and V Kamath, 'Gender Justice and Women Empowerment: Legal Measures in India' (2016) 41(2) Journal of Sharma 140.
[17] See Vignette 4.1.

of course very triggered by the grandfather, and the daughters and the father never directly communicated about this, it was all through the mother. So, all his frustrations he was taking out on the mother too—he threatened to kill the daughters . . . he fractured my client's leg, strangled her. She had audio recordings too. With all this my client went to the police and they refused to file a case and told her to come back the next day. This was after my client had already fled to another city with her daughters because she felt their lives were in danger. So I spoke to the police myself and told them, 'look, she doesn't want to face her husband, but she needs the case for domestic violence to be filed so she will come to the police station for that'.

Some of the things that he [the police officer] said to her, '*keh 25 saal ki shaadi hai, yeh toh mamooli baat hai, yeh toh hota rehta hai, aap 25 saal ki shaadi na chorein bus un ko aik aur mauka de dein* [that it is a twenty-five-year marriage, this is something so trivial, things like this happen, don't leave a twenty-five-year marriage, just give him another chance]'. This is not his job. His job is to register the multitude of offences at play here—fracture, strangulation—it is not his job to give her a lesson on morality or relationships. And then the next day when we went back to the station, he had the guts—while my client is sitting in his office—her husband just walks in! And they [police officers] pressurized her for an hour to reconcile with him.

In front of the police, the husband said, 'Yes, I hit her but I am not an animal, *idhar toh log apne biwion pe tail gera dete hain, un pe aag laga dete hain, maine toh sirf tumhara*— [here, people throw oil on their wives and set them on fire, I have just—]': these were literally his words. This is the kind of discourse; it was an extremely harrowing experience . . . Then the police also pressurized me to leave the room. My client protested and said that she doesn't want her lawyer to leave, but the police said, 'Please, two minutes, let them [husband and wife] talk alone, it is such a small thing it can be easily resolved, don't worry we will supervise'. After twenty minutes I finally went back inside and I even heard the police say to her, '*Aisee cheezain jitne police aur vakeelon se chupayi jayein utna behtar ho ga, mein aap ko personal experience se bata raha hoon* [the more these sorts of things are hidden from the police and lawyers, the better it is. I am telling you from personal experience]'.[18]

[18] Interview with lawyer, Lahore, 13 June 2022 [b]. Parentheses added.

The extract in Vignette 2.2 highlights several themes that reflect the paternalistic gendering strategies used by police officers to subjectivize victims of domestic violence and marginalize their narratives: first, by minimizing the harm caused ('. . . this is something so trivial'); second, by encouraging compromise and reconciliation ('. . . let them talk alone, we will supervise'); and third, by framing their stories as secrets (. . . the more these sorts of things are hidden . . . the better it is').

Minimizing harms

The criminal justice system in Pakistan and elsewhere has continuously failed to recognize the harms perpetrated against women in the private sphere as crimes.[19] Through her research in Australia, Douglas outlines two ways in which law enforcement agents minimize the harms related to domestic violence in police settings.[20] The first is the unwillingness or refusal of police officers to prosecute the crime, or the charging of a less serious offence than the one warranted. During fieldwork in Pakistan, a similar approach was highlighted in interviews, where the majority of complaints relating to domestic violence were not registered and therefore do not make it to trial.[21] Further, in addition to non-prosecution, it was not necessarily charging with lesser crimes but rather simply giving a 'warning' to the perpetrator that was seen to suffice:

> The thing is, our police mindset, we see so much violence in general—I am not justifying anything—but the issue is that *chotay motay thappar jaise* [small slaps and small things like this] are not even considered to be violence. And then again there are multiple factors. For you a slap might be a big thing but for the policeman it is nothing, *matlab sar toh nahi phata* [it's not like the head exploded]. So, they do not see an offence, and the most they can think is to give some warning to the man or ask for an undertaking or affidavit.[22]

[19] See J Stubbs, 'Domestic Violence and Women's Safety: Feminist Challenges to Restorative Justice' in H Strang and J Braithwaite (eds) *Restorative Justice and Family Violence* (Cambridge University Press 2002) 52.

[20] H Douglas, 'The Criminal Law's Response to Domestic Violence: What's Going On?' (2008) 30(3) Sydney Law Review 447.

[21] Interview with police, Karachi 2 August 2022 [c].

[22] ibid. An undertaking or an affidavit refers to a statement signed by the accused that he will not subject the victim to such acts in the future.

One observation I made while visiting police stations was that all acts of violence against women, including but not limited to physical violence, sexual assault and rape, were broadly categorized under 'lady harassment issues'[23] by police officials when speaking to me, and to one another. Blanketing crimes of violence against women under the umbrella of 'harassment', which is legally and in everyday language considered a 'minor' crime, is one way to downplay the level of harm women experience. Similarly, while the reference of 'lesser' harms given in the quote above was that of slaps, it is pertinent to note that, as seen in Vignette 4.2, even bone fractures and strangulations were considered minor due to the familial nature of the relationship between the parties. Just as the father minimized his daughters' sexual assault harms ('so what, it's not that big a deal, it is not like he raped them') and his wife's physical assault harms ('here people throw oil on their wives and set them on fire, I have just—'), police officers used terms such as 'trivial' and 'small' to frame the issue as one that can be 'easily resolved'.

This brings us to the second way in which police personnel minimize harms. Douglas considers this as occurring through negotiations.[24] She provides examples of police officers and prosecutors negotiating with defendants to accept a plea to one charge in exchange for the withdrawal of other charges. In Pakistan, however, this may work differently, as the target of negotiations is not necessarily just the accused but also the victim. When coupled with paternalistic attitudes in policing, these negotiations focus more on the withdrawal or non-issuance of complaints than on plea bargains. As one police officer stated:

> The amount of violence is irrelevant. Doesn't matter whether it was a slap or a blow with a brick; with such husband–wife issues, an FIR is not warranted. *Aakhir agar hum FIR ki taraf gaye toh jo ghar tootne ja raha hai woh waqai mein toot jaye ga* [In the end, if we take it towards an FIR then the house that is already breaking will definitely break]. So we try to save the marriage, we have to save the family. We explain matters to them, help them understand these are *small issues* that can be resolved.[25]

[23] Interview with police, Karachi, 2 August 2022 [a]; Interview with police, Karachi, 2 August 2022 [c].

[24] Douglas (n 20) 451.

[25] Interview with police, Karachi, 2 August 2022 [a] [emphasis added]. The FIR (first information report) is a written document prepared by the police based on information about the commission of a cognizable offence. Examples of FIRs consulted during this research include: FIR 05/22, Karachi West; FIR 13/22, Karachi Central; FIR 16028/21, Gilgit; FIR 232/21,

In some cases, the harm is not just minimized but may be eradicated altogether, which in turn helps justify the non-issuance of complaints. This is done by using gendered allegations that subjectivize the complainant as a 'mad' woman, by suggesting that the harm is 'imagined' or by insinuating that it is a result of her mental state. In Vignette 4.2, for example, 'the final conclusion that he [the father] arrived at was that a faith healer told him that someone had done *kaala jaadu* [black magic] on the girls which affected their mentality and that is why they were falsely thinking that the grandfather had been molesting them'.[26] Similarly, when speaking of a woman who had recently approached the police to file a case of domestic violence, a police officer at the Women and Child Unit to whom I spoke said that she did not feel the need to investigate the case because 'that woman was acting so strange, *bilkul jaise khud se baahir* [as though completely outside of her own body]; we looked at her and thought there was some big mental issue'.[27]

In other cases, the victim's harm may be eradicated by framing it as self-inflicted. During an interview, a victim of acid crime recounted her experience with the police. She had been attacked with acid by her sister's husband, who had proposed to her on numerous occasions. She was eighteen years old at the time, and profusely rejected his advances. Soon after, he threw acid on her near a public shrine. When she went to file a case:

> The police were asking very strange questions, kept asking if I had an affair with him. I was young so they assumed there was some 'scene'—even though I was around eighteen then and he must have been close to forty. They refused to file the case, they kept saying 'we found no evidence' and 'we couldn't find him', such delaying tactics. Even when I went through the court and they were directed to file a case and arrest him, they didn't. They just said they never got the notification from the court. They kept pushing me to compromise. I even told them that there were CCTV cameras where the incident happened, but the investigating officer didn't bother. He just told everyone at the station that I was the one who wanted to marry my sister's husband and he refused,

Ahmad Nagar; FIR 242/20, Islamabad; FIR 266/22, Karachi West; FIR 322/22, Karachi West; FIR 338/22 Karachi Central; and FIR 412/22, Karachi West.

[26] As reproduced in Vignette 4.2; Interview with lawyer, 13 June 2022 [b], Lahore.
[27] Interview with police, Karachi, 2 August 2022 [a].

> so in anger and depression I went mad and threw acid on myself. I hated coming to the station, they all looked at me like I was a dirty woman.[28]

In this narrative, the victim was subjectivized in two ways through narratives that were mediated along gendered lines: first, by insinuating that she was of 'bad' character ('they kept asking if I had an affair with him'); second, by claiming that the victim 'went mad' and threw acid on herself. These allegations were such that she felt she was being looked at as a 'dirty woman' within police premises. By using character allegations that frame the harm as trivial, or self-inflicted due to 'madness' or a figment of one's imagination, it is easier for police officers to refrain from filing cases. Instead, the complainant is either told that her harm is insignificant (or not significant enough to warrant police action), or subjectivized by the police in a way which discredits her narratives. Through such gendering practices, these framings pave the way for the idea that the issues women bring to the police are minor and do not require the issuance of complaints, and therefore 'can be sorted out through counselling'.[29]

Navigating 'duties' through compromise

In Pakistan, police officers consider it their 'duty'[30] to encourage counselling and reconciliation in attempt to reach a compromise between the parties. Doing so is seen to be an 'out-of-the-box approach to help the woman so she can find some peace';[31] however, it is unclear whether this is indeed the kind of help the complainant is seeking. For example, in Vignette 4.2, a lawyer narrated an instance where the police called the complainant's husband to the station to 'supervise' a reconciliation between the two parties without informing the complainant of this, and therefore without her consent. This was done despite the woman informing the police that she was not comfortable meeting her husband, that she had been threatened by him, and that she was fearful of him. When efforts at reconciliation and compromise are understood as 'duties' of law enforcement agents, the consent of complainants is considered irrelevant. One reason provided for

[28] Interview with victim, Islamabad, 7 June 2022 [d].
[29] Interview with police, Karachi, 2 August 2022 [a].
[30] '*Compromise karwana hamara farz hai, nahi?* [Getting a compromise [done] is our duty, no?]' Interview with police, Karachi 2 August 2022 [b].
[31] Interview with police, Karachi, 2 August 2022 [b].

this was because women are perceived as 'emotional' and subjectivized as unable to assess their own best interests. The subtleties in these ideas are similar to assumptions associated with the 'female psyche', as discussed in Chapter 2. Comparably, here too she is constructed as a victim-subject in a way that denies her agency:

> They are emotional when they come, they don't know what's best for them. Sometimes they say that they do not want to compromise and do not want to see the husband so we need to explain to them that *is me in ka bhala hai* [it is for their own benefit].[32]

The paternalistic duty to protect the family system is enshrined in Pakistani society. As Hassan states, a woman who approaches the police as a victim of domestic violence is stigmatized as a 'runaway woman', in a culture where raising her voice and 'saying no' to violence is considered far more deviant than the commission of a crime.[33] In short, she is perceived as a 'bad' woman in need of management. Similarly, the focus on culture—stemming from the State's nationalist discourse—informing the 'duties' of law enforcement actors and legal practitioners was reiterated during interviews:

> When they [complainants] go to the police for a family issue, the police prefer to protect the family and not let it break so they always go for reconciliation. We have a certain culture, we cannot expect the police and courts to turn a blind eye to that.[34]
>
> . . . Police and lawyers are always on the same page about one thing: keep the family intact. This is our culture, it is our duty to protect it. We always encourage that she [the complainant] does not file anything with the police so that she doesn't make the decision to break her house and then regret it.[35]

The duty to protect the family and culture extends even in cases of deceased victims where the victim's family claims she was murdered as a result of domestic violence and the victim's husband or in-laws claim that she died by suicide. While investigation is warranted for all heinous

[32] Interview with police, Karachi, 2 August 2022 [a].

[33] SM Hassan, 'Problems Faced by Women in Police Stations: Need for Police Reforms in Pakistan' (2015) 7(1) Pakistan Journal of Criminology 95.

[34] Interview with lawyer, Karachi, 4 July 2022.

[35] Interview with lawyer, Karachi, 5 January 2022 [a].

crimes, police 'typically let such cases slide'[36] and offer compromise as a way to close the complaint. This is done despite the law granting police officers the right to investigate and conduct a post-mortem examination if the cause of death is suspicious or doubted, even if the husband, as the victim's legal guardian, refuses to sign off on it.[37] A high-ranking police officer whom I interviewed in Karachi felt that choosing compromise over prosecution in such cases was an attempt to reduce the workload of police officers. He said:

> The thing is, if some case is registered then it is a lot of paperwork as well. We are under-resourced, understaffed, and you don't want to register multiple cases where you end up having more paperwork for yourself... More than anything else, how things work here is *bhai hum chutkara kaise pa sakte hain in parents se, koi compromise karwao* [brother, how can we free ourselves from these parents, get some compromise done]. Even if the family backs off, police can technically lodge an FIR through the State, but usually police are so overburdened that they do not bother to pursue it.[38]

Another police officer, however, felt that compromises were a hassle-free way to 'be in peace', particularly if the case was brought to the police's attention after the deceased had been buried:

> Sometimes we have cases where the woman commits suicide, but her family comes to us and says that the husband used to be violent with her and they think that this was a murder case. But in those cases, we have to be careful. Because if we register an FIR, it is a very long process having to exhume the body for medical checks, so we try to explain to the family that this is a difficult process. And we cannot desecrate a grave just because they say so, meaning it's not Islamic and not part of our culture also. Their daughter is already gone, why get into all this hassle?

[36] Interview with police, Karachi, 2 August 2022 [c].

[37] See JJ Nasir, *Guardianship in Relation to Marriage in His Book, The Status of Women under Islamic Law and under Modern Islamic Legislation* (Graham and Trotman 1994). This is despite a Supreme Court judgement in *Shaukat Hussain v the State* [2022] SCMR 1358, which states that in cases where wives have died in their husband's homes, 'a heavy onus is cast upon the latter to satisfactorily explain the circumstances' leading to the death. Also see *Saeed Khan v The State* [2015] SCMR 710.

[38] Interview with police, Karachi, 2 August 2022 [c].

Behtar hai sulah kar ke sukoon mein rahein [better to compromise and be in peace].[39]

Because of the influence that culture has on the decisions of police officials, they may refrain from conducting even murder investigations due to societal pressures. This could come in the form of the accused's family members, or members of the community approaching police officials and requesting them to 'do compromise' because, in the words of one police officer, 'the girl is [mentally] unwell, or she had some illicit affair and then committed suicide and it is a matter of family honour so better to let it go'.[40] Constructing the subjectivities of women victims through such gendered allegations means that 'the society steps in for negotiations, and in 90 per cent of [domestic violence] cases, the *challan* [police complaint or First Information Report] doesn't happen or gets cancelled because the case reaches a compromise and doesn't get to the trial court'.[41] As such, the gendered narratives employed to construct the victim-subject assist the police in negotiating how they understand and consequently act upon their paternalistic duties towards protecting the family structure and sanctity of the private sphere. And policing through a focus on compromise-based approaches can assist in ensuring that private truths remain hidden away as public secrets.

Private truths and public secrets

In her examination of rape trials in India, Baxi considers compromises to be an exposition of secrecy, or in other words, a 'public secret'.[42] In shifting the legal and political terrain, compromises can be seen as shielding the secrecy of familial violence from exposure. Drawing on Taussig, Baxi sees secrecy as 'indispensable to the operation of power rather than as an abuse of power'.[43] Compromises allow for the displacement of stories by positioning them as public secrets, with the concealment of their revelation performing

[39] Interview with police, Karachi, 2 August 2022 [b]. Also see *Yar Muhammad v The State* [2017] PCrLJ 694.
[40] Interview with police, Islamabad, 7 June 2022.
[41] Interview with police, Karachi, 2 August 2022 [c].
[42] P Baxi, 'Justice Is a Secret: Compromise in Rape Trials' (2010) 44(3) Contributions to Indian Sociology 207.
[43] M Taussig, *Defacement: Public Secrecy and the Labour of the Negative* (Stanford University Press 1999) 2.

a 'social justice' that is centred on the 're-insertion of the female subject in the structure of alliance'.[44] Baxi explains these structures of alliance as the marital or familial relations where social order is restored. That is, 'the legal event must be effaced, and the marriage protected from full disclosure of the events'.[45] The consensus on what constitutes social justice is then premised on male-defined notions of honour, and the duty of women in upholding that honour by foregoing their complaints and re-inserting themselves as subjects of familial and communitarian normativities. In other words, she, as a victim, should 'find her way back':

> Mostly there is more to the story. We'll find out from the husband that the wife was having an affair, he saw some messages on her phone and she was talking to some other guy, *aur hote bhi hain, yeh nahi ke mard jhoot bol raha hai* [and this can very much be the case, it's not like the men are lying]. Sometimes there is something else wrong with the woman. Either way, we need to help her find her way back.[46]

If compromises are a way to mask private truths as public secrets, could it then be said that subjectivizing victims through character allegations and gendering strategies plays a similar function? That is, to perform a kind of 'social justice'? Recapping instances from extracts and quotes from fieldwork and interviews reflect ideas that women are either lying or attempting to mislead police officers by bringing forth fabricated stories in lieu of their own misdeeds—either as 'bad' women having illicit relationships with strange men, or as 'mad' women who indicate 'some big mental issue' by acting strange and 'as if outside their own bodies'. As discussed in Vignette 4.1, when referring to the girl in lock-up, I was told by a police officer not to be influenced by her narrative because she was 'not mentally sound'. This was in addition to an assertion that young girls get influenced by Bollywood films and run away to 'contract love marriages'. Similarly, in the extract above, women complainants were subjectivized as being of immoral character based on assumptions that she was 'having an affair' or 'taking to some other guy'. And in Vignette 4.2, women's accounts of molestation within the family were considered a result of black magic which

[44] Baxi (n 42) 208.
[45] ibid. Also see, P Baxi, *Public Secrets of Law: Rape Trials in India* (Oxford University Press 2013) 191.
[46] Interview with police, Karachi, 2 August 2022 [a].

affected their mentality and consequently their recollections of abuse. Relatedly, not investigating allegations of murder allows the alternative explanation of suicide—due to the victim's mental health issues—to take centre stage. These examples and ideas serve to alter the basis of women's complaints, by framing them as products of their own bodies and minds; either as imaginary tales to detract from immoral activities, or as manifestations of mental illness. As such, while compromises may serve to conceal revelations of private truths, using character tropes and 'psy' labels based on gendered discourse to subjectivize women victims may change the very foundation of those revelations.

Comparatively, while compromises are often used as a response to cases of domestic violence, they are also seen as justifications for not filing cases and complaints. When speaking to police officers about the lack of prosecution in cases of domestic violence, the most common reasoning provided was that 'women come but then they leave and most of them never come back',[47] and that 'women approach us and then later they disappear'.[48] The 'disappearance' of women complainants was often explained through an assumption that she had returned to her husband or family, thereby justifying the compromise and reconciliation efforts of the police:

> *In ka relation bhi aisa hay ke din mein jhaggar kar police ke paas aur shaam tak beshak sulah ho chuki hoti hai aur bistar mein phir saath* [the [husband and wife] relation is such that in the morning they're fighting and go to the police [station] and by evening they have reconciled and they're back in bed together].[49]

The idea of 'disappearing women' stuck with me, and I revisited police processes in attempts to locate these women. In Chapter 3, I discussed how women may find agency in using the law as a negotiating tool. However, it was indicated that it was the *threat*—not the *attempt*—of taking legal steps that women spoke of in that context. Those women who approach the police station with the intent to file a complaint of domestic violence are not necessarily looking to reconcile or compromise, but are rather seeking acknowledgement, protection, and at times punishment. As such, it is important to assess more deeply the different stages of police processes and

47 Interview with police, Karachi, 2 August 2022 [c].
48 Interview with police, Islamabad, 7 June 2022.
49 Interview with lawyer, Islamabad, 9 June 2022 [c].

the challenges associated with filing and investigating domestic violence complaints, to explore why women leave police premises, why they do not return, and where they go when they 'disappear'.

'Most of them never come back:' Disappearing women

In exploring gatekeeping approaches and paternalistic attitudes in policing, this chapter has thus far demonstrated the kinds of gendering strategies used by police officials to subjectivize women complainants. By minimizing harms and encouraging compromise and reconciliation in cases of domestic violence, police officers shape the narratives of victims through character allegations emanating from gendered constructions of respectability and suspicions surrounding the 'female psyche'. During this process, many women 'disappear' from the system, either by choosing to withdraw their complaints or, having been deterred by the lack of agency provided to them, by simply choosing not to return:

> Most law enforcement agencies understand this [domestic violence] as a personal, private issue—and they want to limit the issue to that. So they will try to impose reconciliation and keep stressing for it. When the woman arrives at the police station, the police's first instinct is to insist on calling the family and the husband. We as lawyers are always stressing that this is not needed, and that our client's safety is compromised, and she doesn't need to be face-to-face with the man. The woman is already feeling challenged about taking this step, and when you bring the husband or the family, she feels that she has to withdraw the case and she succumbs to the pressure out of lack of choice. And that withdrawal means that the police is happy, and they think 'look, we did reconciliation, we saved the family!'[50]

When women are described as 'disappearing' by police officers, the image that comes to mind is one of women victims fading behind the curtain of a theatrical play. This imagery is similar to the one used by Wall in his work on the ordinary affects of law. Wall considers the way in which the law

[50] Interview with lawyer, Lahore, 14 June 2022 [parenthesis added].

foregrounds certain aspects of the legal scene, while pushing other affects into the background; fading it from view, away from attention and thereby displaced.[51] Yet, he finds that the background is essential to the constitution of the legal scene, for without it the foregrounded aspects made visible would not be possible. Critical legal work therefore requires us to pay attention to the background and explore facets of law which would otherwise go unacknowledged. As discussed previously, the dispositioning of private truths as public secrets through compromise can be seen as one way through which legal affects are pushed into the background. It may however only form part of the gendering practices used by police officers to fade victim-subjects and their narratives from view. To explore how and why women 'disappear' from the system, and the purpose that this serves for the aesthetic and affective relations of the law, we must, as Wall states, 'foreground the background'.[52]

I do this by assessing the experiences of women at three different stages of police procedures, namely the initial reporting of the complaint to police officers, assessments of the information and evidence provided by the complainant, and quandaries relating to medico-legal examinations. Subsequently, I provide a mapping of how cases of domestic violence end up scattered across various civil and family courts, even though they should, by way of current legislation, belong firmly under the criminal ambit. This mapping is presented alongside an examination of how victims of domestic violence are subjectivized through gendered narratives at each procedural stage, and accordingly speaks to the 'disappearance' of women complainants from the legal scene.

Complaint procedures and practices

The first contact that victims have with law enforcement is typically at the police station, when they come forward to seek protection and either register a complaint or request an investigation to file a First Information Report (FIR).[53] In most cases, the victim comes to the station alone, and her first point of contact is the duty officer who asks her initial questions

[51] I Rua Wall, 'The Ordinary Affects of Law' (2019) 19(2) Law Culture and the Humanities 1.
[52] ibid 2.
[53] For police processes, see generally, Police Act 1861 [PAK] and Criminal Procedure Code 1898 [PAK].

to gather information.[54] The duty officer assesses the woman's body for any visible injuries or bruises, and also assesses her mental state. Through an assessment of her responses to questions posed to her, as well as her body language, the duty officer is expected to determine if there is any truth to her story.[55] More problematically, however, the officer will often seek corroborative evidence from the complainant's male guardian or male relative before proceeding. As one lawyer said:

> When she comes to the police station and she is alone, the cases don't go forward at all. They will first tell her to bring her husband or her father or brother or some male relative with her. She alone is never enough. They do not even take her as an individual human being. That is the first problem, because the woman is not allowed to speak. The man she is told to bring with her is the one that is talking for her, and they also say, 'oh, there was a small fight, help reconcile'. No one even takes the woman's official statement. Bring someone else first, a man, only then will they listen to you. If the man says 'yes, she was abused', maybe then the police will write it down. If she is saying it on her own, there is no worth to it.[56]

As discussed in Chapter 2, the reason for a woman's testimony having less worth than that of a man's is due to her 'femaleness' acting as a qualifier. That is, her 'emotionality' and 'female psyche' are attributes that impede her recognition as a legally valid subject.[57] For example, under Zia ul Haq's regime, the laws which regulated offences of *zina* (adultery) and *zina-bil-jabr* (rape) required four adult, Muslim male witnesses to testify to the act of rape in order to prove it.[58] While the Protection of Women Act of 2006 amended these requirements,[59] the reasoning and justifications relating to women's flawed legal capacity remain enshrined in legislation even today, given that Pakistan's Law of Evidence specifies that a woman's testimony is worth half that of a man's in certain matters.[60] Such gendered suspicions

[54] Interview with police, Karachi, 2 August 2022 [b].
[55] ibid.
[56] Interview with lawyer, Lahore, 13 June 2022 [a].
[57] I Nyazee, *Outlines of Islamic Jurisprudence* (3rd edn, Advanced Legal Studies Institute 2005) 39. See also S Toor, 'Gender, Sexuality, and Islam under the Shadow of Empire' (2011) 3(9) S&F Online 22.
[58] Toor (n 57); and SS Ali, 'Law, Islam and the Women's Movement in Pakistan' in SM Rai (ed) *International Perspectives on Gender and Democratisation* (Palgrave Macmillan 2000) 41.
[59] Protection of Women (Criminal Laws Amendment) Act 2006 [PAK].
[60] Article 17, Qanun-e-Shahadat Order (Law of Evidence) 1984 [PAK]

surrounding women's testimonies are also illustrated in police attitudes and practice:

> So many times women come to try and file a fake FIR. This happens so often—that she says her husband abuses her and is threatening her—and we assess her and know she is lying and just being overly emotional because of some little disagreement. We can tell. We know how the female psyche is. That's why we tell her to come back with her husband so we can talk to him and find out what *really* happened.[61]

In subjectivizing the victim in this way, police officers tell women that their complaints cannot be investigated or filed until a man accompanies and corroborates her experiences. For many victims, this is not an option. Khan clarifies that in cases of spousal violence, the perpetrators are the complainants' husbands; and in cases of domestic violence, the perpetrators might be their fathers or brothers. These are the very men whose presence the police institute as a requirement to proceed.[62] Further, women may be reluctant to speak openly about their experiences in the presence of relatives because the disclosure of such 'secrets' are seen as 'sullying the *izzat* [honour]' of the woman and her family, putting her at further risk.[63] There is no expectation for anyone to intervene on behalf of the victim, because such 'private' matters are presumed to be resolved only by the immediate parties involved.[64]

Similarly, when victims call the police from their homes and the reporting police officers pay a visit, it is usually 'the man of the house' who comes out to speak with them.[65] And in doing so, he informs the duty officers that there has been a mistake, and that the woman is fine.[66] I was told that in the majority of cases, police officers consider this information to have more worth than the phone call received previously, simply because '*woh is me parhna nahi chahte, kya pata aurat ke demaagh me kya chal raha hai, kyun aurat aise bol rahi thi* [they don't want to get involved in this; who

[61] Interview with police, Karachi, 2 August 2022 [a] [emphasis added].

[62] See S Khan, 'Disobedient Daughters, Errant Wives, and Others' in *Transnational Feminism and the Moral Regulation of Pakistani Women* (UBC Press 2006) 56.

[63] A Khan and R Hussain, 'Violence against Women in Pakistan: Perceptions and Experiences of Domestic Violence' (2008) 32(2) Asian Studies Review 239.

[64] U Niaz, 'Women's Mental Health in Pakistan' (2004) 3(1) World Psychiatry 60.

[65] Interview with police, Karachi, 2 August 2022 [c].

[66] ibid. The idea of speaking on behalf of women also resonates with the gendered silencing techniques discussed in Chapter 3.

knows what was going on in the woman's mind, why the woman was saying this]'.[67]

Having been subjectivized in a manner that underscores the 'psyche' of women based on their 'femaleness', victims often find themselves unable to meet the prerequisites set by police officials to formally lodge a complaint. As a result, they may leave and be deterred from returning:

> When women see the [police officers'] discouraging and threatening attitudes, they leave. Social pressure plays a big role on the victim. Everyone is telling them that they may have done something that led to this, so [police] telling them that what they say has no meaning unless someone else, some man, comes with them, of course they will leave'.[68]

The assessments relating to the 'female psyche' based on gendering strategies that stem from societal assumptions are visible not only through police practices that expect victims to be accompanied by a man when they approach the station, but also in how the police view the evidence they bring with them. Similar to the ways in which women's testimonies and statements are considered 'weak', her evidence is comparably viewed through the same lens. During an interview, a victim of acid crime recounted that she was told by police officers that her evidence was inadequate because the clothes she gave to them for forensic analysis were drenched in water. Through this, they concluded that her testimony was flawed, and they believed her burns to be 'self-inflicted'[69] and a result of madness[70] (although the reasoning here is unclear). This was concluded despite the victim's argument that when the acid attack happened, 'I was burning so I was only looking for water, and I kept pouring water on myself over and over again to stop the burning, so of course all my clothes got soaking wet'.[71]

Additionally, if the victim tries to present evidence to the police at first instance, they query whether in doing so she is a woman of questionable character who is trying to manipulate them. In one case relating to alleged rape perpetrated by a relative of the victim:

[67] ibid.

[68] Interview with victim support personnel, Karachi, 19 July 2022. Parenthesis added for clarity.

[69] Interview with victim, Islamabad, 7 June 2022 [d].

[70] ibid ('The officer told everyone at the station that I was the one who wanted to marry my sister's husband and he refused, so in anger and depression I went mad and threw acid on myself').

[71] Interview with victim, Islamabad, 7 June 2022 [d].

> Because she brought her clothes as evidence, the police told her, 'This must have been pre-planned. How did you know you had to bring your clothes like this? You are trying to manipulate us.'[72]
>
> . . . And on the other hand, if rape victims do not bring their clothes to the station, then the police say, 'there is not enough evidence to file the case'.[73]

During interviews, police personnel clarified that the only evidence they consider to be 'good' in cases relating to domestic violence comes from medico-legal examinations (MLEs). Any other kind of evidence can be 'easily faked'.[74] If there are marks of violence on the woman's body when she approaches the police, 'it could be self-inflicted'.[75] If she shows pictures or videos of the abuse on her phone, it could be 'photoshopped', and messages and audio recordings too can be 'manipulated'.[76] In focusing heavily on MLEs for evidence in order to file cases of domestic violence, police officers can offload some of the blame that may be attributed to them for the failure to do so, by instead highlighting the shortcomings of medico-legal officers (MLOs):

> Usually MLOs are not available and we keep chasing them through phone calls, and we go and sit there too but they say there is no availability, and particularly lady MLOs are not available . . . You know, for medicals I have also done cases where I have taken women to the hospital at 10am and till midnight I am waiting for the doctor and she is not coming. If everyone else does their job properly then this would not happen, because now all the blame always come on the police. But we are trying to do our job by giving the work onwards but if they don't do it then we cannot either. The blame is not on us, it's on them. No examination means no evidence.[77]

Pakistani researchers have documented numerous instances where police officials have dismissed women complainants of domestic violence at the outset. For example, Bhatti and others speak of the high number of

[72] Interview with victim support personnel, Karachi 19 July 2022.
[73] Interview with lawyer, Karachi 19 July 2022.
[74] Interview with police, Karachi 2 August 2022 [a].
[75] ibid.
[76] Interview with police, Karachi, 2 August 2022 [c].
[77] Interview with police, Karachi, 2 August 2022 [a].

complainants who are not properly advised on the processes or taken to hospital for medical examinations that would provide important evidence for prosecution.[78] And yet, even those victims that do attempt to complete medico-legal examinations in order to proceed with an FIR end up facing numerous challenges during that process, such as unceasing delays, unavailability of women MLOs, and inadequate assessments of victims.

It is pertinent to note that MLEs are considered essential for cases relating to domestic violence, including but not limited to physical violence, sexual assault, rape, acid crimes, and child abuse. When a victim arrives at the police station with a complaint of domestic violence, procedural policies warrant that she is given a letter with instructions to visit the nearest medico-legal services for certification of her injuries.[79] Medico-legal services are only available at public or government hospitals. As one lawyer clarified, 'Private hospitals won't result in MLEs, and if you want an FIR and a criminal case, the MLO's report has a lot more weight and will be taken as proper evidence. The presumption is that you can bribe a private doctor, but you can't bribe a government officer—I am not going to comment on that belief.'[80] Typically, medical examinations are to be done within a few hours, in order to ensure that all injuries are appropriately indexed while the evidence is still 'fresh'.[81] However, this aim is rarely met. In rape cases, for example, it can take an average of sixteen days to conduct a medical examination, and in the majority of cases, the examination is not conducted at all.[82] The main reason for this is the lack of WMLOs (women medico-legal officers) available to conduct exams. In Karachi, for example, there are only nine WMLOs to serve the city of 22 million:[83]

> The problem that a lot of women face is that there are not enough female MLOs available, and they don't want to be touched by male MLOs. Not just in extreme forms of rape etc. but also showing like arm bruises,

[78] N Bhatti, MB Jamali, NN Phulpoto, T Mehmood and FM Shaikh, 'Domestic Violence against Women: A Case Study of District Jacobabad, Sindh Pakistan' (2011) 7(12) Asian Social Science 154.

[79] Interview with medico-legal officer, Karachi, 14 August 2022.

[80] Interview with lawyer, Karachi, 14 January 2022.

[81] Interview with medico-legal officer, Karachi, 14 August 2022.

[82] M Zia, S David and S Randhawa, 'Gap Analysis on Investigation and Prosecution of Rape and Sodomy Cases' (2021) Legal Aid Society 27.

[83] Interview with victim support personnel, Karachi, 14 January 2022. This number was also confirmed during an interview with a woman medico-legal officer in Karachi on 14 August 2022.

> many women are not comfortable being examined by a man . . . We are taught in this society to keep segregation of genders but then you don't have WMLOs on call while a trauma victim is sitting there, waiting. And these delays also mean that bruises could go away, so then what happens?[84]

Given the lack of WMLOs available, victims of gender-based violence have two options: either to be examined by a male doctor with whom they may not be comfortable (bearing in mind that some male MLOs are reluctant and hesitant to examine women victims too), or to leave and come back another day.[85] Both options may weaken their case and their evidence; the former through injuries that are 'left out', and the latter through injuries that start to fade. For instance, a member of victim support personnel I interviewed recounted a case of a girl who was gang-raped by four of her first cousins in her home:

> She was examined by a male MLO. When she told him that she also had bite marks on her breasts, the male MLO asked to see it. How could the girl show it to a male stranger? You cannot expect her to show her breast to some man like that! And of course, the MLO did not write this as evidence in the report, so when she mentioned it during her statement to file the report with the police, they said that she was lying because there was nothing of the sort in the MLO report.[86]

For victims of male violence, the prospect of being examined by a male MLO could act as a deterrent, with many women choosing to leave the process at this stage. On the other hand, if asked to leave due to non-availability of women doctors, many victims may be deterred from coming back at a later date.[87] In addition, the ineffective training of MLOs with respect to violence against women and girls may not necessarily assist in the compilation of evidence, but rather harm it due to lack of thorough examinations:

> The age of injury is such that injuries go through changes sequentially. If the MLO does not know much about the subject and is not able to assess

[84] Interview with lawyer, Karachi, 14 January 2022.
[85] Interview with medico-legal officer, Karachi, 14 August 2022.
[86] Interview with victim support personnel, Karachi, 19 July 2022.
[87] Zia and others (n 82) 30.

> or corroborate the age of injury with the time of incident, the case may fall flat. The case will be lost. They would not be willing to make the extra effort to document the age of injury as required . . . So, there are a lot of things that don't work in our favour—and these are things that are going against the victim. That is why most of the victims drop out during the process.[88]

The lack of thorough examinations by MLOs also extend to post-mortems of victims who are suspected to have been killed through acts of domestic violence, but whose deaths are claimed to be a result of suicide by their husbands and in-laws.[89] Vignette 4.3 below contains an extract from an interview with a medico-legal officer in Karachi which illustrates the procedure and challenges associated with such cases.

Vignette 4.3 Extract from interview with MLO, August 2022, Karachi

Where there is chronic domestic abuse, the scenario we get is that she either ate something and then she died, or that she was not in the right frame of mind, that she was always alone and would not leave her room due to some depression and so she committed suicide. Or there would be some ligature mark and they will say that she hung herself from the fan. And you know, it is always only the husband or the mother-in-law that has seen her hanging. The story we get—so, there is a fresh case right now where they said they found the woman hanging, and that the mother-in-law held her, and the husband cut off the *dupatta* [scarf]. So now we have the *dupatta* which is the ligature material, we have a girl who was supposed to be hanging for almost an hour or two, we have a mother-in-law who might not be feeling too well so she'll avoid us, and a husband whose hand will be shaking when he is signing our papers. These are things that make me think twice about the cause of death.

In such a case, the first thing I would do is to compare the ligature material provided with the ligature mark on the neck. In most instances, they don't match. And then if a body has been left hanging for an hour or so as per the history provided, all the blood would start to settle down towards

[88] Interview with medico-legal officer, Karachi, 14 August 2022.
[89] Judgement, Sessions Judge, 343/20 Islamabad East [Aug 2020].

the hands and feet because of gravity. Then, what happens during hanging is that the glands on both sides of our jaws, the salivary glands, one of them is compressed—and that causes copious amounts of saliva to be dribbling out of the mouth at an angle. And lastly, if a woman is committing suicide, we need to consider her height, the distance from the roof or the fan where the noose was tied, and what she used to jump off. This case that I'm talking about, this girl was found with one of her feet on the ground and the other foot on the bed with the knee turned outwards. And it was claimed that she had committed suicide. How can it be?

She had gotten married three months back, the husband would beat her and sodomize her and she had repeatedly conveyed this to her mother, and the mother kept sending her back and eventually one day, we get a dead body. This is a very common way of disposing of an unwanted girl—to frame it as a suicide due to mental issue. We call it *surkh kabar* [red grave] if it happens within the first year of marriage. But again, many people won't put in the work required. All these steps I mentioned, they won't do it. They'll simply see a mark on the neck and they'll sign it off as suicide without differentiating between strangulation or hanging. Most people want to just close the files when it comes to family matters. MLOs and police both. And the police are also dependent on us MLOs and if we are the ones not doing it correctly, then the police won't have anything to go on either. So, the death of the woman would be registered as a suicide and the body is handed back to the family and case closed. No investigation warranted.[90]

In simply seeing a mark on the neck and signing the case off as suicide, it appears that in a way, MLOs too are subjectivizing the woman and her body. Casper and Donnell argue that while medicine often finds physical explanations for the experiences and injuries of men, women's injuries and experiences are often provided a psychological explanation.[91] The 'psychologising of women's domestic violence experiences' means that medical professionals often perceive the trauma of victims as emotional and psychological, rather than physical or neurological.[92] Similarly, Ballweg's research

[90] Interview with medico-legal officer, Karachi, 14 August 2022.

[91] For more detail, see the use of gendering strategies in the discipline of psychiatry as discussed in Chapter 2.

[92] ST Casper and K O'Donnell, 'The Punch-Drunk Boxer and the Battered Wife: Gender and Brain Injury Research' (2020) 245 Social Science and Medicine 1.

on the 'psychologising of endometriosis' in the late 1990s found that when women approached medical professionals exhibiting symptoms of endometriosis that manifested within the body, they were instead perceived to be patients of somatization, a mental disorder that was seen to primarily affect women.[93] By preferring gendered, psychological explanations relating to the mental state of women over physical explanations of violence, medico-legal officers could be said to be subjectivizing women and their bodies by discounting narratives which may say otherwise. Here too, cases of domestic violence may fall through the cracks.

The reliance on medico-legal examinations, given the quandaries associated with these reports as highlighted above, means that many cases of gender-based violence are either not registered or registered under the wrong offence. A victim of acid crimes shared her experience:

> The MLO examined me after three days. And I had burns but no proper disfigurement because the disfigurement comes later. I had peeled skin and burns at the time. This is what she had written on the examination certificate. On that basis, the police filed it under Section 336A, not 336B. The doctors are not legal experts. But then this is what happens—the other party ended up filing a writ petition to say this is the wrong section for this kind of prosecution and my case got held up.[94]

Further, police officers are quick to close cases by filing them under suicide even if there are complaints by the deceased's family to suggest that the death may have been a result of domestic violence leading to murder. A lawyer I interviewed spoke of a case she recently worked on in Chitral, where a man claimed that his wife suffered from mental health issues and had taken her own life. The MLO who conducted the post-mortem examination made note of the same, after which the police registered the case as suicide. When the lawyer was approached by the family, she got an order from the High Court in Islamabad to send investigating officers to Chitral to speak with the MLO who conducted the examination, as well as with local police personnel. Only then did evidence surface to indicate that the woman had been killed by her husband. The lawyer clarified, 'So, from the

[93] ML Ballweg, 'Blaming the Victim: The Psychologizing of Endometriosis' (1997) 24(2) Obstetrics and Gynaecology Clinics of North America 441; Also see K Young and others, 'Women's Experiences of Endometriosis: A Systematic Review and Synthesis of Qualitative Research' (2015) 41 Family Planning, Reproduction and Health Care 225.

[94] Interview with victim, Islamabad, 7 June 2022 [d].

Islamabad police the determination was that this was not a suicide, this was a murder. But it is a matter of someone making that extra effort, taking the extra step to investigate properly.'[95]

Similarly, in their research on rape cases, Zia and others found that MLOs are often reluctant to clearly state if rape has occurred, and refrain from providing detailed evidence in order to 'avoid being caught in a big contentious trial'.[96] Perhaps that is why research conducted by an organization in Karachi that works on violence against women and girls found large discrepancies between MLO reports and data from the police, with only 30 per cent of cases having FIRs lodged despite having completed medico-legal examinations.[97] This statistic, of course, does not account for the many cases of women who 'disappeared' from the process without having a medical assessment.

The different kinds of gendering strategies highlighted through these three police stages means that cases relating to domestic violence are either not filed, or are filed after multiple delays. At the stage of first instance, women are unable to file complaints due to assumptions surrounding the 'female psyche'. Police requirements to have a man corroborate a woman victim's testimony act as a deterrent to continue proceeding with the case. Second, at the evidence stage, women are discouraged from pursuing the case by police officers who deem their evidence of domestic violence as 'weak', instead insinuating that the woman's injuries are self-inflicted and a result of 'madness' or emotionality stemming from her 'femaleness'. In addition, the evidence she brings with her may also be seen as a tool of manipulation based on tropes relating to her 'bad' character. And third, at the medical examination stage, the lack of WMLOs coupled with the institutional preference for psychological explanations over physical explanations of women's injuries leads to evidence being either incorrectly recorded or not recorded at all. Here too, women may leave and choose not to return due to the difficult, contentious process to which they are subjected.

In the few cases where FIRs do go on to be filed, the delay in doing so is often used as one of the first arguments by lawyers to 'put a dent in the prosecution's case'.[98] As one defence counsel pointed out, 'whenever there is a delay in registration of FIR, it loses the advantage of spontaneity, thereby

[95] Phone interview with lawyer, Rawalpindi, 13 July 2022.
[96] Zia and others (n 82) 30.
[97] Interview with victim support personnel, Karachi, 19 July 2022.
[98] Zia and others (n 82) 22.

raising a potential chance of introduction of a coloured version or concocted story'.[99] Again, this weakens the victim's case and may act as a deterrent to continue proceedings, especially if she is told by police and lawyers alike that her complaint is unlikely to be successful. At this stage too, she may 'disappear'. It is pertinent to note that there is a remedy under Section 22 of the Criminal Procedure Code through which victims and lawyers can move an application to the Justice of the Peace when police officials refuse to register an FIR.[100] However, as one lawyer stated, 'even with Justice of Peace applications—sometimes we also file a formal complaint addressed to the SHO [station house officer] or send an advocate to the police station to get the FIR registered—even through all these means, getting the FIR registered has not been successful'.[101]

As such, when police officers use gendering strategies to gatekeep access to justice, many women complainants 'disappear' or drop out of the police process. In result, only a handful of cases make it to the criminal courts, while others might end up in the civil and family courts:

> A lot of women come to me and they tell me they want to take legal action. When we make the application for domestic violence and take it to the police, the police refuse to register the case and say this is a family matter, we cannot get involved, and tell them to go to the family court.[102]

And yet, having mapped the criminal procedures and practices which underline the challenges and difficulties that women victims of domestic violence face, when I asked a defence lawyer who works across criminal and family courts how allegations of domestic violence are typically challenged in Pakistani courts, he responded:

> Criminal or civil doesn't matter. Look, it is very simple. If the woman was truly in such bad shape and had been beaten up as much as she claims, then why did she not file a complaint? No FIR, no MLE, nothing. So, the burden of proof is not on us. She probably has some mental issue, so she

[99] ibid.

[100] Section 22 of the Criminal Procedure Code 1898 [PAK] regulates instances where there is non-registration of a criminal case by the police, and grants the Justice of Peace powers to make an arrest and/or direct police officers to investigate the matter.

[101] Interview with lawyer, Karachi, 11 August 2022 [b].

[102] Interview with lawyer, Lahore, 16 June 2022 [a].

> makes up these things. That's on her. So as defence counsel, that makes our job easier. We will highlight these things.[103]

The findings and discussion above may answer some of the questions the lawyer posed: why women are unable to file police complaints, why they are unable to get medico-legal examinations done, and ultimately why their cases end up scattered across various courts. The lawyer's assumption that the victim 'makes up these things' because 'she probably has some mental issue' also brings us back full circle to the kinds of character allegations and gendering strategies used by police officers to minimize and at times eradicate the harms of women complainants.

Conclusion

In exploring how women victims of domestic violence are subjectivized through policing, this chapter highlighted the paternalistic attitudes and gatekeeping approaches adopted by police officials. As Franz Kafka put it:

> Before the law sits a gatekeeper. To this gatekeeper comes a [person] . . . who asks to gain entry into the law. But the gatekeeper says that he cannot grant [the person] entry . . . At the moment the gate to the law stands open, as always, and the gatekeeper walks to the side, so the [person] bends over in order to see through the gate into the inside. When the gatekeeper notices that, he laughs and says: 'If it tempts you so much, try it in spite of my prohibition. But take note: I am powerful. And I am only the most lowly gatekeeper. But from room to room stand gatekeepers, each more powerful than the other. . .'[104]

This chapter first examined how the gendered constructions of respectability and social control inform the ways in which police officers understand their 'duty' towards protecting the State-endorsed sanctity of the family structure. In enacting 'formal institutional control', police officers employ gendering strategies that subjectivize victims through character

[103] Interview with layer, Karachi, 15 January 2022.
[104] F Kafka, 'Before the Law' in N Glazer (ed) *The Complete Stories* (Schocken Books 1971) 3, as cited in CR Yung, 'Rape Law Gatekeeping' (2017) 58(1) Boston College Law Review 206.

allegations and claims that minimize their harms and encourage compromise and reconciliation to mask private truths as 'public secrets'. Second, it demonstrated how policing processes and practices construct victim-subjects of domestic violence, in order to not only provide explanations for why some women may 'disappear' from the system, but also map how and why domestic violence cases are found dispersed across various jurisdictions. In illustrating how police personnel are focused more on policing culturally disputed ideas of domestic violence instead of punishing or deterring perpetrators of that violence, the arguments developed contribute to broad-ranging feminist critiques of policing in relation to gender-based violence and abuse.

> A lot of times police officers talk like this, that the woman is *paagal* [crazy] or some *nafsiyati mareez* [mental patient] and has self-inflicted injuries. In my opinion they are foolish people to say that. They have no criteria to make these assessments. I would say lodge the FIR first, then after that you can do the investigation and assess. Always register the FIR. Because if there is a possibility at all that this violence was done to her, then having a FIR is better in terms of serving justice. And the other thing is even if she is mentally unstable, okay we accept it, then that can be proved in the court. They can do psychological assessment. That's why I'm saying that we should register a case regardless, because after that there are many safeguards in place in the court and trial process.[105]

The risk of public disclosure of victims' narratives of abuse and violence is positioned against what Davar refers to as the 'collusion' of the State and disciplinary institutions in protecting patriarchy, in order to ensure that such disclosure does not happen.[106] The 'safeguards' in the trial process spoken of by a high-ranking police offer in the interview extract above may therefore not be as clear cut, as the 'collusion' between the State and other institutions in protecting patriarchal norms and gendering practices is not limited to law enforcement agents. In Chapter 5 I explore how lawyers navigate the cases brought forth by victims, which despite (and/or due to) the hurdles and challenges outlined here find their way to either the criminal

[105] Interview with police, Karachi, 2 August 2022 [c].

[106] BV Davar, 'From Mental Illness to Disability' (2008) 15(2) Indian Journal of Gender Studies 265.

or family courts. While police officials employ gendered allegations and strategies which assist in gatekeeping and consequently marginalize the stories of women victims of domestic violence, lawyers may use gendered allegations and strategies to script those stories as they travel through court processes.

5 Scripting victim-subjects: Lawyerly practices

Paen kokan, meney apny, dewey lokan
[A woman blames others instead of accepting her own faults][1]

Introduction

The courts are awash in storytelling,[2] and yet many stories are the same. There is a pattern in how stories are told and retold, and particularly in how they are scripted. In this chapter, I focus on the scripts commonly applied to women accessing the courts for relief as victims of domestic abuse. As one lawyer said: 'when responding to accusations of domestic violence, we need to make up a bit of a story.'[3]

> The attitudes of advocates here is, *aap fikr na karein mein us ko suli peh lakta doonga* [don't worry, I'll hang her from the gallows]. Sometimes even the client says that this didn't happen, this isn't true, but the advocates will say, '*par humein yeh likhna pare ga* [but we have to write this]'.[4]

During early interviews, a couple of lawyers referred to the use of 'templates' in legal drafting and suits. At the time, I didn't think much of it. I assumed the templates they were referring to were formatted drafts to fill in relevant details of the case, considered a standard legal practice. As interviews progressed, however, I realized that the templates being spoken about

[1] A Punjabi proverb. See M Shahbaz, *Saday Akhaan [Our Proverbs]* (Aziz Book Depot 2004) 121.
[2] AG Amsterdam and J Bruner, *Minding the Law* (Harvard University Press 2002) 110.
[3] Interview with lawyer, Karachi, 5 January 2022 [a].
[4] Interview with family judge, District and Sessions Courts, Karachi, 5 August 2022.

Domestic Violence in Pakistan. Daanika Kamal, Oxford University Press. © Daanika Kamal 2025.
DOI: 10.1093/9780198953470.003.0005

were in fact fully drafted. They already contained certain 'facts' about the case—albeit lacking in specifics—along with the grounds for the suit and/or allegations against the other party. Practitioners also referred to these pre-drafted suits as 'scripts', and described them as being used by lawyers in a one-size-fits-all approach in cases relating to domestic abuse:

> The thing is, they all use pre-existing templates and they all have the same grounds that they use. Pre-existing drafts exist for almost every type of case but family law particularly. When you are a junior lawyer specially, you'll be given a draft by your senior and [told] to adjust the facts of the case. But 80 per cent of the lawyers get these suits directly from the draftsmen at the courts and there is no adjustment . . . They use it as a script.[5]

These boilerplate pre-drafted suits are easily available in Pakistani courts through draftsmen who charge lawyers a fee for the service, ranging anywhere from 500 to 1,500 rupees per suit.[6] My interactions with a draftsman in Karachi assist in illustrating their role and provision:

> Some call us draftsmen, some call us stenos, but our job is to make the jobs of lawyers easier. Lawyers are very busy and do not have time to draft suits over and over again. Many of them do not have access to a computer or a printer. They come to us and tell us the nature of the suit, as well as the names of the parties and we add them into the draft suits that we have and print it out for them to file . . . The drafts have always been there, it is a normal part of the practice, everyone has the same ones. If we are smart, we keep two or three versions with different grounds, and the lawyer can choose which one they would like . . . *Jitna purana vakalat hai, utne puranay yeh bhi hain* [the drafts are as old as the practice of law] . . . It is a good money-making business. You do not need to have a legal background . . . *Drafts toh asaani se mil jate hain. Buss computer le keh save kar lein aur phir un ko edit karte rahein* [drafts are easily available, just save them on the computer and keep editing them].[7]

[5] Interview with lawyer, Karachi, 1 August 2022 [parenthesis added].

[6] Court observation, Karachi, 5 July 2022. One lawyer said the average cost in ICT was between 1,000 and 3,000 PKR (Interview with lawyer, Islamabad, 13 July 2022).

[7] Court observation, Karachi, 5 July 2022. 'Stenos' may be referring to stenographers, although the role of draftsmen does not seem to align with the role popularly associated with stenographers.

While I was observing the draftsman at work, multiple lawyers approached him, of which a few stopped by just to have a chat and two asked for the draftsman's services. One case related to a property dispute, and the second related to dissolution of marriage due to cruelty. When the latter task was complete, I asked the draftsman to walk me through the process for this request. He said: 'for allegations of cruelty it is easy; the draft is ready. First, we know the allegation is false. All suits to file *khula* say cruelty. Second, there are only one or two things we put in response to these allegations; this is what lawyers expect'.[8] And yet, when more deeply questioning the lawyerly practice of using such boilerplate text in my interviews, most practitioners would simply respond that 'it's routine practice, it's what lawyers get from the draftsmen',[9] as though absolving themselves of responsibility for the content of those drafts. This prompted me to reflect on the implications of such practices, and I made note of a few questions which I go on to address over the course of this chapter: Where do these drafts come from? Why was it assumed that the claims of 'cruelty' or domestic abuse were false? What are the kinds of allegations that lawyers expect in pre-drafted suits when responding to these claims? And does the lawyer intend to bring any proof for these allegations during the court process?

This chapter accordingly identifies and examines the kinds of character allegations and gendering strategies employed by lawyers that 'script' women victims of domestic violence. By 'script', I mean that legal actors adopt certain practices in a one-size-fits-all approach, in an attempt to subjectivize complainants in particular ways.[10] This includes not only the actual script or text used in case filings, but also the common practices in which lawyers engage to narrate and enact that script. I develop this argument in two phases. First, I explore the kind of boilerplate text included in pre-drafted legal suits that are filed in response to women's claims and petitions. This text, which practitioners refer to both as 'scripts' and as 'templates', predominantly allege that the complainant is of immoral, 'bad' character, and/or that she is 'mad' and suffering from some form of mental ailment. Second, I present an assessment of techniques used by legal actors

[8] ibid.

[9] Interview with lawyer, Lahore, 17 June 2022 [b]; similar ideas were shared during a phone interview with a lawyer from Peshawar (1 July 2022) and during a phone interview with a member of legal aid personnel in Sialkot (28 June 2022).

[10] Smart has also used the term 'scripted' to refer to accounts that undergo legal processes to translate everyday experiences into legal relevance. See C Smart, *Feminism and the Power of Law* (Routledge 1989) 11.

to build on these scripts, in an effort to shape the credibility of the complainant in the courtroom. These lawyerly practices include performative, restrictive questioning tactics, and the presentation of peculiar forms of 'evidence' for the scripted claims. Identifying the features and naturalizing effects of such character allegations further allows an examination into the strategic use of suggestibility, and whether these practices construct the victim-subject of domestic violence in a manner that not only subjectivizes her but also secures her in the field of that subjectification, setting her up to be viewed by the judiciary through the lens of the allegations applied to her.

One-size-fits-all: Boilerplate text in legal drafting

In *Decoupling*, Michelson explores the use of 'highly standardised and scripted boilerplate'[11] in divorce cases in China. The case files and judgments he examined contained 'recycled and rehashed' paragraphs used by legal actors in a copy-paste manner.[12] This meant that most of the text remained unchanged, and specific facts of the case were regularly excluded. Scripting legal documents through boilerplate text enabled them to be applied 'to almost any case after filling in a few blanks', such as litigants' names and pertinent dates.[13] Michelson's findings from China bear close resemblance to legal practices in Pakistan. The use of boilerplate text in and through pre-drafted suits is particularly visible in *khula* and divorce cases, where women seek dissolution of marriage due to acts of domestic abuse.[14] In the following sections, I investigate how these boilerplate texts are incorporated into lawyerly practices, examine the contents and allegations included within these texts, and explore how this one-size-fits-all approach can be viewed as a gendering strategy that helps legal actors construct victim-subjects of domestic violence.

A family judge I interviewed explained that the use of pre-drafted suits is an integral part of everyday legal practice. Particularly in family cases, she said, 'the grounds are always the same; they are always copy-pasted'.[15] These

[11] E Michelson, *Decoupling: Gender Injustice in China's Divorce Courts* (Cambridge University Press 2022) 237.

[12] ibid 224, 328.

[13] ibid 301.

[14] As mentioned in Chapter 1, acts of domestic abuse and violence are commonly bracketed under the term 'cruelty'.

[15] Interview with family judge, District and Sessions Courts, Karachi, 5 August 2022.

grounds refer to 'the women's character' and 'her mental state, that she is in the need of a doctor'.[16] In the judge's experience, she had seen multiple instances where the suits contained spelling errors in the names of the parties involved, and sometimes even the names of litigants were not changed in the boilerplate drafts used:

> The advocate did not even bother reading the draft. The name of the party was wrong throughout the case . . . When the client appeared, he said that this is not my name, so the entire litigation got tied up. They don't bother to read the draft. Many litigants cannot read or understand English either. Sometimes they don't even know what is written in the suit.[17] It is the responsibility of advocates to check this, but they do not care. I think they are lazy, want to reduce work, so they go to draftsmen and print out such templates to file.[18]

Another family judge I spoke to had a different view. For him, such 'designed templates' were necessary because the court requires specific formats, without which the case 'cannot be maintained'.[19] When I asked him about the difference between using a 'template' to ensure consistency in formatting versus using pre-drafted suits containing scripted allegations that are unadjusted to the facts of each individual case, he said, 'I think that in order to get necessary ingredients to file a case, allegations are always levelled and included'.[20] Earlier in our interview, the judge had mentioned that a woman does not need a reason to file for divorce, and can simply say she doesn't want to continue the marriage. And so, I asked for clarification regarding what the 'necessary ingredients' may entail. He explained, 'the law guides us as to in what circumstances a *khula* can be granted'.[21] The Dissolution of Muslim Marriages Act states a number of grounds on which a Muslim woman is entitled to file for a divorce.[22] Examples include: if the

[16] ibid.

[17] This point was also reiterated during another interview: 'I have seen cases where the lawyer is having a discussion during the hearing and outlining these allegations and even the husband goes into shock, because even he does not know what the lawyer is saying. The lawyer does it on his own because it is a common practice in our legal field.' Phone interview with legal aid personnel, Sukkur, 27 June 2022.

[18] Interview with family judge, District and Sessions Courts, Karachi, 5 August 2022.

[19] Interview with family judge, District and Sessions Court, Karachi, 4 July 2022.

[20] ibid.

[21] ibid.

[22] The Dissolution of Muslim Marriages Act 1939 [PAK], s 2.

husband has been neglectful and failed to provide for her; if he is impotent; or if he treats her with cruelty.[23] The latter, he said, 'is the easiest and most common'.[24]

In practice, however, most lawyers I spoke to agreed that the inclusion of such grounds is not necessary, because 'even if a woman says she doesn't like her husband's face, that is enough for a successful seeking of *khula*'.[25] And while the judge agreed with this sentiment, he rationalized the inclusion of allegations by saying:

> Yes, she doesn't need a reason, she can simply say she doesn't want to continue with the marriage. But in our society, she won't do that because she has people to answer to. If she does not put allegations on the man, then the man will badmouth her—that for no reason she broke the family. And in terms of proof he will say, look, she didn't put any allegations on me, so she is the defaulter.[26]

Rationalizing the inclusion of allegations based on administrative rules of formatting and the need to get 'necessary ingredients' to file a case helps justify the use of pre-drafted suits, thereby solidifying the practice further.[27] For example, one lawyer mentioned that she was unable to file a one-page dissolution of marriage suit. The court clerk told her it was 'too short', to which she replied, 'no, this is sufficient because what concerns this specific case is all I will put—why should I use the template with all these allegations?'[28]

The lawyerly practice of using pre-drafted suits has led to a popular presumption, in family cases relating to domestic abuse, that all *khula* suits filed by women complainants allege cruelty—falsely—to meet legal procedural requirements. And based on this presumption, lawyers argue that it is 'only fair' that the boilerplate suits used by the defence also include allegations:

[23] ibid s 2 (viii). As discussed in Chapter 1, acts of 'cruelty' by the husband include habitual assault, associating with women of evil repute, or attempting to force his wife to lead an immoral life.

[24] Interview with family judge, District and Sessions Court, Karachi, 4 July 2022.

[25] Interview with lawyer, Islamabad, 9 June 2022 [a]. The idea that, '*Kaafi hai keh us ki shakal nahi achi lagti* [It is enough that you don't like his face]' was also repeated in other interviews, such as: Interview with lawyer, Karachi, 5 January 2022 [c]; Interview with lawyer, Lahore, 13 June 2022 [a].

[26] Interview with family judge, District and Sessions Court, Karachi, 4 July 2022.

[27] Order VII of the Code of Civil Procedure 1908 [PAK] outlines the format to be used in plaints.

[28] Interview with lawyer, Karachi, 4 July 2022.

> I am really sorry to say—you are a woman—that 90 per cent of these domestic violence in *khula* cases are false. You don't know the real story; the woman is typically being aggressive, or she is interested in some other man so she says that he does violence . . . The lawyer will do what he needs to protect the client. So, if the defence is putting allegations, it is only fair because the woman is also falsely accusing her husband of abuse.[29]

Similar to discussions in Chapter 4, here too a key ingredient relates to suspicions surrounding the 'female psyche'.

I was advised by lawyers that the quickest way to differentiate between suits that are drafted based on the facts of the case and those that are filed using pre-drafted boilerplate scripts is the lack of specificity in the text. 'The language used will be generic, with blanket statements. The allegations will be there but with lots of terms added as fluff, and there will be nothing specific about the relationship between [the parties] or specific incidents—you can tell that the lawyer did not engage with the client at all.'[30] While some lawyers distanced themselves from the practice of 'scripting' women, saying that they knew it happened but they themselves did not engage in it, others were quite open about the benefits of the practice. One lawyer explained that because the law is an oversaturated profession, one needs to take as many cases as possible to make a living. Lawyers do not have time to engage with every single client, and the availability of draftsmen and ready-made suits therefore makes this possible.[31] Another lawyer justified the inclusion of allegations in pre-drafted suits by positing that it is in line with what the defendants want and expect:

> Men come to me about filing a case against their wives and say '*is ko ragra lagana hai, theek thaak ragra lagana hai*' [you need to put her through the wringer, give her a really hard time]. I'd say, '*jab tumhari biwi thi, tab tumne lagaya nahi ragra, mujhe keh rahe ho ke ragra lagao* [when she was your wife you didn't give her a hard time, now you are telling me to]'. We are lawyers and we do whatever it takes. If we are told to assassinate their character . . . of course we will do it. We just need to see

[29] Interview with lawyer, Islamabad, 9 June 2022 [c].
[30] Interview with lawyer, Lahore, 17 June 2022 [a] [parenthesis added].
[31] Interview with lawyer, Karachi, 11 August 2022 [b].

> if there is a way to make it relevant to the case—mostly it is and it helps the case.[32]

The judicial, formalistic approach to law allows practitioners to focus more on following the rules than on inquiring the nature of those rules. In other words, they focus on techniques which extract and apply seemingly universal statements whose values of 'truth' are detached from the context of their making.[33] Delgado claims that the responsibility of perpetuating practices lies with the prevailing mindset, which members of the dominant group use to justify those practices. He proceeds to demonstrate the process through which a 'stock story' is often used to offer a seemingly plausible or acceptable explanation for actions and decisions in legal settings. This stock story is one which 'the institution collectively forms and tells about itself. It picks and chooses from among the available facts to present a picture of what happened: an account that justifies the world as it is.'[34] Stock stories can then act as a 'cure'.[35]

Similarly, 'stock stories' may come to form in response to suits filed by women relating to domestic abuse, as there are two main allegations that are reproduced in the boilerplate text of pre-drafted suits, visible in case files, and consistently mentioned during interviews. As touched upon earlier, the first relates to the woman's character (that she is immoral, associates with strange men, does not fulfil the man's sexual rights, and is disobedient), and the second relates to her mental state (that she is aggressive, is psychologically disturbed, or has a psychiatric condition). At times, the two allegations are intertwined (that she is disobedient *due* to her 'mental issues').[36] For example, a legal aid worker told me about a case he worked on where a woman's shoulder had been dislocated due to marital abuse. In response to these claims, the woman's husband submitted a written statement alleging that she 'was having an illicit affair with some man who put a *taaweez* [amulet] on her and she became mentally unstable, that is why she was filing for divorce'.[37]

[32] Interview with lawyer, Karachi, 5 January 2022 [a]. The literal translation of '*ragra lagao*' would be to rub; I have tried to provide the best fitting translation, but it does not wholly capture the essence of what was said.

[33] See KH Ng, *The Common Law in Two Voices: Language, Law and the Post-Colonial Predicament in Hong Kong* (Stanford University Press 2009) 254.

[34] R Delgado, 'Storytelling for Oppositionists and Others: A Plea for Narrative' (1988) 87 Michigan Law Review 2411.

[35] ibid 2413.

[36] Phone interview with lawyer, Peshawar, 1 July 2022.

[37] Interview with victim support personnel, Lahore, 15 June 2022.

The practice of scripting women through boilerplate text in a one-size-fits-all approach is not limited to *khula* or divorce cases, but often also seen in other cases relating to domestic abuse. When women file for child custody on the basis of violence,[38] for example, similar scripts are used in the written reply.[39] I often questioned the root of these pre-drafted suits and the kinds of allegations they contained. Where did they come from? One lawyer suggested that someone got hold of a draft many years ago and shared it amongst the legal fraternity.[40] Another lawyer suggested that they may have come from samples in old textbooks on conveyance or legal drafting, which were copied and disseminated until someone thought to make a business out of it.[41] 'Even if you have ten lawyers coming to you daily and all you're doing is changing a name and printing it out, that is 10,000 rupees per day. It's a proper business', she said.[42] However, a judge to whom I spoke put it more succinctly, in a manner which resonates with Delgado's theorizing of prevailing mindsets: 'The society we live in, this is in the society roots. That is where the templates come from. That is where the allegations come from. The societal roots will always speak.'[43]

'Bad' woman, 'mad' woman

In Chapter 2, I spoke of how the social control of women can (re)produce social order through both formal, institutional control, as well through normative control in close relationships. The moral regulation of women through gendering strategies adopted by the State promotes ideas of what

[38] Custody applications analysed for this research where claims of domestic violence featured prominently include: Guardian and Ward judgment, Family Court 1708/19 Karachi South (Jul 2021); Guardian and Ward application, Family Court 2313/21 Karachi Central (Jan 2021); Guardian and Ward judgment, Family Court 50/22 Karachi Central (Apr 2022); and Guardian and Ward judgment, High Court 419/21 Lahore (Sept 2021).

[39] As discussed in Chapter 1, the welfare of the child is the prime consideration in custody cases, with significant weight given to the character and mental capacity of the proposed guardian (see Guardian and Wards Act 1890 [PAK], s 17). For example, in Guardian and Ward judgment, Family Court 1093/22 Karachi Central (Apr 2022), it was stated 'that the respondent is mentally sick she torture the minor ward when she became angry on any petty matter, she even not take care of the minor ward and her health [sic]'. Also see, S Ishaque and MM Khan, 'The Best Interests of the Child: A Prevailing Consideration within Islamic Principles and a Government Principle in Child Custody Cases in Pakistan' (2015) 29(1) International Journal of Law, Policy and Family 86.

[40] Interview with lawyer, Karachi, 11 August 2022 [a].

[41] Phone interview with lawyer, Rawalpindi, 13 July 2022.

[42] ibid.

[43] Interview with family judge, District and Sessions Courts, Karachi, 5 August 2022.

is permissible and aids in understanding the kinds of character allegations prescribed to women in cases of domestic violence. For example, Khan's work on the moral regulation of Pakistani women[44] uses Corrigan and Seyer's argument as a cornerstone, which proposes that the nation is grounded in relations of domination and subordination with a set of socially produced notions that are 'simultaneously descriptive and moral'.[45] This suggests that moral regulation is 'a project of normalizing, rendering natural, taken for granted, in a word "obvious," what are in fact ontological and epistemological premises of a particular and historical form of social order'.[46] Similarly, the practice of subjectivizing women through gendered allegations reflects the ways in which bodies are subjugated and identities are shaped through disciplinary regimes in order to produce docile subjects.[47] This resonates with what Allen posits: that legal discourse brings in sexual and gender-based divisions not only into 'what the law can legitimately "do," in terms of particular provisions and procedures, but also more profoundly, into what it can reasonably argue'.[48] Bearing this in mind, an example of the boilerplate text used in pre-drafted suits to allege that a woman is of 'bad' character is as follows:

> . . . That the plaintiff is not entitled for any relief as claimed by her as she proved herself disobedient wife. The plaintiff never fulfilled her duties of being an obedient wife neither did the plaintiff performed house chores . . . Plaintiff neither allowed to fulfil her husband matrimonial rights [sic].
>
> . . . The defendant loves the plaintiff from core of his heart and kept her like a Queen/Malika. The defendant provided all the necessities of life to the plaintiff [sic].[49]

This extract comes from a reply to a suit filed for the dissolution of marriage and recovery of maintenance and dowry articles on the basis of cruelty, where the complainant alleged both physical and financial abuse by her

[44] S Khan, *Zina, Transnational Feminism, and the Moral Regulation of Pakistani Women* (UBC Press 2006) 56.

[45] P Corrigan and D Sayer, *The Great Arch: English State Formation as Cultural Revolution* (Basil Blackwell 1985) 4.

[46] ibid 6.

[47] AL Stoler, *Race and the Education of Desire: Foucault's History of Sexuality and the Colonial Order of Things* (Duke University Press 1996).

[48] H Allen, *Justice Unbalanced* (Open University Press 1987) 30.

[49] Reply filed to suit for dissolution of marriage and recovery of maintenance and dowry articles. See Dissolution of Marriage, Civil and Family Court 744/22 Karachi Central (Mar 2022).

husband. In response, the allegations relating to her character seem to be used as an excuse (or perhaps a justification) for her treatment, in addition to the denial of that treatment—as if to say, I didn't do it, but even if I did, she is not liable to relief.[50] Riaz and Begum claim that as per Shariah law, if a wife is immoral, is disobedient, or has a health condition, then the husband is no longer accountable for her maintenance. They say: 'it is a just and balanced right that when the husband is made liable for maintenance then in return the wife is made to be obedient to her husband.'[51] It is also pertinent to note that character allegations are commonly used as a means to discredit female witnesses in Pakistan.[52] As noted in Chapter 2, Article 151 of the Qanun-e-Shahadat Order, '*impeaching credit of witness*', included an explicit section relating to sexual offences to say, 'when a man is prosecuted for rape or an attempt to ravish, it may be shown that the prosecutrix was of generally immoral character'.[53] While this clause was omitted through an amendment to the criminal laws in 2016,[54] evidence of a victim's 'bad' character continues to be used in litigative practices. In a 2017 rape case, for example, the judge noted that the complainant was 'a lady of easy virtue and hence corroboration of her statements was needed'.[55] In the same judgment, it was later said:

> I do agree with the learned counsel for prosecution that simple penetration is sufficient and positive report of swabs and DNA are not a requirement of the law but I would say that when a victim is *enjoying bad character* then these things are important to believe her version.[56]

As discussed in previous chapters, painting women as immoral and of bad character is an age-old, familiar patriarchal technique within and beyond the law, which primarily focused on the woman's body as the site at which

[50] This was alluded to as a tactic: 'They have to deny [the abuse], of course, but will also say things and attack her character to reduce her credibility and increase their own.' Interview with lawyer, Lahore, 16 June 2022 [a] [parenthesis added].

[51] S Riaz and S Begum, 'Non-Maintenance Creates a Right of Separation: A Comparative Study of Court's Practices and Shariah Law' (2021) 4(1) IQAN 21.

[52] S Omar, 'Dissolution of Marriage: Practices, Laws and Islamic Teachings' (2007) 4(1) Policy Perspectives 91.

[53] Article 151(4), Qanun-e-Shahadat Order (Law of Evidence) 1984 [PAK].

[54] See s 16, Criminal Law Amendment (Offences Relating to Rape) Act 2016 [PAK].

[55] Judgement, Sessions Court [2017] OSC 124, as cited in FY Bokhari, 'Accountability for Rape: A Case Study of Lodhran' (2018) Centre for Human Rights, University College Lahore 1, 41.

[56] ibid [emphasis added].

these contestations were deliberated.[57] The inclusion of the woman's mind into assessments of her character, by infusing subjective labels from the 'psy' disciplines, appears to be a more recent approach within Pakistani courtrooms. In other words, 'these are those terms that were always used in *aam zabaan* [everyday language], *keh yeh toh paagal hai* [that she is mad]—very dismissive things to do, to discredit her in society—that are now codified as examples of mental illness in the drafting of suits'.[58] An extract from case files assists in illustrating the kind of boilerplate text and allegations relating to a woman's mental state that are found in legal documents:

> . . . That the defendant has extended extreme love and affection to the plaintiff since marriage but unfortunately the plaintiff could not acknowledge or appreciate the love and sacrifices made by the defendant and due to her psychological disturbances always argued, quarrelled, misbehaved, maltreated, taunted, and extended abusive language towards the defendant and his family. It is worth mentioning here that the aforementioned attitude and behaviour of the plaintiff towards the defendant is a matter of routine for the plaintiff.
>
> . . . The plaintiff never physically, mentally or by any other means whatsoever abused or tortured the plaintiff . . . rather has always shown ultimate love and care considering the psychological condition of the plaintiff. The plaintiff has never turned out to be an obedient/respectful wife.
>
> . . . It is also worth mentioning it is the defendant who has requested with extreme love and submissiveness to the plaintiff and her father to get herself consulted from a good psychiatrist and go through a psychiatric/psychological test as her irrational, abrupt, attitudinal and mental behaviour demands the same, which hyperactive/overly reactive the plaintiff [sic] and instead of understanding that the advise is purely for our better future, but has always considered such suggestion as negative with construing that the defendant is calling the plaintiff a wrathful/mad person [sic].[59]

[57] N Yuval-Davis, *Gender and Nation* (Sage Publications 1997).
[58] Phone interview with lawyer, Rawalpindi, 13 July 2022.
[59] Written statement [respondent], Dissolution of Marriage, Family Court 1223/22 Islamabad West (May 2022).

This extract is from a written response to a case of dissolution of marriage that alleged physical and sexual abuse by the complainant's husband. The lawyer working this case told me that her client had recently found out that her husband had been sexually abusing their ten-year-old daughter as well, but requested to keep that information off the legal record for the sake of her daughter's '*izzat*' [honour]. 'She said, if they can malign me with this type of character assassination, imagine what they would do to my daughter.'[60] Interestingly in this extract, the discussion of a woman's 'psychological disturbance' is followed by a testament of her lack of obedience as a wife. The two allegations—of being a 'bad' woman and a 'mad' woman—appear to have converged.

Scripting victims through gendered allegations that frame them as 'bad' and/or 'mad' women is often accompanied by another technique: the character enhancement of men. Hartley's research on domestic violence trials specified a few techniques that lawyers use to enhance the character of defendants. The first is that the defendant is a 'good guy' (or that he did 'nice things' for the victim) and the second is that the defendant loved the victim.[61] As seen in the extracts above, statements included in boilerplate scripts adopt a similar trajectory ('the defendant loves the plaintiff from the core of his heart and kept her like a Queen/Malika'). Comparably, one lawyer spoke of a domestic violence case in which she was involved where 'the husband said, "I don't look at any other woman, I don't gamble, I don't drink, I don't smoke", like great, good for you, you are a good Muslim man, what does that have to do with anything? Does it give you a licence to beat her up?'[62] Both techniques—the character assassination of victims and the character enhancement of defendants—are based on dampening the credibility of the former and increasing the credibility of the latter.

Further, Watkins speaks of facets of lawyering which operate to bring about distinctions between those on the inside of the law and those on the outside.[63] Perhaps that is why, when questioned about the practice of using pre-drafted suits, one lawyer told me that I should not get 'hung up' about

[60] Fieldwork notes, Family Court, Islamabad, 9 June 2022.
[61] C Hartley, 'He Said, She Said: The Defense Attack of Credibility in Domestic Violence Felony Trials' (2001) 7(5) Violence Against Women 523, 524.
[62] Interview with lawyer, Lahore, 13 June 2022 [b].
[63] D Watkins, 'Recovering the Lost Human Stories of the Law: Finding Mrs Burns' (2013) 7(1) Law and Humanities 71.

such everyday legal practices.[64] Scheppele writes that 'we' (the lawyers) are the insiders, whose versions count as facts, and 'they' (the litigants) are the outsiders, whose versions are discredited and ultimately disbelieved.[65] Those whose stories are believed have the power to create fact. As such, in using a one-size-fits-all approach, the lawyerly practices prevalent in Pakistani courtrooms assist legal actors in scripting facts and subsequently in litigating the credibility of women complainants of domestic violence. In doing so, they remind the dominant group, 'we', of its identity in relation to outgroups, which in turn provide it with a form of shared reality in which its superior position is seen as natural.[66] In a male-dominated arena, 'we' may encompass both the legal fraternity and men at large.

'We just plant a seed, God waters it for us': Litigating credibilities

Credibility can take on multiple meanings: to be truthful, believable, trustworthy, and convincing. In short, it is to be someone that can be taken seriously. Women, however, are often seen as less credible witnesses in the justice system. Schafran helps us understand why this may be case. Particularly in domestic violence cases, she posits that women are perceived to lack credibility in three arenas.[67] First, they are seen to lack 'collective credibility' because they belong to a societal group that is generally assumed as being less credible. Second, they are viewed as lacking 'contextual credibility', which relates to the ability of being able to put oneself in another's shoes. In cases of domestic abuse, specific instances of assault are taken out of the larger relationship context, leading to evaluations of the claim in a vacuum.[68] And third, Schafran says that women are perceived to lack 'consequential credibility' or the ability to have their 'harms and injuries taken seriously, not devalued or trivialised'.[69]

[64] '*Aap is peh kyun atki hui hain, yeh toh aam practice hai, is se pareshan na hon* [why are you hung up on this, this is routine legal practice, don't worry about it so much].' Interview with lawyer, Islamabad, 9 June 2022 [c].

[65] KL Scheppele, 'Foreword: Telling Stories' (1988) 87(8) Michigan Law Review 2079, 2080.

[66] Delgado (n 34) 2412.

[67] LH Schafran, 'Credibility in the Courts: Why Is There a Gender Gap?' (1995) 34 Judges Journal 40, 42.

[68] Hartley (n 61) 512.

[69] Schafran (n 67) 41.

It is pertinent to note that cases of domestic violence are emblematic of credibility in law, where the (typically) female victim and male perpetrator are offering two opposing versions of events in a 'he said, she said' manner.[70] The conflicting narratives may

> put in place a suspicious cognitive set that colours how we will interpret the words of another. It leads us to look for signs of deception, irrationality, or incompetence and thus leads us to seek out evidence of inconsistencies, to magnify those we suppose ourselves to have found, and to focus on them in our assessment of the story as a whole.[71]

As such, there is a great amount of consideration given to the perceived legitimacy of a woman's testimony[72] and her personal trustworthiness.[73] And in determining the credibility of her account, any trait which poses as a defective power of observation, recollection, or communication is admissible.[74] Similarly, in Pakistani law, the general rule relating to the veracity or reliability of a witness is that their statement 'must be in consonance with the probabilities fitting the circumstances of the case and inspire confidence in the mind of a reasonable prudent person . . . if there is one infirmity which impeaches the credit of a witness, it is enough to make the entire statement doubtful'.[75] Further, scholars working on gender-based violence have noted that defence attorneys spend 'considerable time in cross-examination attempting to expose inconsistencies in the survivors testimony' because they feel that 'inconsistency creates suspicion of the woman'.[76] Put differently, it is to 'punch a hole in the survivor's story' because doing so can lead to her being disbelieved in the court.[77]

[70] D Epstein and L Goodman, 'Discounting Women: Doubting Domestic Violence Survivors' Credibility and Dismissing Their Experiences' (2019) 167(1) University of Pennsylvania Law Review 399.
[71] K Jones, 'The Politics of Credibility' in L Antony and C Witt (eds), *A Mind of One's Own: Feminist Essays on Reason and Objectivity* (Routledge 2002) 159.
[72] S Ramon, 'Intersectionalities: Intimate Partner Domestic Violence and Mental Health within the European Context' (2015) 4(2) A Global Journal of Social Work Analysis, Research, Polity, and Practice 76.
[73] Epstein and Goodman (n 70) 406.
[74] JH Wigmore, *A Treatise on the Anglo-American System of Evidence in Trials at Common Law* (3rd edn, Little Brown and Company 1940).
[75] Prosecutor General, 'Veracity of Witness or Reliability' *Government of the Punjab* <https://pg.punjab.gov.pk/veracity_of_witness_or_reliability> accessed 20 October 2022.
[76] L Madigan and NC Gamble, *The Second Rape: Society's Continued Betrayal of the Victim* (Lexington Books 1991) 102.
[77] ibid.

A lawyer I interviewed agreed with this sentiment, contending that the character assassination of women through pre-drafted suits and otherwise is a 'defence strategy, a tactic, and the easiest thing to do because all men pander to the gallery'.[78] Such allegations serve to dampen the veracity and credibility of the woman's narrative and shift the blameworthiness in those accounts from the accused to the victim. In 2020, for example, a woman was gang-raped in front of her children on a motorway in Lahore while waiting for assistance after her car developed a mechanical issue. In a press conference, the investigating officer said that the incident took place because 'the victim was travelling late at night without her husband's permission'.[79] Such testament of blameworthiness is accorded to both 'bad' women and 'mad' women, as a study in Pakistan found that 76 per cent of respondents consider that patients with mental illnesses have 'only themselves to blame'.[80] In assessments of fact-finding, the law is inclined towards accounts that have low blameworthiness and high credibility. Accordingly, the law is cautious of narratives that appear to have low credibility and high blameworthiness. While gendering strategies that use allegations relating to a woman's character assist in increasing her blameworthiness as a litigant, 'psy' labels can assist in reducing her credibility. Smith suggests that labelling a victim as 'disordered' in legal settings is either done to suggest that the victim's trial testimony is not to be believed, or to suggest that her original perception of events was inaccurate and the product of such an illness.[81] Similarly, a lawyer I spoke to explained:

> Look, women's credibility is always diluted in the courts—that is always what happens. They would even use examples of her yelling or her crying to try and prove this. But I mean, if I was frustrated, even I would yell and cry—that doesn't mean that I have some mental issue, you know? They basically want it to come down to '*yeh theek nahi hai is ki na suno* [she is not okay (mentally), don't listen to her]'. They want to dilute her testimony completely. It is a credibility issue.[82]

[78] Interview with lawyer, Lahore, 15 June 2022 [b].

[79] N Siddiqui, 'Motorway Rape Occurred Because Victim Travelled "Late Night Without Husband's Permission", CCPO Tells Senate Panel' *Dawn News* (28 September 2020) <https://www.dawn.com/news/1582117> accessed 26 October 2022.

[80] F Naeem, M Ayub, Z Javed, M Irfan, F Haral, and D Kingdon, 'Stigma and Psychiatric Illness. A Survey of Attitude of Medical Students and Doctors in Lahore, Pakistan' (2006) 18(3) Journal of Ayub Medical College 46.

[81] DM Smith, 'The Disordered and Discredited Plaintiff: Psychiatric Evidence in Civil Litigation' (2009) 31 Cardoza Law Review 788.

[82] Interview with lawyer, Lahore, 17 June 2022 [a].

In her analysis of women's experiences of sexual assault, Teurkheimer coined the term 'credibility discounting'. She explains that credibility discounting happens when 'a faulty preconception [. . .] reduces a speaker's perceived trustworthiness or diminishes the plausibility of her account'.[83] In Chapter 2, I provided examples from Pakistani literature that discussed how character tropes and 'psy' labels may impact the way someone is perceived, and the credibility they are awarded (or denied) through that perception. Those examples demonstrate how the rhetoric related to psychiatric illnesses, for example—such as lacking agency and being uncredible and untrustworthy—may be invoked simply through the use and application of 'psy' labels on victims. In conjunction with the low credibility awarded to women more generally, as posited by Schafran above, this raises a few questions: In scripting women through character allegations in this manner, what kinds of gendering strategies are employed in lawyerly practices? Particularly, is simply using labels and adjectives to frame women complainants as 'bad' and/or 'mad' sufficient to subjectivize litigants? And where evidence is provided, what is the nature of that evidence and how is it navigated by legal actors in the courtroom?

Perceptions and oral tactics

Research conducted by Jalil and others at two public sector universities in Pakistan surveyed the perceptions of students about whether a woman's character is 'good' or 'bad' based on her visible personality characteristics.[84] In addition to choice of clothing and the ease with which they interacted with members of the opposite sex, they found that boys judged the character of girls as immoral or 'bad' based on 'bold temperaments' and insubordination.[85] As discussed in previous chapters, all three of the ideas here—clothing, interaction with men, and insubordination—are indicative of respectability tropes typically used in gendering practices. The key focus is on perception.

[83] D Tuerkheimer, 'Incredible Women: Sexual Violence and the Credibility Discount' (2017) 166(1) University of Pennsylvania Law Review 14.

[84] A Jalil, QK Mahmood, A Usman and A Ahmad, 'Qualitative Analysis of Feminine Morality and Visible Personality Characteristics among Young Adults' (2020) 54 Quality and Quantity 887.

[85] ibid 900.

Even within the law, perceptions can have significant influence. For example, when questioned about the low conviction rate in rape cases, a Sessions Judge said: '*Aadhi toh habitual hoti hain, prostitutes hoti hain. Shakal se nazar aa jata hai* [half are habitual, they are prostitutes. You can see it on their face(s)]'.[86] Similarly, there is a common perception amongst legal actors that 'you can tell when you look at someone how their character is, and the mental is part of the character'.[87] This idea was reiterated on numerous occasions during interviews with lawyers:

> *Woh toh mujhe psycho hi lag rahi thi* [she was looking 'psycho' to me].[88]
>
> *Us ki toh shakal dekh kar pata chal gaya tha ke yeh zehni tor pe kamzor hai* [you could tell she was mentally weak when you looked at her].[89]
>
> *Us ko dekhte hi main us aurat ki psyche samajh gaya* [as soon as I saw that woman, I understood her psyche].[90]

What does a 'psycho' woman look like? When asked, lawyers were unable to provide a set criterion. Rather, it was suggested that 'one can understand the intention and mental character of such women through experience'.[91] It was proposed that judges too do not require much evidence of such allegations because their judicial experiences enable them to perceive women in real time: 'they too can see it on the [women's] faces'.[92] These perceptions come from observing women's expressions, behaviour, mannerisms, and ways of speaking. However, physical characteristics may at times be incorporated. One judge I interviewed said he was 'convinced' that a woman litigant in a case he presided over was mentally disordered due to her 'abnormally large head'.[93]

Alden considers the rhetoric of public opinion as having an impact on both courtroom practices and legislative decisions, clarifying that this rhetoric is largely informed by cultural myths and ideas that circulate through popular culture and discourse.[94] Perhaps that is why lawyers themselves

[86] Interview with lawyer, Lahore, 16 June 2022 [a].
[87] Interview with lawyer, Karachi, 5 January 2022 [a].
[88] ibid.
[89] Interview with lawyer, Lahore, 16 June 2022 [b].
[90] Interview with lawyer, Karachi, 5 January 2022 [c].
[91] Interview with lawyer, Karachi, 5 January 2022 [b].
[92] Interview with lawyer, Karachi, 15 January 2022.
[93] Interview with family judge, District and Sessions Court, Karachi, 4 July 2022.
[94] A Alden, *Disorder in the Court: Morality, Myth and the Insanity Defence* (University of Alabama Press 2018) 3.

consider the use of labels and corresponding perceptions to be sufficient in subjectivizing litigants for the purpose of gendered allegations, and engage in oral tactics to help shape these narratives. In doing so, they select specific aspects of women's experiences and use the boilerplate text in predrafted suits as a script to be enacted for spectators. To help illustrate, one lawyer explained how he adopts oral tactics to build on scripted narratives during custody battles, which in turn subjectivizes the complainant as a 'mad' woman:

> Now if I state that, '*dekhain is ka rawwaiya kaisa hai, aik dum hyper ho jati hai, is ka koi pata nahi kab deemagh ghoomein aur yeh psycho ban ke bachon ko maarne lage* [look how her behaviour is, she suddenly becomes hyper, and you don't know what to expect, when her mind turns and she becomes psycho and starts hitting the children]'. I can say this verbally, and the judge will assess. We know people's psyche *aur hum bhi logo ki nafsiyaat se khel rahe hote hain* [and we are also playing with/messing with people's minds]—meaning, a girl can be standing quietly and saying nothing and if I say, 'look, she is suddenly getting hyper', then of course she will react and shout and say 'what do you mean, I am not being hyper', and the judge makes a note of this and gives his observation on this. This is also a kind of proof [of mental instability], is it not? It serves the lawyer's purpose.[95]

In another case, a victim of acid crime recounted her experience with the legal fraternity. In a fit of rage, her husband had attacked her with acid in the middle of the night. Her two-year-old son had been sleeping next to her and died as a result of the acid that had splashed on him during the attack. When the victim was testifying in court, the defence lawyer claimed that women are very emotional by nature, and the victim was suffering from the trauma of her son's death and therefore dealing with a mental breakdown. As a result, he purported, she was mistaking the attack, and her testimony could not be trusted.[96] Here too, the lawyer used oral tactics to shape how the complainant was perceived in court, helping to construct her as an uncredible, 'mad' victim-subject.

[95] Interview with lawyer, Lahore, 16 June 2022 [a].
[96] Interview with victim, Islamabad, 8 June 2022 [e].

By generating clusters of ideas through which women's stories are scripted, these examples indicate that oral interactions and perceptions play a large role in the kinds of character allegations, gendering strategies, and lawyerly practices used to subjectivize women. During court observations, I too witnessed such practices at play during a *khula* [divorce] case. When the hearing commenced, the judge requested the complainant to remove her mask so that he could see her properly. She responded to say that she felt uncomfortable doing so, as she has elderly parents at home and wanted to protect them from any possible transmission of illness. To this, her lawyer said, '*Judge ki baat ko izzat dom utaar do paanch minute ke liye, kuch nahi hota* [give respect to what the judge is saying, take off the mask for five minutes, nothing will happen]'.[97] The defendant's lawyer, standing on the other side of the bench, added: '*Yeh miya ki baat kabhi nahi maanti, ab judge ki kya baat mane gi* [She never agreed to/listened to what her own husband would say, do you think she will listen to the judge?]'.[98] Here, the oral tactics used by legal actors aimed to subjectivize the plaintiff as a disobedient, 'bad' woman. Such lawyerly practices can therefore encompass multiple character-based allegations:

> The other party try to say things that would make you aggressive and angry and derail you so that you are acting in a way that even the judge stops to think whether the false allegations they are putting on your client are true. In one case they asked my client about her second marriage—there was no second marriage—but they just wanted to derail her so she would react in a certain way and they could tell the judge, 'See, her mental state is not good, she is unable to keep her emotions in check, this is not a good environment for children to be raised in'.[99]

In addition to lawyerly practices that shape perceptions through oral strategies, lawyers may also build on the scripted, 'stock' story by using restrictive questioning tactics in conjunction with the presentation of peculiar forms of 'evidence'.

[97] Court observations, Sessions Court Karachi (South), July 2022.
[98] ibid.
[99] Interview with lawyer, Lahore, 17 June 2022 [a]. The case being spoken of is related to custody and guardianship, where allegations of domestic violence surfaced.

Restrictive questioning and peculiar forms of 'evidence'

The majority of research conducted into courtroom questioning and cross-examination finds that witnesses and litigants are prevented from 'telling their own stories'.[100] As Tiersma notes, the question-and-answer format 'allocates control to the questioner; in this case, the examining lawyer'.[101] As touched upon in Chapter 3, with a narrative, 'the story-teller herself decides how to tell her tale',[102] but in courtrooms, the lawyer becomes the primary narrator of the story. And in adopting this role, one of the key methods used by lawyers is limiting the respondent to providing one-word confirmatory responses—'yes' or 'no'. These kinds of closed-ended, restrictive questions are of the type classified by Woodbury,[103] employed by lawyers to construct specific narratives that contradict the experience of legal parties and challenge the credibility of witnesses. In Pakistani courts, yes/no questions are primarily employed by lawyers to subjectivize victims during cross-examination in cases relating to domestic violence. And to ensure that they remain on script, this is done in conjunction with the allegations and labels applied to the complainant through boilerplate suits, and any evidence they may bring forward for the claims. A case from Lahore helps illustrate.

In 2021, a man attempted to rape his stepdaughter, aged seven. Because the victim was a minor, the complaint was filed by her mother, the wife of the defendant. She too had been physically abused by the defendant but had chosen to pursue a case for the violence inflicted on her daughter and not for that inflicted on her. During trial, the defence lawyers felt it more advantageous to discredit the mother as the main complainant in the case. Their stance was that '*maan ki zehni haalat theek nahi hai, is liye hum iska nafsiyati ilaaj bhi karwa rahe hain aur diwaayan bhi le rahi he, toh is wajah se, matlab ke, yeh ghalat inzaam diya hai aur parcha hum par jhoota ho gaya* [the mother's mental state is not good, we are getting her mental (psychiatric) treatment and she is taking medicines too, that is why she is mistaken and this false accusation has been put on us]'.[104] To support these claims, the defence team brought in members of the respondent's family as witnesses

[100] See J Cotterill, 'Collocation, Connotation, and Courtroom Semantics: Lawyers' Control of Witness Testimony through Lexical Negotiation' (2004) 25(4) Applied Linguistics 513.
[101] P Tiersma, *Legal Language* (Chicago University Press 1999) 159.
[102] ibid 160.
[103] H Woodbury, 'The Strategic Use of Questions in Court' (1984) 48(3–4) Semiotica 197.
[104] As narrated by a lawyer during an interview, Lahore, 13 June 2022 [a].

to testify to the mother's 'aggressive' and '*laraku*' [bellicose or rebellious] nature. In addition, they presented a pharmacy receipt for medication as evidence of the treatment she was taking for said mental illness. The question that the lawyer asked the complainant during cross-examination was simply, 'is this your receipt? Yes or no?' She responded yes. The lawyer for the complainant was unaware of the existence of this slip and therefore was unable to counter-argue on the spot. After the hearing, she realized that the receipt was not for a medication that treats any mental ailment, but in fact for an emergency contraceptive pill dated eight months prior. While recounting this case to me, the lawyer added: 'It's such a strange thing, even my client did not think they would bring this up. It was from eight months ago and irrelevant. How could we have prepared to counter this? She did not even know how they found it.'[105]

In some cases, women may not be fully informed of the nature of the medication they are taking. One lawyer recalled a case where her client was seeking full custody of her child due to numerous instances of domestic abuse. The defence team claimed that she was unfit for childcare because she took medication for her mental ailments. During cross-examination, the defence lawyer showed a paper slip to the litigant and asked, 'do you take this medicine, yes or no?' She responded that she was unable to read or write. The lawyer then brought out a medicine sachet and asked the question differently: 'look at this, have you ever taken this medicine, yes or no?' When she remained silent, the judge prompted her to respond, and she said yes. Later, she came to her lawyer and said, '*mujhe yeh dawa pilayi gai hai jab abortion hua tha, yeh log kuch bolne hi nahi dete* [I was made to take this medicine when I had an abortion,[106] these people don't allow you to even say anything]'.[107]

Further, while observing the courts, I noticed that when a litigant attempted to provide background information during cross-examination, she was interrupted in one instance by the lawyer questioning her and in another instance by the judge himself. In both cases, she was firmly requested to keep her answers short and curt.[108] Answering a question in 'yes'

[105] ibid.

[106] It is common to use the term abortion interchangeably with miscarriage in Pakistan. The lawyer on this case thinks it was given to her client to force an abortion/miscarriage when they found out she was carrying a daughter and not a son: Interview with lawyer, Karachi, 14 January 2022.

[107] As recounted by a lawyer during an interview, Karachi, 14 January 2022.

[108] Court observations, 10 June 2022, Islamabad; Court observations, 4 August 2022, Karachi.

or 'no' often lacks the necessary context, which may explain why lawyers commonly use this tactic to subjectivize the litigant:

> If she is not giving us the answers that we want, we change the subsequent questions in order to get it. Sometimes the judge catches us and tells us not to do it, but good lawyers find a way to do it. For example, I was the defendant for the husband in a *khula* case and he told me to say that the girl was having an affair with a man who lives in Dubai. So, I asked her, did you go to Dubai—yes or no—she said yes. I asked, were you having a relation with that man—yes or no—she said no. So, then I changed the next question and asked, did you stay in Dubai for fifteen days—yes or no—she said yes. And then I asked, was the man in Dubai—yes or no—and she said yes. See, I got my answer. That was sufficient for the judge to understand that there was a relationship with that man. My purpose was served, so I did not need to go into any more detail.[109]

What this questioning left out was that the man lived in Dubai, and therefore was in the city while she was visiting on holiday. There was nothing to say that she was in fact having an illicit affair with him, but it was the suggestion of its plausibility that stuck. As termed by Clark, lawyers use a conscious manipulation of 'conceptual perspective' to construct scenarios in court.[110] Clark explains this as 'the speaker's presentation of an object, relation or event, through choice of words to the addressee, such that some properties of the referent are included, and others excluded by each choice'.[111]

Similarly, in the other examples provided above, 'medicine' was included as a referent for the 'psy' label, but the nature or relevance of those medications to the 'psy' label was excluded. In view of this, I often asked lawyers why the nature of various medicines are not questioned or elaborated upon, to deem whether they are in fact relevant to the allegations being contested. The responses are summarized as follows: the judge does not have time to go into so much detail for every case, and want to dispose of it as soon as possible;[112] the judge does not have the knowledge or expertise to be able to differentiate between different medications (hence the presentation of

[109] Interview with lawyer, Karachi, 5 January 2022 [a].
[110] EV Clark, *Word Choice and Conceptual Perspective* (Koninklijke Nederlandse Akademie Van Wetenschappen 1998) 5.
[111] ibid.
[112] Interview with lawyer, Karachi, 5 January 2022 [d].

a medication, *any* medication, suffices);[113] and if it is disputed, it is just as easy to get fake prescriptions of relevant medications and submit them in court, so why bother to engage further?[114] As a result, the unsubstantiated allegations are rarely questioned or penalized, making the sheer volume of boilerplate scripts containing mental health-related allegations a relatively easy way for women's cases to be undermined. For this reason, in cases where women are experiencing anxiety or depression as an *outcome* of the violence they experienced, their lawyers choose to keep this off the official record:

> You would expect this to be proof [of the violence]—if she is crazy, it is because you made her crazy. But we cannot discuss this in the court, because once you go to see a doctor, that piece of paper can always be used against you. It's used as proof of your mental illness, not as proof of the violence you experienced. That prescription is a stain on you. Better not to bring it up.[115]

This further reflects the uncomfortable tension between the use of 'psy' labels to undermine women's claims and the complex relationship that often exists between domestic abuse and mental health, with the latter potentially causing or aggravating mental health symptoms.[116] The use of 'psy' labels as a narrative strategy can then be seen as doing a disservice to that complexity, where, as we see above, aspects of victim's needs and harms being kept off the official record also means that those needs and harms are not recognized.

In instances where the complainant can respond in more than one-word answers, thereby providing context for the claim and 'evidence' presented in the court, the defence strategy changes. For example, one lawyer recalled a case of a woman who filed for *khula* [divorce] after an abusive

[113] Interview with lawyer, Karachi, 8 January 2022.
[114] Interview with lawyer, Islamabad, 9 June 2022 [c].
[115] Interview with victim support personnel, Lahore, 15 June 2022.
[116] See S Oram S, H Khalifeh and L Howard, 'Violence against Women and Mental Health' (2017) 4(2) Lancet Psychiatry 159; C Humphreys and R Thiara, 'Mental Health and Domestic Violence: "I call it symptoms of abuse"' (2003) 2(1) The British Journal of Social Work 209; V Munro and R Aitken, 'From Hoping to Help: Identifying and Responding to Suicidality amongst Victims of Domestic Abuse' (2020) 26(1) International Review of Victimology 29; T Afifi and others, 'Mental Health Correlates of Intimate Partner Violence in Marital Relationships in a Nationally Representative Sample of Males and Females' (2009) 24(8) Journal of Interpersonal Violence 1398.

marriage of five years. The defence team claimed that the plaintiff's allegations of abuse were mistaken on account of the influence that her prescription medications for mental illness have on her soundness of mind. As evidence, they presented a prescription for birth control medication. During cross-examination, the woman admitted that she took medication daily, but went on to say that the medicine was prescribed to her by a doctor due to heavy bleeding during menstruation and not because of any mental illness. Her lawyer too, 'rebut[ted] it aggressively', due to which she was told by the judge 'not to prance *such things* around so openly in court'.[117] When the litigant's response affected the credibility of the defence's evidence, they adapted their claim to say the medicine 'was evidence of bad character' because 'only a woman of questionable mind and questionable character would feel the need to take medication of *such nature*'.[118] The lawyer on this case added: 'That is the thing, they would go to her room and find some tiny medication and bring that in as some big evidence.'[119] Here, it appears that a different property of the referent was included, adapting conceptual perspectives to construct a slightly varied narrative. Given that women who take contraceptive pills are considered indecent and immoral in Pakistan,[120] the litigant's subjectification through such gendering practices correspondingly fluctuates from 'mad' woman to 'bad' woman.

As demonstrated by the discussion above, there appears to be a pattern in the medications chosen to be presented as 'evidence' of mental illness. They primarily relate to women's sexuality and sexual health, in the form of abortion pills, emergency contraceptive pills, or birth control pills (also referred to as 'period medicine'[121]). In the same way that character allegations relating to the body are linked to respectability politics and a woman's sexuality and femininity[122] (for example by alleging that she is having illicit affairs), allegations relating to her mind adopt a similar tone. As signalled earlier, it seems that these two allegations can be intertwined to form two sides of the same coin. And when such allegations are presented alongside

[117] Interview with lawyer, Lahore, 15 June 2022 [c] [emphasis added].
[118] ibid.
[119] ibid.
[120] See for example F Younas, M Naseem and M Mustafa, 'Patriarchy and Social Media: Women Only Facebook Groups as Safe Spaces for Support Seeking in Pakistan' (Information and Communication Technologies and Development Conference, 17 June 2022, New York).
[121] See *SR Abbas v SS Sattar* [2015] YLR 489 as discussed in Chapter 2.
[122] See M Zia, 'A Pilot Study on Honour Killings in Pakistan and Compliance of Law' (Aurat Publication and Information Service Foundation 2011).

performative oral tactics, peculiar forms of evidence, and restrictive modes of questioning, they help serve the lawyer's script and present an alternative set of facts which litigates credibilities in the courtroom and shifts the balance of blameworthiness. From the analysis presented, it also becomes evident that a common strand of the lawyerly practices used to subjectivize women is the power of suggestion. As one lawyer said: 'we just plant a seed; God waters it for us.'[123]

The power of suggestion

In *Rewriting the Soul*, Hacking 'fears' that 'we have very little understanding of the working of "suggestion", a word . . . that so often stands for a question mark rather than for a clear idea.'[124] While he considers this a fear, it is also a warning of the harm that suggestibility may have on autonomous judgment. Suggestions, particularly when deliberate, can create response expectancies not only in how individuals behave to produce an outcome but also in how behavioural responses are cognitively viewed by others.[125] In Pakistani courts, the allegations applied to victims of domestic violence, particularly those which make use of 'psy' labels, are often posed as suggestions. This is done both through language choices in legal drafting and through oral discourses of commentary and questioning:

> Usually calling a woman psychologically weak is just a casual practice and it is used by lawyers as a suggestion when they are talking. They are even written as suggestions: 'it is incorrect to suggest that the appellant did this' or 'it is suggested that the plaintiff is like this', and *there is nothing wrong with that*.[126]

'There is nothing wrong with that' indicates that lawyers consider a suggestion to be just that—a proposal or a possibility. In framing allegations as such, they do not need to necessarily bring evidence for the claims. This is aligned with text analysed in case files, where character allegations that

[123] Interview with lawyer, Islamabad, 9 June 2022 [a].
[124] I Hacking, *Rewriting the Soul: Multiple Personality and the Sciences of Memory* (Princeton University Press 1995) 267.
[125] RB Michael, M Garry and I Kirsch, 'Suggestion, Cognition and Behaviour' (2012) 21(3) Current Directions in Psychological Science 151.
[126] Interview with lawyer, Islamabad, 9 June 2022 [a] [emphasis added].

employ 'psy' labels may be entered into the record as suggestions or requests. For example, a legal notice sent to a woman who sought a divorce due to cruelty states:

> ... You always forced my client to obey your nonsense wishes due to your mental issues. Instead of being humble, you keep on threaten[ing] my client [with] serious consequence, which suggests your malafide intention or psycho behaviour towards your husband.
>
> ... That it came into my knowledge that you are mentally sick just after few weeks of marriage you started with a dominating tone, arrogant attitude and ambiguous behaviour towards my client.
>
> ... Under the circumstances you are requested to get treatment from doctors regarding your mental issues [*sic*].[127]

Campbell considers suggestions to be neither an abstraction nor a question mark, but rather animated concepts which give meaning and specific causal efficacies through their use in social practices.[128] Corresponding to this, a recurring theme during interviews with lawyers was that framing allegations relating to a woman's character and mental state as suggestions is intentional. The purpose is twofold. The first objective that suggestibility serves is to shift the court's focus by 'planting a particular seed of doubt in the mind of the judge'.[129] Second, suggestions are often used as 'bargaining chips' to get women to agree to demands and negotiations.[130] When examined alongside other lawyerly practices which help construct victim-subjects of domestic violence, the strategic use of suggestibility can too be seen as a gendering strategy. To help illustrate, a lawyer and a member of victim support personnel who work at an organization focusing on sexual violence shared details of a recent case relating to incest:

> There was a girl whose father was sexually assaulting her since she was twelve years old till the age of twenty-five. The father kept her in isolation. His wife had taken a divorce and he found jobs for his sons as

127 Legal notice sent to the plaintiff relating to Dissolution of Marriage, Family Court 424/22 Karachi East (January 2022).

128 S Campbell, 'Relational Remembering: Suggestibility and Women's Confidential Records' in CM Koggel, A Furlong and C Levin (eds) *Confidential Relationships: Psychoanalytic, Ethical and Legal Contexts* (Rodopi 2003) 152.

129 Interview with lawyer, Lahore, 16 June 2022 [c].

130 Phone interview with lawyer, Lahore, 28 July 2022.

> labourers in other cities so they would not come home. During this period, she conceived seven pregnancies of which four were born and the father sold them out, and others she was unable to take to term due to ongoing sexual violence. He would isolate her, [sexually] abuse her and assault her, and showed her nothing of the outside world, no relatives, nothing. He would also move from one neighbourhood to another every few months. You know, some neighbours would sometimes see her through a window and ask why she is isolated, and he would say that she is suffering from a mental illness and that's why he has to keep her indoors and take care of her.[131]

Due to a complication during her seventh pregnancy, the girl was taken to a hospital, where she was eventually able to get help. When the case made it to court, the father maintained the allegation that his daughter, the complainant, was suffering from a mental illness. When the prosecution requested proof of this allegation, the defence stated that the medical examination specified that she had been pregnant for eighteen weeks, but during questioning in court, she had said 'yes' when asked if she had been raped twenty weeks ago. Because the dates did not match up, they suggested that her testimony was flawed and uncredible, and evidenced mental unsoundness. The prosecution responded that 'it can take time for a woman to get pregnant after being subject to sexual intercourse',[132] but the suggestion had already planted a seed of doubt in the courtroom.

Assessing the credibility of a litigant in legal contexts is often confused with another term, 'competence'—both of which are arguably impacted by allegations that make use of 'psy' labels. Competence is the capability or capacity of an individual to serve as a witness and to 'sufficiently observe, recollect and recount an event'.[133] A witness's competence is typically presumed, unless it is suggested that their capacity is impaired—either due to age or due to a psychological problem. Unlike competence, credibility does not concern the physical characteristics of a witness, but they are linked in that a suggestion that questions a witness's competence may in turn impact

[131] Interview with lawyer, Karachi, 19 July 2022; interview with victim support personnel, Karachi, 19 July 2022.

[132] Interview with lawyer, Karachi, 19 July 2022. I speak about legal language and the (problematic) litigative practice of using 'subject to sexual intercourse' to refer to the offence of rape in Chapter 6.

[133] R Rosenthal, 'Suggestibility, Reliability and the Legal Process' (2002) 22(3) Developmental Review 337.

her credibility.[134] As one lawyer said, 'suggestions are used purposefully so that women get out of their mental balance and act in a particular way or say particular things. The same way it is normal for doctors to see blood, it is normal for lawyers to do this and make such statements. It is just our profession.'[135]

A woman I interviewed recalled an interaction with lawyers who engaged in suggestibility. She had been the victim of an acid attack in her home and underwent numerous surgeries to treat burn-related facial disfigurements and the loss of eyesight in one eye. During her trial, she said that she had covered her face with a *dupatta*, both because she felt ashamed of the disfigurement and because she wanted to retain her modesty in court. The defence lawyer tried to use this to subjectivize her by telling the judge, 'She is not mentally stable, she has no sense of what she is saying . . . Look at her hiding her face, there is nothing there, she is lying, nothing of this sort happened'.[136] The victim professed her apprehension at taking off her *dupatta*, but she had a choice to make: to either be painted as a 'bad' woman by taking off her veil in a public place, or to be painted as a 'mad' woman by not. She chose the former. 'I removed the *dupatta* from my face and told the judge, look at me, see for yourself, look at what that man did to me. That shut up the lawyer, but I did not like it at all',[137] she said.

Another victim of acid crime had been attacked by a neighbour for refusing his marriage proposal shortly after she was widowed. The defence lawyer in this case suggested that the acid attack was self-inflicted by the victim due to grief stemming from her husband's death. When the prosecution rebutted this claim by asking 'do you really think anyone in their right mind could burn themselves like this?', the defence replied: 'exactly, she is not in her right mind, that is what we are suggesting.'[138] When framed as suggestions, anecdotes and labels regarding a woman's character or mental soundness were often spoken of as 'planting a seed' to be germinated in the minds of judges. In other words:

[134] ibid 334.
[135] Interview with lawyer, Islamabad, 9 June 2022 [a].
[136] Interview with victim, Islamabad, 8 June 2022 [d].
[137] ibid. Another victim of acid crime similarly recalled that the defence lawyer suggested that she had covered her head and face with dupatta because there was 'nothing to show'. Rather, she had covered herself when attending court due to shame stemming from the burns and disfigurement. Interview with victim, Islamabad, 8 June 2022 [c].
[138] Interview with victim, Islamabad, 8 June 2022 [a].

> It is so that the judge starts viewing the behaviour of the women through a certain lens. It would be unfair to say that all judges do, but many would. If you turn up in a family court dressed in trousers and a sleeveless shirt and look fashionable, and give the impression of a modern woman, and they say that you are a *badchalan* woman [of bad conduct], you think that won't make a difference?[139]

It was interesting to note that in cases where the victim's lawyer is also a woman, these 'suggestions' may extend to her as well. The legal counsel for a domestic violence shelter referred to multiple instances where her character had been maligned in similar ways. In one case, the defence team told the judge: '*yeh toh lag ta hai woh hain jee, "mera jism meri marzi walay", Aurat March walay* [it seems like she is one of those "my body my choice" ones, the Aurat March women]'.[140] This statement made the judge stop and ask the lawyer who she is, what the nature of her work was, and under what jurisdiction the victim was being kept at the shelter. This suggestion served to create doubts about the conditions being contested in the court, shifting the focus of the case and changing the subsequent questioning and narrative. 'It was no longer about the victim or the circumstances she was testifying to, but about her lawyer's character and line of work.'[141]

While suggestions can be used to effectively subjectivize women by creating doubts relating to their testimonies, they could have a similar effect even on deceased victims. In cases where the death of the victim is alleged as suicide by the accused, and as murder resulting from domestic violence by the victim's family,[142] lawyers engage in suggestibility through other means. In the absence of medical evidence, for instance, the defence team may bring in screenshots of old emails or pictures that the victim had saved

[139] Interview with lawyer, Lahore, 16 June 2022 [c].

[140] As discussed in Chapter 2, *Aurat March* refers to Pakistan's current women's movement. For a brief account of public discourse surrounding the movement, see D Kamal, 'Networked Struggles: Placards at Pakistan's Aurat March' (2022) 30 Feminist Legal Studies 219.

[141] Interview with lawyer, Lahore, 14 June 2022.

[142] Relevant cases include: *A Ali v The State* [2014] MLD 965 LHC; *Basharat Ali v The State* [2017] PCrLJ 689; *Basit v Asghar Jan and others* [2018] PCrLJ Note 116; *Haji Qasim Khan v Kabir Khan and others* [2018] YLR 282; *Hakim Zada v The State* [2015] PCrLJ 1171; *Peeru Ram v The State* [2019] PCrLJ 325; *Qabil v The State* [2020] PCrLJ Note 13; *M Amin Ahmed v Gul Daraz* [2019] SCMR 1451; *M Zahid Khan v The State* [2019] PHC 244; *Sarfraz v The State* [2020] PLJ CRC 1059; *Raja Waqas Shafique v The State* [2015] MLD 22; *Manzoor Elahi v Session Judge* [2016] PCrLJ 211; *Mst Sarwari and others v The State* [2018] YLR 728; *Muhammad Dildar v The State* [2018] YLR Note 83; and *Yar Muhammad v The State* [2017] PCrLJ 694.

on her phone to suggest that she was experiencing depression and took her own life.[143] At other times 'they bring records of text messages which suggest some apprehension and are interpreted as signalling that the woman was under some pressure or stress and so committed suicide'.[144] By psychologizing the deceased in this way, such suggestions and propositions bring in doubts, and 'once you have a doubt, the benefit of it will always go towards the defence'.[145]

Additionally, presenting allegations as suggestions to script victims of domestic violence may serve a bargaining purpose, in that they pressurize victims to agree to demands and negotiations. As described by one lawyer, it is as if to say, 'if you don't do this, then we will continue to malign you in the court'.[146] Framing allegations relating to a women's character and mental state as suggestions can then give defendants leverage over court proceedings. A conversation I had with a litigant in the civil courts of Karachi while she was waiting to have her case heard assists in understanding how such suggestions may play out as bargaining chips. She had been subjected to violence on multiple occasions and was pregnant with her first child when her husband deserted her. Soon after, she found out that he had taken on a second wife without her consent. She pleaded for him to return, unsure how she would manage to support her child financially on her own. He responded through a legal notice which stated that he thought she was psychologically unstable, and suggested that she get herself medically checked. The notice added that if she did as he suggested, he would return to take care of her. And so, she went to the doctor to 'satisfy' her husband, and sent him pictures of her appointment slip to prove that she had done as he had asked. He did not return. When she eventually filed a case for maintenance a few months later, he brought those same pictures to court as evidence that she was mentally unstable, visiting a psychiatrist, and therefore not liable for maintenance. After the hearing, he told her that if she gave birth to a son and did not grant him full custody, he would share these images during custody proceedings too, and 'snatch' the child from her.[147] Here, not only did the appellant gain leverage over the current maintenance case by using

143 Interview with lawyer, Lahore, 13 June 2022 [b]
144 Phone interview with lawyer, Rawalpindi, 13 July 2022.
145 Interview with lawyer, Islamabad, 9 June 2022 [c].
146 Phone interview with lawyer, Lahore, 28 July 2022.
147 Interview with victim, Karachi, 4 July 2022. In a similar tone, in response to allegations of domestic abuse in *Saba Akhtar v Imran Ashraf* [2021] CLC 1165, the appellant filed an application to direct his wife to 'get herself medically examined' and be 'declared sexually and physically fit.'

suggestibility to get his wife to agree to his demands, but he could potentially gain leverage over other prospective cases as well:

> Even if these allegations don't have an effect on the current case of *khula* [divorce] or maintenance per se, it would have an effect on the later custody cases for example. Because at that time, they reiterate all these allegations—that we also said this during the *khula* case. So, it is a tactic for future strategy and future cases . . . It comes from the fact that the position of women in society is so weak, it is so easy to discredit her, that men are able to get away with anything with no one questioning them.[148]

Lastly, it is pertinent to note that suggestions in relation to the 'psy' labels can also be, and commonly are, used as a delay tactic. As one lawyer explained,

> He [the respondent] has been doing as many delaying tactics as possible . . . He came to court and said to give him more time to convince her to forgive her. He did not want reconciliation and never approached her [the client] for reconciliation. After the last hearing date, we finally sat down with him and his lawyer to see what he wants, and he said he wants her to get a psychiatric test. That '*yeh apne hawaas mein nahi hain, hum written mein likh keh request karein ge keh yeh psychiatric test karwayen* [she is not in her right mind, we will request in writing that she get a psychiatric test done]'. This is also another delaying tactic, because he knows by the time he files a written reply and then we file another one, more weeks will pass.[149]

Ring refers to delays in legal processes as a tool of legal regulation.[150] Given that trial processes in Pakistan are lengthy, sometimes spreading over a period of a few years even in family and civil matters, the lack of case disposals in a timely manner has been overwhelmingly linked to lawyers seeking adjournments on false grounds and using delay tactics in the interest of their client.[151] Using character allegations as 'suggestions' may therefore assist

[148] Phone interview with lawyer, Lahore, 28 July 2022.

[149] Interview with lawyer, Islamabad, 9 June 2022 [b].

[150] S Ring, 'On Delay and Duration: Law's Temporal Orders in Historical Child Sexual Abuse Cases' in S Beynon-Jones and E Grabham (eds) *Law and Time* (Routledge 2018) 93.

[151] R Shah, S Khan, S Farid and A Shah, 'Delaying Tactics Used by Lawyers in Dispensation of Civil Justice in Lower Courts of Pakistan' (2014) 6(2) Pakistan Journal of Criminology 113.

in such lawyerly practices and strategies, because they serve the same purpose as those of stock stories and boilerplate, scripted narratives, in that they aim to present an alternate account to that of victim-subject of domestic violence—an account that justifies the world as it is, and is in effect a 'cure'.[152]

Conclusion

I was often told that the best way to summarize legal processes relating to cases of domestic violence in Pakistan is that 'the victim turns into the accused'.[153] This chapter investigated how and why that may be so. It argued that legal actors use character allegations as gendering strategies to script women victims as they travel through the courts. First, by using pre-drafted boilerplate suits in a one-size-fits-all approach, women are labelled as 'bad' and/or as 'mad' in response to their claims of domestic violence. Second, lawyers build on such scripted narratives by presenting peculiar forms of evidence and engaging in performative and restrictive questioning techniques. In doing so, they subjectivize women in a way that increases their blameworthiness and reduces their credibility. In addition, lawyers make strategic use of suggestibility to shape how women complainants are perceived in the courts. As such, victims are scripted not only by the pre-drafted suits that are applied in a boilerplate manner in response to their claims, but also by gendering strategies used by lawyers attempting to enact that script through the court process. And when cases of domestic violence are scripted in this manner, the resulting effect is that,

> they [the defence] pressurize the victim to either withdraw the case or to negotiate with them to reach an out-of-court settlement. We know that victims face character assassinations at home, at police stations, at the courts, so by the time they get here they are so tired, their capacity to deal with the same allegations over and over becomes slim. At some point they just think it's enough. It is easier to withdraw the case and try to go on living whatever little of their lives they have left. It is easier than being constantly maligned and waiting for a judgment, not knowing

[152] Delgado (n 34).
[153] Interview with lawyer, Lahore, 16 June 2022 [a].

> what that judgment will be, when they will get justice, or if they will get justice at all.[154]

In Chapter 6, I delve more deeply into how lawyerly practices play out in the courtroom. Particularly, I investigate the use of anticipatory performances as a gendering strategy, which looks more closely at how legal actors view the role of the judiciary and perform to the judge as audience. In doing so, Chapter 6 assesses the distortion of stories and narratives that may come to form when litigation is carried out as a scripted performance for spectators, and the role this plays not only in how victim-subjects of domestic violence are enacted, but also in how their cases are adjudicated.

[154] Interview with legal aid personnel, Islamabad, 7 June 2022 [a].

6
Enacting victim-subjects: Anticipative performances

Zan, zar tay zameen, tinen fasad di jar
[Women, gold, and land: all are apples of discord][1]

Introduction

In examining cases of domestic violence that survive the apathy and antipathy of the justice system, Waheed finds that 'judicial discretion is all-determining in Pakistani law'.[2] Section 308-F of the Pakistan Penal Code (PPC) has often been cited as giving the judiciary express permission to assess cases 'not only under the statutory provisions of law but also under the injunctions of the Quran and Sunnah'.[3] Waheed argues that such discretionary provision gives the judiciary a rather difficult task of determining issues before them in relation to their own interpretations and biases towards certain social and religious norms. This in turn, may supersede recognitions of penal laws, particularly in relation to violence against women.[4] As recounted during an interview with a lawyer:

> One thing I have to say right off the bat is that the domestic violence law is a great start, but there is so much to be desired in the law itself and of course, one of the first hearings for a domestic violence case that I went to, the reader looks at the petition, laughs at the judge and says, '*Yeh kis*

[1] A Punjabi proverb. See M Shahbaz, *Saday Akhaan [Our Proverbs]* (Aziz Book Depot 2004) 232.
[2] M Waheed, 'Domestic Violence in Pakistan: The Tension between Intervention and Sovereign Autonomy in Human Rights Law' (2004) 29(2) Brooklyn Journal of International Law 962.
[3] S Burney, 'Crime or Custom? Violence against Women in Pakistan' (1999) Human Rights Watch 45.
[4] Waheed (n 2) 960.

Domestic Violence in Pakistan. Daanika Kamal, Oxford University Press. © Daanika Kamal 2025.
DOI: 10.1093/9780198953470.003.0006

> *kism ke kanoon bana diye hain* [what kinds of laws have they made]', and the judge chuckles. It will be a long time before they even think about it as a real thing. And a large part of them even considering [the domestic violence petition] was for my sake, just for them to get me off their backs or to get the client off their backs.[5]

In *Feminism and the Power of Law*, Smart discusses the struggle between 'new' and 'old' contrivances of power.[6] She argues that the law may retain its 'old' power by 'exercising new contrivances of power in the form of surveillance and modes of discipline'.[7] Put differently, the 'old' order may employ strategies to reassert its power over legal changes and reform, thereby diluting the transformative potential of reforms by hindering effective implementation. The belittling of domestic violence in the quote above, deeming it as unnecessary or perhaps unworthy of being codified by law, is a sentiment that could be attributed to the pushback of 'old' power against legal reform. For example, Bucha and Aqeel cite a case of a woman who had filed charges of domestic violence against her husband. After a hearing, she was beaten by her husband within court premises. When the woman's lawyer made the judge aware of what had happened, the judge responded that 'as long as she was his wife, he could treat her in whatever way he chose',[8] adding that 'the Quran gives the man this right'.[9]

Abu-Odeh notes that the judiciary and legal actors share 'the essential nationalist ideology of striking a balance between tradition and modernity'.[10] In her analysis of domestic violence and honour killings, she concludes that the judiciary delivers a cultural message by reminding women that private violence is still sanctioned in some forms because in doing so, it keeps the management of gender and sexuality—as endorsed by the nationalist project—in check. Further, as members of the ruling male elite, the judiciary makes 'concessions' to men, in order to avoid facing the expected 'wrath and resentment' resulting from the system being pushed towards (an intolerable) liberalization.[11] The influence of societal beliefs and

5 Interview with lawyer, Karachi, 1 August 2022.
6 C Smart, *Feminism and the Power of Law* (Routledge 1989).
7 ibid 17.
8 S Bucha and A Aqeel, 'Battered Lives' *Newsline* (March 2002) <https://newslinemagazine.com/magazine/battered-lives/> accessed 3 January 2023.
9 ibid.
10 L Abu-Odeh, 'Crimes of Honour and the Construction of Gender in Arab Societies' (2011) 2(1) Comparative Law Review 27.
11 ibid 47.

'old' contrivances of power on judicial discretion can therefore have an effect not only on whether acts of familial abuse are recognized as such in Pakistani courtrooms, but also on how women complainants are perceived and viewed by the court. As such, lawyers often tailor their arguments and storytelling narratives in cases relating to domestic violence by anticipating judicial responses:

> We know how they [the judges] think and the kinds of judgments they give, so lawyers know what to say to get them in their favour . . . We leave a lot to the discretion of the judge. Especially if the judge is somebody who has a gender bias or view, or someone who is not willing to be informed by laws or changes in culture or status quo, that discretion can be very dangerous. Judges can choose to look at the information and run with it in either direction and then justify it on judicial discretion.[12]

Towards the end of Chapter 5 I discussed how lawyerly practices are catered towards judges and their courtrooms, by using strategies that build on allegations framing women complainants as 'bad' and/or as 'mad' in order to 'plant a seed' that germinates in the minds of judges. In other words, it is 'so that the judge starts viewing the behaviour of the women through a certain lens'.[13] This indicates an element of performativity present in the courtroom. In viewing the judge as an audience, the lawyerly practices employed to script and enact victims of domestic violence can be seen as a performance which anticipates judicial reactions, and indeed judicial discretions. Performance, here, is defined as what Schechner calls 'restored' or 'twice-behaved' behaviour: acts that have been rehearsed, or that consciously evoke formal templates or scripts that can be repeated, re-enacted, and recreated.[14] The inclusion of the evocation of formal templates in this definition of performance also forms a link to the lawyerly practice of using boilerplate texts and scripts in pre-drafted suits, as discussed in Chapter 5.[15]

12 Interview with lawyer, Karachi, 11 August 2022 [a] [parenthesis added].

13 Interview with lawyer, Lahore, 16 June 2022 [c]; Interview with lawyer, Islamabad, 9 June 2022 [a].

14 R Schechner, *Theatre and Anthropology* (University of Pennsylvania Press 1985) 36.

15 For example, one lawyer said: 'the practice here is that the lawyers never really make their case documents themselves. Any domestic violence related suit that comes, the workers [draftsmen] that are sitting at the courts, they just copy-paste the same wordings and give them to the lawyers to file. I see this all the time, the same words and the same sentences being repeated.' Phone interview with legal aid personnel, Sukkur, 27 June 2022 [parenthesis added].

Julie Stone Peters' work explores the role of legal performance and theatricality in constituting meanings within and outside the courtroom.[16] She argues that the ultimate performativity of the law is 'producing the frameworks of subjecthood and subjectivity through discursive acts'.[17] Performance, then, is intrinsic to the way in which law produces itself, and the way it produces specific outcomes. This chapter similarly assesses how legal actors view the role of the judiciary and perform to the judge as audience. First, the chapter presents a relational analysis which considers how the ideas of 'playing to the judge' and 'playing the victim' anticipate judicial reactions and discretions. Particularly, I examine the distorting effects that occur when litigation is performed for spectators through character allegations and gendering strategies, and the role this plays in how victim-subjects are enacted and consequently perceived. Second, this chapter looks at the role that language plays in the subjectification of women complainants. Through an interplay of language and performance, I argue that the constructed subjectivities of victim-subjects may then circulate as forms of legal knowledge, not only reframing their narratives but ultimately affecting the adjudication of their cases.

Playing to the judge, playing the victim

During fieldwork, numerous interviewees talked of 'playing to the judge'[18] and 'playing the victim',[19] both in terms of how legal practitioners advise their clients to behave in court and in how they shape case narratives when communicating with the judge.[20] As one lawyer said, 'One needs to play to the judge. Always think of the judge as someone who doesn't know anything, and you can sway him left or right.'[21] In doing so, one must appeal to the 'judge's sensibilities'.[22] A common example provided during interviews

[16] JS Peters, *Law as Performance: Theatricality, Spectatorship and the Making of Law in Ancient, Medieval and Early Modern Europe* (Oxford University Press 2022).
[17] JS Peters, 'Legal Performance Good and Bad' (2008) 4 Law Culture and the Humanities 181.
[18] Interview with lawyer, Karachi, 11 August 2022 [a]; Interview with lawyer, Lahore, 17 June 2022 [b].
[19] Interview with lawyer, Lahore, 16 June 2022 [c].
[20] Interview with lawyer, Karachi, 11 August 2022 [b].
[21] Interview with lawyer, Karachi, 14 January 2022.
[22] Interview with lawyer, Karachi, 1 August 2022.

was that of the Restitution of Conjugal Rights (RCR), which is frequently filed as a countersuit when women initiate court proceedings against their husbands for domestic violence. RCR is an antiquated law; a colonial legacy introduced by the British first under English ecclesiastical jurisdiction and later through civil jurisdictions.[23] It was a legal remedy that could be employed by either spouse if the other was not fulfilling their obligations under the marital contract. However, in present-day Pakistan, it is predominantly filed by men as a tool to intimidate their wives in court.[24] Used as a gendering strategy, the RCR decree helps men present a certain story to the judge, contesting their wives' allegations of domestic violence by saying, 'I would never do that, I want to maintain marital life; she is being irrational, erratic, emotional, or unreasonable'.[25] Lawyers consider the judicial mobilization of RCR to be 'automatic', which speaks to Schechner's definition of performance being 'restored' or 'twice-behaved' behaviour:

> Whenever a woman files for *khula* on the basis of cruelty, the other side will automatically file a counter suit known as the Restitution of Conjugal Rights. This is where the husband says that he loves his wife and wants her to come home, and the woman is a deserted wife and left the house against his will because she has some mental issue, or some psychological ego problem, and is not fulfilling her Islamic marital duties. This is despite that he is likely physically torturing her. And then the effect is that the judge sees that Restitution of Conjugal Rights suit and says, '*magar yeh toh ghar bharsana cha raha hai toh aap chali jayein* [but he wants to build a marital home with you, you should go (back home)]' and then judges are also trying for reconciliation. They even take them into their chambers and try to make the woman see sense. The judges see the woman as having a mental issue, stubborn and not knowing what is best for her, and the man they see as the saviour because who else would marry a woman like that?[26]

By anticipating judicial responses and playing to the judge's sensibilities, the RCR suit presents the notion that men are being 'gracious' in accepting

[23] See generally, SA Cheema, 'Islamisation of Restitution of Conjugal Rights by the Federal Shariat Court of Pakistan: A Critique' (2019) 58(4) Islamic Studies 535.
[24] Interview with lawyer, Karachi, 6 January 2022.
[25] Interview with lawyer, Karachi, 11 August 2022 [b].
[26] Phone interview with lawyer, Peshawar, 1 July 2022.

'bad' and/or 'mad' women, because they are giving these women the prospect or assurance of marital relations, when society is unlikely to deem them worthy of it. In the interview extract above, the lawyer anticipates the judge's response to these suits ('the judges see the woman having a mental issue . . . and the man they see as the saviour because who else would marry a woman like that'). This is not too far off from actual judicial reactions, as an interview with a judge illustrates. When discussing a case where a woman's sexual images had been circulated by her intimate partner without her consent, he said:

> My last posting was with the cybercrime unit, and in 90 per cent of those cases they were related to the modesty of women [sic]. But you know, I think it is true that these women first themselves compromise their privacy. If she was sharing her privacy and her private moments and private parts with some man then of course, if you have given them access to that privacy yourself, then the other party would be innocent or even think of himself as aggrieved . . . There was one case like this. And the woman was intimate with him, *aur woh apnana chahta tha* [and he wanted to marry her] and he was willing to give all his wealth to her. In my experience, when a woman has compromised her privacy by choice, then she should not have any reason to not marry that person. I thought that was very mighty of the man, he showed so much grace. The same girl whose private pictures and videos were being circulated on social media and even in the phone shops—here this is what happens—he was showing so much grace to offer to marry her even after that. So what if he had made those pictures viral? You know, it is *apnane ki baat* [the offer to marry her]. He showed grace and no one else would marry her. I was very concerned and really wanted to give him relief in that case. He did not deserve to be punished for the grace he showed. But unfortunately, I got transferred so another judge took over.[27]

In the interview extracts shared above, the stories presented to the judge reflect similar character allegations to those found in the boilerplate predrafted suits discussed in the previous chapter. Presenting women as 'bad' or 'mad' allows for a reframing of narratives which anticipates judicial reactions, by suggesting that it was the men that were aggrieved by women,

[27] Interview with family judge, District and Sessions Court, Karachi, 4 July 2022.

not the other way around. Through the RCR, this is illustrated by the man's insinuation that the woman deserted him and is not fulfilling her conjugal obligations[28] due to her 'mental issue'; and in the latter case, the lawyerly practices appealed to the judge's sensibilities by contending that men would 'of course' feel aggrieved when they were 'given access to that [woman's] privacy'. In playing to the judge as audience, there is a performative role in legal practices that shapes the subjectivities of litigants. Such reframing of narratives suggests that in playing *to* the judge, particularly in cases of domestic violence, it is important that the woman also plays *as* the victim.

Christie describes the 'ideal' or most credible victim in gender-based violence as one who is weak, who is respectable and blameless, and who has been victimized by a big, bad offender with whom she has no prior relationship.[29] He goes on to note that the victim must be able to command just enough power to establish herself and her identity as an 'ideal' victim, yet 'be weak enough to not become a threat to other important interests'.[30] In other words, she needs to find a balance in how she presents herself as a victim. Given that victims of domestic violence predominantly have some sort of relationship with the perpetrator, most often through marriage, they already approach the court as victims that are perceived as having lesser credibility. Further, in shaping the subjectivity of women victims in the courtroom, legal actors such as lawyers and judges not only have the margins to invoke (or indeed revoke) victimhood, but often monopolize the expertise of speaking for the victim, thereby depriving victims of the agency and voice of speaking for themselves.[31] In doing so, performative techniques are employed to enact victims through gendering strategies, anticipating how judges perceive victims and how they ultimately adjudicate cases of domestic violence. In Chapter 5, I outlined some of these lawyerly practices—such as the use of restrictive questioning tactics and suggestibility—which help to build on character allegations that frame

[28] For example, an extract from an RCR suit states: '. . . her unwillingness to return is absolute negation on her part to perform her duties as a Muslim wife and in spite of best efforts advanced by plaintiff and his well wishes she is not ready to perform her obligation of conjugal rights, in fact plaintiff loves the defendant from [the] core of his heart, hence this suit for restitution of conjugal rights.' Suit for Restitution of Conjugal Rights, Family Court Islamabad (West) 38/18 (Aug 2018).

[29] N Christie, 'The Ideal Victim' in EA Fattah (ed), *From Crime Policy to Victim Policy* (Palgrave Macmillan 1986) 18.

[30] ibid 21.

[31] C Schwobel-Patel, 'The Ideal Victim of International Criminal Law' (2018) 29(3) The European Journal of International Law 714. For a related assessment of 'active' versus 'passive' victims, see Chapter 3.

woman complainants as 'bad' and/or 'mad' women, and present them in a certain (often unfavourable) manner:

> It is the judge's job to make a note of the woman's behaviour and way of speaking and make a decision accordingly, so such allegations and lawyer strategies have an effect on the judge because he sees the woman and what she is saying *through* that allegation. If she gets frustrated or fed up with these allegations, then the judge will make a note that she was acting out or has some mental psychological issue. It removes any sympathy that the judge may have had for her. So of course, it can affect the outcome of the case.[32]

It is pertinent to note that there is 'an overwhelming notion [in society] that women who come to courts are not good women, so by standing in the court, she is already seen as having a questionable character'.[33] Amidst such gendered discourse and practices, lawyers representing women who have been subject to domestic violence must carefully advise their clients on how best to present themselves during hearings. Similar to Christie's assessment of the 'ideal' victim, they need to adopt a balance. Because as one judge said, 'I will be honest—in our legal system, I have seen that those [women] who show themselves to be the most *mazloom* [oppressed/victimized] are actually those who are not, and those who show themselves as too confident are trying to manipulate the justice system'.[34]

There were two instances during fieldwork that highlight these ideas. The first instance was when I was observing a case for the recovery of dowry articles in the family courts in Islamabad. The case had been filed by a woman who had been granted a *khula* a few months prior on the basis of cruelty. The woman's lawyer, standing next to her client, told the judge that the respondent's team had been consistently engaging in tactics to delay proceedings, and the delays in returning her client's belongings were only exacerbating the abuse she faced during her marriage. The judge, however, granted the respondent's request for a new date, stating '*do haftay mein kuch nahi hone wala* [nothing will happen in two weeks]'. The complainant then spoke herself, telling the judge that she had been present at every hearing

[32] Phone interview with legal aid personnel, Sukkur, 27 June 2022 [emphasis added].
[33] Interview with lawyer, Islamabad, 9 June 2022 [a].
[34] Interview with family judge, District and Sessions Court, Karachi, 4 July 2022 [parenthesis added].

to date, and that she felt increasingly threatened and at risk from her ex-husband the longer this case was prolonged. She added: '*mein adaalat baar baar aa rahi hoon, woh nahi aate, yahan aisa mohol banaya hua hai ke aurat ki izzat hi kharab hojati hai* [I have been coming to the courts over and over, they do not show up, the kind of environment (that has been built) here is that a woman's honour is impacted]'. The judge replied, '*izzat ki baat aap pehle sochteen* [you should have thought about the matter of honour earlier]'.[35]

In another instance, I was standing outside a courtroom with the lawyer I was accompanying for the day. Shortly before the scheduled time for the hearing, her client arrived wearing a long, full-sleeved *kurta* on top of jeans, and the lawyer asked if she had a *dupatta* [scarf] with her. When the client responded to say that she had left it in her car, an associate was asked to quickly find a *dupatta*, because '*yeh jo judge hain, in ke saamne behtar hai chaadar pehen ke jayein* [for this judge, it is better to wear a veil / large scarf when you go before him]'. The lawyer then asked the client if she remembered what they had previously spoken about, and the client nodded and recalled four points: First, deny the allegations, but don't overreact and stay calm. Second, show some emotion but do not cry. Third, speak confidently but in low tones. And lastly (she smiled as she said this), bring a *dupatta*.[36]

As per the guidance given by lawyers to their clients, it appears that a fine balance needs to be struck to accurately 'play the victim'. In a manner akin to what Christie spoke of, women must command just enough power to assert their identity as a victim, without appearing as a threat to other important interests. In the example above, the client was advised by her lawyer that she must deny the allegations the other party presents but should only do so in a composed manner. That is, she should react but not overreact. Similarly, she must show some emotion but should not cry, and she must speak confidently but in low tones. In playing the victim, she must find a balance between 'not enough' or 'too much', because 'they always say *keh aurat ko to bas dekh kar pata chal jata hai* [that you can tell what is what just by looking at the woman]'.[37] During fieldwork it appeared that this sentiment is accorded both to how victims are expected to behave, perform and present themselves in front of the judge during case hearings and to judicial expectations of how victims are expected to respond at the time of

[35] Court observations, 10 June 2022, Islamabad.
[36] Court observations, 9 June 2022, Islamabad.
[37] Interview with lawyer, Karachi, 11 August 2022 [a].

the violent act they were subjected to. This indicates temporal continuity in judicial perceptions relating to the gendered enactment of narratives, beginning even before the case is brought to the courtroom.

Enacting victimhood: Too much or not enough?

In 2018 a woman accused a man whose house she used to work at of rape. The judgment for the case stated that the victim's 'story' was not credible, and consequently was disbelieved by the court that ruled in favour of an appeal. The reasoning provided in the order was that the victim's account of the perpetrator's behaviour at the time of the crime was 'not expected from a prudent mind'. The judge's disbelief, associated with the (male) 'prudent mind', was not necessarily relating to whether or not a man would rape, but rather the particular location that a man would choose for that rape:

> For committing a forcible rape/zina, the appellant chooses a room of his house while in [the] very next room his wife and children were allegedly sleeping. Such story is always hard to believe: that appellant/convict would dare to commit the offence of forcible rape/zina in [the] presence of his own wife and children in very next room when there was always a possibility of his wife and children com[ing] to such place . . . Thus, such story was never safe to be taken as natural and confidence inspiring and was never strong enough to hold the conviction . . . such attitude and behaviour is not expected from a prudent mind.[38]

In assessing the veracity of the claims—based on an understanding of what it means to be a man of 'prudent mind' when committing the offence of rape—the judge places undue focus on a gendered notion of rationality.[39] In previous chapters, I discussed the ways through which the legal capacity of

[38] *Muhammad Khan v The State* [2020] PCrLJ Note 10. It is pertinent to note that the offence of rape is used interchangeable with 'zina' (used to signify sexual relations outside of marriage, such as adultery) by the judge. I discuss the implications of this in the next section of this chapter, '"A dispute of family nature": Language in the courtroom'.

[39] O Smith and T Skinner, 'How Rape Myths Are Used and Challenged in Rape and Sexual Assault Trials' (2017) 26(4) Social and Legal Studies 447. A similar judicial approach can be found in *Muhammad Younis v The State* [1989] PCrLJ 1747, where the judgment specified that 'the appellant had two children from his deceased wife and when he took the extreme step of taking her life by giving her repeated knife blows on different parts of her body, *she must have done something unusual to enrage him to such an extent*' [emphasis added].

women is constantly placed in comparison to that of men, with the former being deemed as inherently defective due to the 'female psyche'. The veracity of a woman's testimony has been left to the discretion of judges,[40] who use their own understandings of rationality, based on (and comparative to) male models of legal capacity and credibility,[41] to assess the trustworthiness of the female witness. This can either take form by assessing how the testimony of women complainants portray and present the actions of the male perpetrator, as seen above, or by using a male understanding of rationality to assess the presentation of the victim's response to alleged acts of violence.

For example, reported judgments spanning a twenty-year period help to better understand how the presentation of the victims' behaviour at the time of the violent act is judged against what is considered to be a 'rational' or 'normal' response to such acts. In a 2016 sexual assault case at the Supreme Court, the judgment suggested that the offence in question was 'highly improbable' because the two women victims 'did not raise hue and cry'.[42] In a 2002 judgment relating to wrongful confinement, the court found the victims to be rational and therefore credible as it 'observed that their conduct was quite natural because soon after they were dropped by accused persons . . . they raised hue and cry'[43] (perhaps inadvertently stating that had they not done so, they may have compromised their credibility as witnesses).[44] Similarly, in a 1993 case of abduction, the lack of 'hue and cry' raised by the woman victim resulted in the accused getting bail.[45] The Federal Shariat Court has also previously overturned a lower court's conviction of rape on the grounds that medical examiners 'did not observe any injury on the thighs, legs, elbows, arms, knees, face, back and buttocks of the victim', holding that 'she [the victim] was bound to sustain injuries . . . as she was *supposed to put up resistance*'.[46]

These judgments seem to require women victims to act a certain way, by either 'putting up resistance' or 'raising hue and cry' when subjected to acts of violence. More importantly, it is the performative optics associated with

[40] Burney (n 3) 58.

[41] I Nyazee, *Outlines of Islamic Jurisprudence* (3rd edn, Advanced Legal Studies Institute 2005) 39.

[42] *Muhammad Nawaz v The State* [2016] SCMR 267, as cited in M Zia, SO David and S Randhawa, 'Gap Analysis on Investigation and Prosecution of Rape and Sodomy Cases' (2021) Legal Aid Society 69 [parenthesis added].

[43] *Bashir Ahmed v The State* [2002] PLD SC 775.

[44] Zia and others (n 42).

[45] *Mahmona Hamayun v Abdul Hakim and 2 others* [1993] SCMR 893.

[46] *Bahadur Shah v The State* [1987] PLD FSC 11 [parenthesis and emphasis added].

how the victim's response to violence is framed by lawyers in the courtroom that inform the judge's adjudication of the case. The performativity of gender is then a key consideration in judicial expectations and determinations of how victims 'should' behave.[47] At the district court level, similar gendering strategies are used—even by judges—to interject the testimonies of women and dismiss their claims. Burney reports that during a case relating to abduction and sexual assault, when the complainant testified that she had been forced by the defendant to board a train at gunpoint, the judge interrupted her testimony to say that he found it unbelievable because 'even a goat would have struggled under the circumstances'.[48] These discretionary judicial responses are therefore often based on how women ought to be and have been, and how women ought to act and have acted. In doing so, it ignores the idea that the 'actions being portrayed as "irrational" (for example, not struggling or putting up resistance) could also be framed as a logical response to trauma or fear', or perhaps a drive for survival.[49] Instead, based on male models of 'rationality', it is how the victim of gender-based violence is presented, and the judicial understandings of those gendered presentations, that play a large role in how cases are adjudicated. As one lawyer said:

> Optics matter. Optics make a difference. That's why if you ever visit the family court *aadhi toh aurtein bechari ban ke ayi hui hoti hain, sar pe dupatta, dakha hua munh* [half the women come looking poor and miserable, covering their head with a *dupatta* and hiding their faces]. I mean, a judge also commented one day that these new young women lawyers come here with open hair and wearing bright nail polish, and that they should not be wearing makeup. I also tie my hair and don't wear any makeup but like, sometimes I have nail polish on and when this conversation was happening, of course I hid my hands. So, in this line of work, appearances matter. And in domestic violence cases, it matters even more. Because domestic violence is justified across social strata.[50]

In line with this sentiment, lawyers with whom I spoke recounted experiences of their clients being subjectivized by judges based on how they

[47] J Butler, *Gender Trouble: Feminism and the Subversion of Identity* (Routledge 1990).
[48] Burney (n 3).
[49] Smith and Skinner (n 39). Also see Z Lodrick, 'Psychological Trauma: What Every Trauma Worker Should Know' (2007) 4(2) British Journal of Psychotherapy Integration 18.
[50] Interview with lawyer, Lahore, 16 June 2022 [c].

presented themselves or how they were presented by lawyers in the courtroom.[51] In one case, a young woman had fled her home due to threats of domestic violence and a forced marriage, and sought refuge at a domestic violence shelter. Her parents filed a habeas corpus petition soon after, stating that their unmarried daughter was at the shelter unlawfully. When the woman was summoned to the court, her lawyer recalls:

> She was just wearing lipstick—that's all. And the judge actually commented, saying, '*Aap ne apne maa baap ko itna tang kiya hua hai aur aap yahan lipstick aur makeup laga kar aa gayi hain* [you have been creating so many issues for your parents and here you have come wearing lipstick and make up]'. The judge is thinking why is she happy, how is she happy—after making her parents come to court and causing them so much grief with her actions, and here she is wearing make up! So, there is character assassination from the judge too, right?[52]

Further, in a custody case filed on the basis of domestic abuse, the mother's character was dampened by alleging that she was 'working full-time with a showbiz/modelling agency'.[53] It was contended that 'the appellants belong to a pure religious family having a tradition to wear hijab by young girls, and the respondent is attached with showbiz industry that is fatal for the brought up of the minor [sic]'.[54] As evidence, the appellant's lawyer presented a picture of the mother that was printed in a magazine. In fact, because she worked for a jewellery designing company, she had gone to an exhibition as a guest, where her picture was taken and printed alongside those of other attendees.[55] Her lawyer clarified: 'the husband and his lawyer took that picture and added it to the suit to say, look, she does modelling for *ghatiya* [disgraceful] magazines . . . Time and again the judge would keep asking me if she was modelling. He was convinced. I had to argue the same thing over and over again and it went on for ages.'[56] Here, by anticipating judicial responses, lawyerly practices organize and narrate stories in a manner which helps to construct and enact the victim-subject as a 'bad' woman.

[51] On being judged according to norms of gendered respectability, see T Serisier, *Speaking Out: Feminism, Rape and Narrative Politics* (Palgrave MacMillan 2018).
[52] Interview with lawyer, Lahore, 14 June 2022.
[53] Statement [appellant], Guardian and Ward Application 419/21, Lahore (Sept 2021).
[54] ibid.
[55] Interview with lawyer, Lahore, 17 June 2022 [a].
[56] ibid.

My reason for providing these examples is to help establish a trend in how considerations relating to the way in which women victims are presented before the judge play a role in judicial responses and assessments of credibility. It also helps highlight the social and cultural norms by which these considerations are informed. A similar approach is undertaken when victims are subjectivized through gendered allegations that make use of 'psy' labels in the courtroom. For example, one lawyer to whom I spoke recalled that he was previously asked by a judge to counsel a woman because she 'looked' as though she had a mental issue:

> One thing they [lawyers] do is that they make her out to be mentally disordered, they talk about her mentally. In one case, there was a woman who was about nineteen years old, and it had not even been six months since her marriage. She filed a case of divorce due to cruelty, and I knew the judge who was taking care of that case, so the judge called me and told me to give some counselling to the woman because the husband said she had a *mental issue*. The judge even said that she is very stubborn and not agreeing to reconciliation and *looking very mentally disturbed to him*.[57]

Here, it appears that it was the woman's stubbornness and unwillingness to compromise and reconcile with her husband that was seen as evidence of her lack of rationality, and consequently her 'mental issue'. Perhaps she tipped the balance—by asserting her agency in not compromising, she no longer presented herself as an 'ideal' victim, but as a threat to larger interests and to the role of judges as 'custodians of the morals of Pakistani citizens'.[58] And as a result of legal actors using anticipative performances to frame the victim as 'mad', the judge too felt that she was 'looking very mentally disturbed to him'.

As discussed in the previous chapter, I wasn't provided very clear answers when, in response to ideas that 'one can simply tell by looking at the woman if she has some mental issue',[59] I asked interviewees what that appearance or presentation entails. Primarily, it was suggested that this was determined based on the judge's discretion; drawn from their personal knowledge,

[57] Interview with victim support personnel, Sukkur, 27 June 2022 [parenthesis and emphasis added].

[58] A Zia, 'My Body, Allah's Choice: Islamic Laws and Sexual Autonomies in Pakistan' (2022) 23(2) Australian Journal of Asian Law 95, 99.

[59] Interview with lawyer, Karachi, 5 January 2022 [c].

experience, and, as Geva puts it, judicial observations in relation to what is considered 'common sense'.[60]

> Judges will read the paperwork, observe the victim and see how she speaks and acts and they assess her themselves. If the judge thinks that the victim looks very mentally unstable then he could ask for a psychiatrist to assess, but that is at the judge's discretion and usually it is not done nor is it needed. The judges have enough experience to assess someone's mental soundness and mental issues.[61]
>
> No, such [medical expertise or assessment] is not needed. They [judges] can do it themselves. No one else is brought in. That level of technicality is not needed and not approached, from what I have seen. These judges have experience; they can observe and themselves determine whether the allegation is true, and if the woman is mentally unstable or if the husband is just saying it.[62]
>
> The judge will assess. The judge will look and listen, and he will be able to determine who is telling the truth and if she is indeed *paagal* [crazy]. The judge has the experience to assess on his own. He does not need anyone else, it's just using common sense, that is why he is the judge![63]

A judge to whom I spoke expressed a similar sentiment to those of lawyers above. While she was aware that lawyers tend to use boilerplate texts in suits that contain 'generic' allegations, she said that the 'allegations relating to the woman's morality or her mindset and mentality are not always false'.[64] And so it is important for judges 'to not disregard it completely, because even if the allegation in false in some cases, it does not mean it is false in all the cases, and it could have an effect on the outcome [of the case]'.[65] Rather, she said, judges should assess the behaviour of the woman, keeping in mind that because emotions and sentiments are attached, people always say or do something that 'gives it away . . . you can feel something as a judge,

[60] AS Geva, 'Judicial Determination of Child Custody when a Parent Is Mentally Ill: A Little Bit of Law, a Little Bit of Pop Psychology, and a Little Bit of Common Sense' (2012) 16(1) UC Davis Journal of International Law and Policy 78.
[61] Interview with lawyer, Karachi, 19 July 2022.
[62] Interview with lawyer, Karachi, 15 January 2022.
[63] Interview with lawyer, Karachi, 5 January 2022 [d].
[64] Interview with family judge, District and Sessions Court, Karachi, 5 August 2022 [parenthesis added].
[65] ibid.

something clicks'.[66] Here too, there is an element of performativity that comes into play, as it appears that judges determine the veracity of claims by assessing how victims perform before them. How these performances are viewed, particularly in relation to allegations that the victim is a 'bad' or 'mad' woman, are influenced by public discourse relating to the politics of respectability and the 'psy' disciplines that are largely informed by discourse that circulates through popular culture.[67] For example, in Chapter 5, I mentioned that a judge told me that he observed a woman complainant and found her to be mentally disordered due to her 'abnormally large head'.[68] Later in the interview, the same judge also suggested that those who have 'mental issues should not be moving freely around in society. They should be confined or if not confined, then at least restrained.'[69]

In *Decolonizing Global Mental Health*, Mills provides an excerpt of descriptions of what social workers look for when trying to 'see' mental illness. She terms this the psychiatric field of visibility, where 'long matted hair, uncut and dirty nails, grimy clothing . . . talking to oneself, laughing or singing wildly' were examples of visual signifiers and appearances evoked in South Asia in the construction of 'mad' subjects.[70] It is not surprising that, like the descriptions here, interviewees used similar adjectives when speaking of women complainants whom they perceived as being psychologically unstable in the legal system. Most of these adjectives were consistent with the feminine sex role stereotype,[71] with 'psy' labels being used as gendering strategies, such that conceptions of mental illness, such as irrationality, illogicality, and emotionality, were largely assigned to women.[72] For example, one lawyer said that the judge made note of a litigant 'throwing arms around wildly, going totally hysterical'[73] when being cross-examined by the defence. Another lawyer said that a judge called him to his chambers to 'discuss the case' and at one point said that his client '*thori si psycho lag*

66 ibid.

67 A Alden, *Disorder in the Court: Morality, Myth and the Insanity Defence* (University of Alabama Press 2018) 3.

68 Interview with family judge, District and Sessions Court, Karachi 4 July 2022.

69 ibid.

70 C Mills, *Decolonizing Global Mental Health: The Psychiatrization of the Majority World* (Routledge 2014) 81.

71 P Chesler, *Women and Madness* (Doubleday 1972) 56.

72 N Potter, *Mapping the Edges and the In-between: A Critical Analysis of Borderline Personality Disorder* (Oxford University Press 2009) 167; CE Cooper and PL Sweet, '"Daddy Issues" and Diagnoses: Gendered Weaponisation of Mental Health in Intimate Relationships' (2024) Violence Against Women 2 <https://journals.sagepub.com/doi/10.1177/1077801224 1277894> accessed 2 October 2024.

73 Interview with lawyer, Lahore, 16 June 2022 [b].

rahi hai, bilkul aankhein bhaar ke baat kar rahi thi [looked a bit psycho due to how wide she opened her eyes when she spoke]'.[74] The most common association with the 'mad' victim-subject, however, brings us back to the idea of performativity. This idea is that women complainants are 'overly emotional and doing drama'[75] in the courtroom:

> Think about it this way: sometimes if this allegation comes and I [the judge] can tell that something is off about the woman—that maybe there is some truth to It—and if there is a custody case, then if the woman is in fact with a mental problem and manipulative character, and she comes and does drama and *hangama* [commotion] in court, then I can see that it would have an effect on the well-being of the child.[76]

This is not to say that all judges would negatively subjectivize women based on gendered allegations. Rather, it is to illustrate that anticipation of judicial reactions and discretions may play a role in how women are presented in relation to these allegations by legal actors. In some instances, based on their observations of the woman's presentation in the courtroom, judges may in fact use their discretion to dismiss the character allegations and 'psy' label applied to her:

> Recently I had a custody case where both the husband and wife were PhDs. They had been separated due to allegations of cruelty. The husband took the plea that the mother was not mentally fit for custody. And he shared screenshots of messages to the court, that she was addicted to some medication. I personally didn't consider that too much because I could assess her myself. She was a PhD, meaning marvellous, remarkable achievements. She was not working so could give due time to [the] child, and she was normal. She responded to me properly and spoke very well in English, so I had no reason to question her mental soundness.[77]

Through a survey of district courts in Lahore, Siddique found that litigants who were uneducated or had limited education were far less familiar with English comprehension (if at all) than those who were educated. Education

[74] Interview with lawyer, Islamabad, 9 June 2022 [c].
[75] Interview with lawyer, Lahore, 17 June 2022 [b].
[76] Interview with family judge, District and Sessions Court, Karachi, 5 August 2022 [parenthesis added].
[77] Interview with family judge, District and Sessions Court, Karachi, 4 July 2022.

levels and familiarity with the English language therefore go hand in hand.[78] As per this interview extract, it appears that both the woman's level of education and the language she spoke during the hearing played a role in how the judge perceived her 'mental soundness'. With the former, however, it was pertinent for the judge to specify that while the litigant had 'marvellous, remarkable achievements' as a PhD scholar, she was not a working woman and therefore was able to give 'due time' to the child. In many ways, this projects an image of the 'ideal' woman transmitted through popular culture. For example, a study by Ashfaq and Shafiq examined gendered images on Pakistani television dramas to find that the most common presentations of 'good' women are those who are educated but also homebound; not career-oriented, and finding fulfilment in their responsibilities as daughters, sisters, or mothers.[79] Similarly, I observed a case of divorce on the basis of cruelty where the judge told a complainant, '*aap parhi likhi lagti hain, itni choti se baat peh ghar nahi begharte* [you look educated, you shouldn't break the family home due to such small things]'.[80]

Khurshid speaks of '*parhi likhi*' [educated] women in Pakistan as having regulated empowerment.[81] That is, empowerment and regulation are not oppositional but rather interconnected, where the empowerment of women, through education, also constitutes stricter adherence to the gendered norms of sexuality.[82] If education levels play a role in perceptions of mental soundness (that is, a woman is seen to be 'normal'), she must also adhere more strictly to gendered norms as a 'good' mother, in order to balance the 'ideal' woman and, therefore, the 'ideal' victim. This is also illustrative of the link between 'bad'/'mad' woman and 'good'/'normal' woman.

An even more interesting observation, however, was that for the judge, the litigant conversing in English amounted to a perception of mental soundness. This idea was also reiterated during another interview with a lawyer:

> Once I did a case of a girl. She was from a rich family. And her mother—due to some domestic disputes—the mother had gotten her forcibly

[78] O Siddique, *Pakistan's Experience with Formal Law: An Alien Justice* (Cambridge University Press 2013) 137.

[79] A Ashfaq and Z Shafiq, 'Contested Images of "Perfect Women" in Pakistani Television Dramas' (2018) 55(1) Journal of the Research Society of Pakistan 60.

[80] Court observations, Karachi, 4 August 2022.

[81] A Khurshid, 'Does Education Empower Women? The Regulated Empowerment of *Parhi Likhi* Women in Pakistan' (2017) 48(3) Anthropology and Education Quarterly 252.

[82] ibid 254.

> admitted to some mental institute. Her friend got in touch with me and asked for my assistance. I met her, and she was looking absolutely normal, she was even talking normal. It was a property dispute, and the property had their joint signatories. The girl was unmarried, so the mother wanted to make sure she did not get the property. Now, when I took the case to court through a habeas petition for illegal detention, my colleague and I heard the lawyer from the other side say to the mother, '*larki se kuch aisa kaho jis se yeh hyper ho jaye, kyunke judge phir observation dein ge* [say something to the girl such that she would go "hyper" so that the judge can give his observation on it]'. So, I told my client that no matter what the judge asks you, you need to respond in English. And yes, the judge got frazzled when she did this! The mother would stand there and say '*yeh zehni mareez hai* [she is a mental patient]' and the judge responded '*chup karein, aap ko behtar pata hai ya mujhe?* [keep quiet, do you know better or do I?]' And he gave an observation that she is mentally normal.[83]

I asked the lawyer what he meant by the judge getting 'frazzled' when his client responded in English. What is the relevance of speaking in English in the courts, and it's link to perceptions of mental soundness? He clarified, 'We have given English a superiority in our society: those who speak English are considered to be educated, smart, and normal. Especially for judges in the lower courts. There is an idea of status that comes into play as well, and all of this is linked with a level of mental soundness.'[84] Literature from anthropology of law in postcolonial contexts offers some insight into this idea. For instance, Bhabha proposes the idea of 'mimicry' as a disciplined, conscious imitation of the white man by the colonized and native.[85] Western education, and particularly language, are a means through which the native is trained to behave and think like the white man. He becomes a mimic who can respond in English and argue rationally rather than sentimentally, which would be a stereotypical 'native' form of argumentation.[86] As such, English situates itself as the language of logic, of reason, and therefore of rationality. In the example above, the lawyer anticipates that the judge would extend this idea (that speaking in English signifies reason and

[83] Interview with lawyer, Lahore, 16 June 2022 [a].
[84] ibid.
[85] H Bhabha, 'Of Mimicry and Man: The Ambivalence of Colonial Discourse' (1984) 28 Discipleship: A Special Issue on Psychoanalysis 125.
[86] PK Nayar, *Postcolonialism: A Guide for the Perplexed* (Continuum 2010) 28.

rationality) to the perception of mental soundness more broadly. This, of course, has the potential to impact women litigants more than men, as the former are those whose mental state and 'rationality' is being more significantly questioned and assessed in the courtroom.

English is the language of Pakistani law. Some call it 'the language of justice'.[87] Legislation, regulations, and reported judgments are written in English, with little to no effort to translate them into Urdu or other native languages. It is therefore not surprising that the justice system can be inaccessible in many ways, not only because one requires a certain level of English comprehension as a vital prerequisite to that access, but also because even for those who have basic comprehension of the language, the English used is an 'archaic'[88] or 'old fashioned' form that many are unable to understand.[89] This may play out in different ways – not only for litigants, but also for lawyers and judges themselves. As seen in Chapter 5, for lawyers this could lead to a higher use of boilerplate text in legal drafting (sometimes with litigants themselves not knowing what is contained in those suits[90]), indicating an interplay of language and performance; where language is used to draft the script, and performances are used to enact that script. And for judges, this interplay not only impacts how they perceive and subjectivize victims, as discussed above, but it may also lead to differences in how crimes relating to gender-based violence are reframed through language within the court, and ultimately how proceedings are recorded and adjudicated.

'A dispute of family nature': Language in the courtroom

A judgment from Lahore states that 'the courts do not function in a vacuum and must take due notice of social and moral environments prevailing in society . . . the norms and social values of our society have to be kept in view while considering such matters'.[91] The idea of 'commonsense justice',

[87] O Siddique, 'The Language of Justice' *The Express Tribune* (27 February 2022) <https://tribune.com.pk/story/342487/the-language-of-justice> accessed 26 January 2022.
[88] Interview with lawyer, Karachi, 11 August 2022 [b].
[89] Siddique (n 78) 135.
[90] As one judge said, 'Many litigants cannot read or understand English either. Sometimes they don't even know what is written in the suit', Interview with family judge, District and Sessions Courts, Karachi, 5 August 2022.
[91] *Farman Ali v Abid Ali* [1995] PLD 364.

as phrased by Finkel, talks of the way in which judges are able to situate morality above the judicious use of logic in their reading of evidence and presentations of case narratives.[92] Commonsense justice is what 'ordinary people think is just and fair. It is embedded in the intuitive notions'[93] that the guardians of justice, such as jurors and judges, bring with them to the courtroom:

> Now if the judge who is dealing with all these cases isn't bothered to investigate properly then he would rely on his own discretion and what he sees . . . If the judge is bothered, or more gender-neutral or gender-favourable or sensitized, then they would take a different approach, but most are generally sympathetic towards men, and they will go in that direction.[94]

These notions can be used by judges to presuppose guilt and innocence. They allow for the isolation of various understandings and indeed, social categories which materialize through the use of language and go on to govern the case at hand.[95] For example, in cases where a woman is murdered by her husband or family member and it is framed in the courts as suicide,[96] labelling the victim as a patient of depression which led her to take her own life helps to exonerate the accused, and ultimately depoliticizes the death. In *Abdul Aziz Bhatti v The State*, for example, the husband was accused of murdering his wife with a shotgun 'due to delay in providing meals', and an appeal was granted based on the husband's claim that his wife had committed suicide.[97] Similarly, in relation to domestic violence, such presuppositions of innocence are mostly towards the defendant, with

[92] NJ Finkel, *Commonsense Justice: Jurors' Notions of the Law* (Harvard University Press 1995).

[93] ibid 2.

[94] Interview with lawyer, Karachi, 11 August 2022 [a].

[95] S Zaman and M Zia, 'How Much Rape Is Rape? Understanding Normative Assumptions within Rape Victimology in Pakistan', in N Hussain (ed) *Disputed Legacies: The Pakistan Papers* (Zubaan Books 2019) 155.

[96] For examples of such claims, see *Adam Khan v The State* [2018] MLD 1007; *Adil Khan v The State* [2019] CrLJ 852; *Abdul Khaliq v The State* [2009] PLD 33; *Muhammad Ismail v The State* [2017] PCrLJ 1130; *Nadeem Abbas v The State* [2017] PCrLJ 1669; *Wahid Khan v Mohabat Khan* [2020] PCrLJ Note 135; *Naseer Ahmed v Khair Bibi* [2017] MLD 2068; *Sheer Muhammad v The State* [2020] PCrLJ 864; *Syed Muhammad v The State* [2019] YLR 337; *Syed Tahir Shah and others v The State* [2018] CrLJ 242. In the case of *Ali Hassan v Station House Officer* [2015] YLR 2474, it was said that the deceased committed suicide because she was 'annoyed with her husband.'

[97] *Abdul Aziz Bhatti v The State* [2019] YLR Note 49.

language playing a role in how offences are presented and ultimately reframed to allow for that disposition.

In Chapter 4, I spoke of how police officials use 'lady harassment issues' as an umbrella term in everyday language to refer to offences relating to gender-based abuse and violence. By doing this, police officers were downplaying the level of harm associated with crimes such as rape or domestic violence by equating them to the more 'minor' crime of harassment. As my research progressed, however, it appeared that this practice—of using legal language which reframes the offence in a multitude of ways—was also adopted by lawyers and, most significantly, by judges. And in doing so, it subjectivized women complainants, because the performative reframing of their narratives through language at best can minimize the violence endured, and at worst may eradicate the commission of an offence altogether.

A good illustration of this is domestic violence, which, despite being a legal term adopted through legislation across various provinces in Pakistan, is still not referred to as such in the courts. Predominantly, it is referred to as a 'family matter' or a 'dispute of family nature'. For example, when I interviewed a woman who had been the victim of an acid attack by her brother-in-law, she recalled that the judge started laughing in the middle of her testimony and interjected to ask the room, '*ais tarhan day khaandaani maamalat noon court ich liyawan de ki zaroorat hai* [what's the need to bring family matters like this to court?]'.[98] This was despite the victim having visible burns and scarring on her face, neck, and right arm, as well as medical reports testifying to the injuries she sustained during and after the attack. Similarly, one lawyer recalled a case she had worked on:

> In the [domestic violence] case I was mentioning, the police refused to file the case and so I took it to the Sessions Court and asked the judge to issue a direction to the police to register the FIR. When that was refused, we went under a writ petition to the High Court to say that the police's refusal to register an FIR is a violation of my client's fundamental rights. The Sessions Court judgment says clearly that it is a 'family matter'. He [the judge] has clearly written in the order that it is a family matter, which is actually crazy because we listed out all the offences—theft, assault, and forced abortion. When the pregnancy was already six months

[98] Interview with victim, Islamabad, 7 June 2022 [d].

in, they forced the woman to abort it because they found out it was a girl. This is domestic violence as per the law.[99]

The judgment corresponding to the case spoken of above states: 'Prima facie, there is *a dispute of family nature* between the parties and petitioner wants to redress her grievances at this forum which is not permissible under law'.[100] In reframing the domestic violence crimes of forced abortion, assault, and theft, amongst others, as a 'dispute of family nature', the judge used his discretion and authority to state that these 'grievances' could not be redressed in 'this forum', or in other words through the courts. Through this (re)presentation, the offence of domestic violence was reframed as a 'family matter' or 'a dispute of family nature', with language being used to eradicate the commission of an offence. As the lawyer on the case rightly pointed out, crimes within the family are still crimes, and 'cannot be an excuse for non-prosecution under the law'.[101]

A couple of the lawyers to whom I spoke explained that judges use language that reframes criminal offences relating to domestic violence because they are 'very [uninterested] in studying the more recent laws, especially at lower court level'.[102] That is to say, many judges will push back in instances relating to domestic violence because either they do not agree with the law, or they simply do not care to know how to navigate it. This is despite 'a spectacular judgment from the High Court on how judges need to take domestic violence seriously and respond to it—and you would think that because the High Court has said it, then the lower court guys need to get in line, but it still doesn't mean anything to them'.[103] Recall that in Vignette 2.1 a lawyer had shared the Sindh Domestic Violence Act with the judge prior to the hearing but 'he did not have the law in his file or chambers and seemed unfamiliar with key provisions',[104] and when she 'tried to walk him through the relevant provisions . . . he lost interest pretty quickly and said enough of his time has already been wasted'.[105]

[99] Interview with lawyer, Lahore, 15 June 2022 [d] [parenthesis added].
[100] Judgment, Sessions Judge, 8928/22 Lahore (Feb 2022) [emphasis added].
[101] Interview with lawyer, Lahore, 15 June 2022 [d]; Writ Petition No. 26687/22 (Apr 2022) LHC.
[102] Interview with lawyer, Karachi, 1 August 2022.
[103] ibid.
[104] See Vignette 2.1, in relation to Criminal Revision Application No 10/2019 (Jan 2020) Karachi West; Interview with lawyer, Karachi, 6 January 2022.
[105] Interview with lawyer, Karachi, 6 January 2022.

These ideas resonate with Smart's theorizing of the struggle between 'old' and 'new' contrivances of power,[106] and also speaks to the interplay between language and performance as theorized by Peters. By using different legal terms than those codified by legislation, legal actors reframe narratives and produce frameworks of subjectivity through discursive acts that performatively work to produce specific (favourable) outcomes.[107] While law may dictate the *form* of performance, it is the performative enactment by legal actors—through language and expression—that governs that form to produce ontological effects and naturalized assumptions of what constitutes legal truths.[108]

The offence of rape is another example which helps illustrate. Under Pakistani law, rape is *zina-bil-jabr*, whereas the offence of *zina* is defined as a man and woman wilfully having sexual intercourse outside the bounds of marriage.[109] However, lawyers and judges alike continue to use the term *zina* for the offence of rape. In doing so, the term used in court indicates that the dispute relates to consensual sexual relations as opposed to the criminal offence of rape, which has also led to the latter being spoken of more generally as 'subjected to sexual intercourse':

> Look, rape is *zina-bil-jabr*, and it is committed on someone. But the judges will not say rape, they'll say 'subjected to sexual intercourse'. But you know sexual intercourse is a voluntary act and rape is without consent. You cannot call it sexual intercourse! It's like not saying murder but saying 'piercing a body leading to death'. The same way, you don't say 'he deliberately took somebody's property and left without asking them', you say it was theft. These are offences with names in the law, so why is it different for rape? Why do we mince our words and not use the correct terminology when it comes to violence against women?[110]

[106] See Smart (n 6).

[107] See Peters (n 17).

[108] See J Butler, 'Performative Agency' (2010) 3(2) Journal of Cultural Economy 147; and Peters (n 16).

[109] Offence of Zina (Enforcement of Hudood) Ordinance 1979 [PAK]. Currently, the offence of 'fornication' is found under s 496B of the PPC and defined as follows: 'a man and woman not married to each other are said to commit fornication if they wilfully have sexual intercourse with one another.'

[110] Interview with lawyer, Karachi, 11 August 2022 [a]. For example, in *Amanullah v the State* [2009] PLD SC 542, the Court said, 'no reasons could be offered as to why the prosecutrix who had admittedly been *subjected to sexual intercourse*, should have spared the actual offender' [emphasis added]; and in the case of *Nasreen Bibi v Farrukh Shahzad* [2015] SCMR 825, the Court stated that 'the petitioner was a virgin lady and according to medical evidence was *subjected to sexual intercourse*' [emphasis added].

While the examples of murder and theft provided above are good comparison points, it is pertinent to add that one lawyer to whom I spoke even referred to a case of murder as 'a brother who had *sacrificed* his sister'[111] due to connotations surrounding 'honour' killings. In addition, the re-framing of offences through legal language can cause complications in cases of attempted crimes. In thinking of rape as being 'subjected to sexual intercourse', attempted rape may no longer find space in that legal language. For example, in a case where a girl aged ten was sexually assaulted in a domestic setting, the medical examination report stated that it found evidence for an attempted rape but insufficient evidence to implicate the accused. However, despite witness testimonies and a statement by the medical officer, the judge only focused on specific aspects of the report. In equating rape to 'being subjected to sexual intercourse', the lack of sexual intercourse leaves no room for an offence. He accordingly gave a judgment which stated that 'the facts of the case itself look to be imaginary and unbelievable under the circumstances'.[112] In dismissing the case in this way, the judge minimizes and perhaps eradicates the violence that the girl endured. Choosing to use the word 'imaginary', too, subjectivizes the victim, by insinuating that her testimony was a (false) product of her mind.[113] Instead, the judge could have recognized that an attempt to rape did indeed occur, but that there was insufficient evidence to prove that it was the accused who committed the offence.

Language can accordingly assist in presenting case narratives in a manner that aligns with and perhaps performs societal attitudes and beliefs stemming from socio-cultural and religious norms and practices. By 'coaching it down, the legal language used here has a tendency to either minimize the violence or not recognize it, by hiding it under other terms which are more generally accepted [in society]'.[114] On the other hand, however, there may be times when judges are in fact very rigid about the language used and specified in the law, if doing so enables them to reach the favourable legal decision based on those same attitudes and beliefs. For instance, when recounting a case of rape involving a transgender person,[115] one lawyer I interviewed said:

[111] Interview with lawyer, Islamabad, 9 June 2022 [c].
[112] Zia and others (n 42) 45.
[113] See a similar discussion in Chapter 4.
[114] Interview with lawyer, Karachi, 11 August 2022 [b] [parenthesis added].
[115] Section 5 of the Protection of Women (Criminal Laws Amendment) Act 2006 [PAK] specifies that 'a *man* is said to commit rape who has sexual intercourse *with a woman* under circumstances . . .' [emphasis added]. However, the offence of rape has since adopted more

> In 2019, I had a case of a transgender person who had been raped and sexually assaulted. Someone had invited them to dance at a wedding or some celebration, and then those people started drinking and they physically beat them and sexually assaulted them. The case came to me to file an FIR. Now, it was tricky for me, and I thought it was best to go under s 377 [of the PPC]—unnatural offences—but it states that it is only an offence if it is carnal intercourse against the order of nature with any 'man, woman, or animal'. The transgender [person] that came to me, their ID card stated 'X' and so they did not fall under the specifics of the law. The police refused to register the case, saying, read the law, it does not fall under this section as an offence. So I came back and then filed a writ petition with the court, but the judge also told me to go home. He said have you read the section? I said yes, this is why I have come to you. The judge said this cannot be done, and so no case could be filed.[116]

In Pakistan, there continue to be widespread debates about the legality of transgender rights. Many political segments of society, as well as legislators, claim that transgender rights contradict Islamic teachings and pave the way for homosexuality and same-sex marriage, both of which are prohibited in the country.[117] Transgender persons continue to experience stigma, being viewed by others as 'sexually deviant, morally corrupt, unnatural or mentally disordered',[118] which could implicate how they are perceived in the court, and ultimately inform judicial reactions. In this case, a transgender persons' identity card specified a third gender, denoted by 'X'. As such, they were neither a man nor a woman for the purposes of the legal definitions of sexual offences provided by way of legislation, and were consequently unable to register a police case for their assault. In instances of domestic violence and rape, as discussed above, legal language and definitions were

gender-neutral language through s 2 of the Criminal Law (Amendment) Act 2021, extending the law to both male victims and transgender victims.

[116] Interview with lawyer, Lahore, 16 June 2022 [a].

[117] A Rashid and U Rashid, 'Constitutional and Legal Guarantees for Transgender in Pakistan: Reforms and Failures in Law' in G Guney, D Davies and P Lee (eds), *Towards Gender Equality in Law* (Palgrave Macmillan 2022) 79; Additionally, see S Zaman, 'Pakistan's Progressive Transgender Law Faces Opposition 4 Years Later' *Voice of America* (28 September 2022) <https://www.voanews.com/a/pakistan-s-progressive-transgender-law-faces-opposition-4-years-later-/6768168.html> accessed 26 January 2023.

[118] S Winter, M Diamond, J Green, D Karasic, T Reed, S Whittle and K Wylie, 'Transgender People: Health at the Margins of Society' (2016) 10042 The Lancet 390, 394.

deserted by judges so as to minimize or eradicate the commission of the offence. Here, the judge opted to adhere to legal language so strictly as to disallow a transgender victim from seeking redress for their sexual assault. In other words, legal language was selectively used in a manner that envelops attitudes and beliefs to reframe offences and narratives within the courtroom to bring out an anticipated and desired judicial outcome.

In addition to the lack of interest, and perhaps unwillingness, associated with studying recent laws, which was provided as reasoning for why judges use different terminology and language for offences relating to gender-based violence, a second explanation was also provided during fieldwork. This relates to the comfort, or rather discomfort, that judges have with the English language more generally, and with English terms relating to domestic violence in particular. Here too, legal actors selectively use language to perform to the judge as audience, anticipating that the judge would have a 'language disability':

> Bear in mind that you are also playing to the judge—if you try to change the words then the judge might not understand. Even when we have cases, we first find out who the judge is and think, will he be able to understand the arguments that we are trying to make. You forget that the judges also have this language disability—all our pleadings are in English, right, they understand certain amounts of them. But many of them are people who have not received an English education, they have working knowledge of English and that's it, and the English language has stuck as our legal language since the British. So even if the oral arguments are in Urdu, the judgments are all in English. So, you need to plead in a way that the judge understands. In the same way, putting in new definitions that he may not understand would end up doing a disservice to your client. If I say, 'she is a victim of psychological abuse because her husband has exhibited a pattern of jealousy and gaslighting', the judge will be like what the hell is this and he won't be able to understand it, as opposed to if I say, 'the man mentally tortured her for three years'. In the lower courts especially, the judges do not have the basic—or beyond basic—understanding of the [English] language. And they will only write what they know.[119]

[119] Interview with lawyer, Karachi, 11 August 2022 [a] [parenthesis added].

Revisiting the transcripts of these interviews reminded me of an interaction I had when accompanying a state prosecutor to the courtroom of a family judge to request a meeting. The judge was not present at the time, and I was introduced to the court clerk in the hope that he would be able to fit me into the judge's schedule over the next few days. The court clerk greeted me, and then looked at the state prosecutor and said, '*yeh toh England se PhD kar rahi hain, kisi parhe likhe judge se milwayen* [she is doing her PhD from England, you should make her meet some educated judge]'.[120] There appears to be a general presumption in the legal system that judges, particularly those in lower courts, are not educated; and there also appears to be a conflation of the comfort levels of judges speaking in English with their level of education. I previously discussed how a judge perceived litigants speaking in English as being educated, rational, and therefore 'mentally sound'. Perhaps it is this 'language disability'—and the way the legal system may perceive judges because of it—that leads to them forming this equivalence in their discretions when adjudicating cases of domestic violence.

Such discomfort with language and the role it plays in reframing legal narratives may also pose issues relating to the lack of accurate data recording in courtrooms. Because the legal language of the justice system is English, all court documentation is (typically) in English too. On the other hand, the language barrier of legal actors means that in many instances, oral arguments and proceedings are done in Urdu. As a result, there is a transcription process through which much of the context of those proceedings is, quite literally, lost in translation. This too can implicate the character allegations and gendering strategies used within the courtroom:

> What the woman says in the court is never recorded accurately. When you look at the papers of what she said, it is written as a statement, and the questions she is asked are not recorded. And that statement is first translated from Urdu into English, and it is written by hand, so it is also summarized by the court clerk sitting over there. And so, a lot of what she says in a narrative, that value is gone and her story is gone—the context and the actual words that she is saying, all of that disappears. And the issue is that a judge looks at a hundred cases a day. When he is looking at the file, he only sees the summary of what the woman said, which is based off of another man's perspective of what she said—I say

[120] Court observations, Karachi, 4 August 2022.

> man because the court clerks are all men. That recording is a big issue for me. It could either influence the judge too much or not influence them enough.[121]

The process through which case files are prepared, particularly in relation to the recording of court proceedings, not only presents a summary based on the recorder's interpretation of the victim's words, but also undergoes a process of translation. In addition to the testimony being interpreted through the same public discourse that other legal actors may be affected by, the lack of familiarity with certain terms used in the law may mean that the language adopted during that transcription is not accurate. For example, if the victim testifies that she had been raped and the recording of her testimony states that she was 'subject to sexual intercourse', her testimony is at risk of being reframed not as a violent act but as a consensual one when it is presented to the judge for decree. This process can also be significantly implicated alongside the anticipative legal performances adopted in the courtroom. As discussed in Chapter 5, the boilerplate character allegations applied to women complainants of domestic violence are typically accompanied by lawyerly practices such as restrictive questioning techniques. In subjectivizing women victims as 'mad' through allegations that make use of 'psy' labels, for example, this means that if she answers 'yes' when shown a medical receipt and asked whether or not she has taken that medicine, the recording of court proceedings would state that the litigant 'admitted to taking medication' without specifying the nature of those medicines. As such, it could feed into the judge's perception and discretion regarding the allegation applied to her, as neither the context of that medication nor its relevance to her mental state is provided in the recording.

At other times, arguments are not recorded at all. This could lead to difficulties in challenging or questioning the impartiality and discretion of judges. In other words, if the oral arguments and their transcriptions are not accurately reproduced in case files and judgments, it is far more difficult for lawyers and litigants to identify and challenge the biases that may have informed judicial reactions and case outcomes where character allegations and societal discourse are used to frame legal narratives:

> In a domestic violence case that I did, at the appeal level, the lawyer on the other side did not even contest the evidence. His view was that the

[121] Interview with lawyer, Karachi, 11 August 2022 [a].

> beating my client was subjected to was permitted in Islam anyway. He said that he didn't care what the domestic violence law says, it was permitted in Islam and so his client was not guilty of anything. This argument was not even noted in the file, and the judge did not even note this argument in the judgment.[122] Our hearings are not recorded or properly transcribed, so from a lawyer's point of view and a research point of view it is so difficult because what the case file or the case judgment says is so different from what goes on in the courts.[123]

These practices can lead to the constructed subjectivities of victim-subjects continuing to be circulated as forms of legal knowledge. This is because apart from the very limited reported judgments, most legal data remains unused both for the purposes of research and for the purposes of case law by judges. In many ways, the limitations associated with case law management can be beneficial for the performative gendering strategies used by legal actors to enact victim-subjects of domestic violence, with little to no judicial evaluations being conducted to remedy these practices.

As one lawyer said, 'there is also a lot of misreading and nonreading of case files by judges, and a lot of inherent bias is present even in judgments. They have a predisposed mind when it comes to cases relating to the family.'[124]

Conclusion

This chapter investigated the use of anticipatory performances as a gendering strategy that enacts victim-subjects of domestic violence in the courtroom. Through a relational analysis, it looked at how the ideas of 'playing to the judge' and 'playing the victim' anticipate judicial reactions and discretions, and outlined the effects that character allegations have on how victims are perceived in the courtroom. I also examined the interplay between performance and language to argue that complainants are subjectivized as 'bad' and/or 'mad' women through a reframing of their narratives which aims to either minimize their harms or eradicate

[122] Criminal Petition 457/17 Magistrate, Karachi West (Feb 2019).
[123] Interview with lawyer, Karachi, 6 January 2022, in relation to Criminal Revision Application No. 10/19, Karachi West (Jan 2020).
[124] Interview with lawyer, Lahore, 17 June 2022 [b].

the commission of an offence altogether. These ideas are summarized by a judge's concluding thought at the end of our interview:

> I would just like to add—you know, I did a gender workshop, and in terms of our laws I think we have overreacted in creating all these women legislations in line with international ordinances. Are they necessary? Do we really need them?[125]

Zaman and Zia find that by way of application of the law, the politics of gender-based violence are enacted in the justice system in various ways.[126] Three aspects particularly resonate. First, they posit that legal negotiations serve to discipline society by privileging discourse around protection and social identities. This comes to form through the analysis which illustrated judicial favouring of 'old' contrivances of power, by pushing back against legal reform. Second, they argue that language is used to construct alternative narratives. Similarly, this chapter assessed how judges selectively use language to bring about desired outcomes. And third, they find that the justice system aims to create a uniform truth which 'annihilates all other truths'.[127] In other words, the constructed subjectivities of victim-subjects of domestic violence may then circulate as forms of legal knowledge.

The adjudication of domestic violence cases through anticipative performances can lead to a number of outcomes. For instance, judges may adopt similar practices as those explored in previous chapters, by persuading victims to either compromise or withdraw their cases:

> They [judges] will just tell the husband not to do it again and then tell the woman, look, he is saying he won't do it again. In one case a judge also said that '*aap affidavit inse le lein, aur anghoota kya aap dasson unglian lagwa lein ke woh aainda in par haath nahi uthain ge* [get an affidavit from him, forget one thumb print, get all ten fingers done that he won't raise his hand on her again]'[128] and my client was like '*haath kya yeh toh mujhe frying pan aur kenchi se bhi maar chuke hain* [what hands, he has even used frying pans and scissors to hit me]'. They try everything they

[125] Interview with family judge, District and Sessions Court, Karachi 4 July 2022.
[126] Zaman and Zia (n 95) 161.
[127] ibid 162.
[128] Affidavits in Pakistan are undertakings or oaths, typically affixed by a signature and one thumb impression.

can to make the woman go back with the husband, or to withdraw the case.[129]

Additionally, particularly in cases where women are alleged as being mentally unstable, judges maintain the idea that returning home to their families will be 'easier' for them. This too mirrors performative presentations, such as the notion that men are protecting socio-religious norms and culture by being 'gracious' in accepting 'bad' and/or 'mad' women. As one lawyer recalled:

> I had a case [where] the woman was taking a *khula* [divorce] because of domestic abuse. They said she was a *nafsiyati mareez* [mental patient]. But even the judge tells the woman to let it be, to compromise, to think of her children—and the mindset is that even the judges tell women that your husband will keep filing some counter case or a custody case and as a *nafsiyati mareez* you wouldn't get custody, so why do you want to get involved in all this? The judge didn't even bother to check if she is actually sick. Their advice to women is to just keep going the way you have, it will be easier for you.[130]

Many times, victims succumb to the pressure to compromise and end up withdrawing their cases.[131] At other times they may be granted relief through the civil courts in the form of *khula* or divorce, for example, but the criminal acts to which they were subjected remain ignored. Given that the judge is only expected to adjudicate on the case at hand—the extent of which is to grant the dissolution of marriage or not—even when men confess to the crime of domestic violence in open court and justify it with the 'bad' character of their wives, that admission is not recorded in legal case files, nor is it further deliberated on in any way:

> In our society, when the husband has been domestically violent with the wife, they tend to justify it. They justify it by Islam, that the religion

[129] Interview with lawyer, Lahore, 13 June 2022 [b].

[130] Interview with lawyer, Karachi, 19 July 2022.

[131] A number of the criminal petitions consulted during this research which related to acts of domestic violence were withdrawn by complainants during the legal process. For example, see, Criminal (Misc) Application 328/17, Sessions Judge Jacobabad (Sept 2017); Criminal (Misc) Application 383/15 Sessions Judge Jacobabad (Sept 2015); Criminal Petition 1/16, Sessions Court Jacobabad (May 2017); Criminal Petition 318/14, Sessions Court Jacobabad (Nov 2014); and Criminal Petition 52/14, Sessions Court Jacobabad (Jul 2014).

> gives them permission. One client, the husband tore open her head with a metal rod, and he said that she was having an affair and he has permission to do this by Allah and that he did the right thing. And those statements are said in open court during proceedings, and nothing happens with them—because the decision for the judge is only to the extent of *khula* or no *khula*. Who is going to do something about this?[132]

In Chapter 7, I draw on the main findings of empirical work to offer a concise account of how character allegations function as a gendering strategy to construct victim-subjects of domestic violence. In doing so, I identify four cross-cutting conclusions that shed light on how such allegations work to mould the subjectivity of women complainants and alter their narratives, and how this relates to secondary victimization outcomes. I also present a vision for the way forward which acknowledges the limitations of the law, while retaining 'cautious optimism'[133] about the transformative potential of legal reform to prioritize the narratives and safety of women and accommodate for the iterative relationship between domestic abuse and mental health in legal processes.

[132] Interview with lawyer, Lahore, 17 June 2022 [a].
[133] V Munro, *Law and Politics at the Perimeter: Re-evaluating Key Debates in Feminist Theory* (Hart 2007) 72.

7

‘Bad’, ‘mad’, both, or neither?

Aurat ki aqal gadi pechay
[In the nape rests a woman’s wits][1]

Introduction

Before domestic violence was clearly defined in legal terms through criminalization, it was often interpreted within the framework of ‘psy’ disciplines. Psychological theories of domestic violence developed through a focus on individuals and their relationships, attributing dysfunctions and abusive acts within those relationships to defective personality types.[2] Social factors here were secondary; attention was instead diverted to ‘abnormal’ facets of personality. The development of concepts such as ‘female maladies’, for example, sought to explain abuse in intimate relationships being caused by deficiencies in women’s psyche, suggesting that violence against women was self-induced. The idea of ‘female masochism’ or ‘finding pleasure in pain’[3] was similarly considered a core component of female psychology, with ‘psy’ disciplines claiming that women secretly desire male aggression.[4] Victims of domestic violence were accordingly ‘assumed to have played a crucial role in their own victimisation’.[5]

The emphasis on pathology in psychological theories of domestic violence often led to a preference towards mental health responses rather than criminal justice interventions.[6] By framing violence as a result of personal

[1] A Punjabi proverb. See M Shahbaz, *Saday Akhaan [Our Proverbs]* (Aziz Book Depot 2004) 155.
[2] MD Pagelow, *Woman-Battering: Victims and Their Experiences* (SAGE Publications 1981) 19.
[3] L Woods, ‘Litigation on Behalf of Battered Women’ (1979) 5(1) Women’s Rights Law Reporter 7, 12.
[4] S Brownmiller, *Against Our Will: Men, Women and Rape* (Simon and Schuster 1975) 15.
[5] L Shultz, ‘The Wife Assaulter’ (1960) 6(1) Journal of Social Therapy 103.
[6] M Bard and B Berkowitz, ‘Training Police as Specialists in Family Crisis Intervention: A Community Psychology Action Program’ (1967) 3 Community Mental Health Journal 315, 317.

Domestic Violence in Pakistan. Daanika Kamal, Oxford University Press. © Daanika Kamal 2025.
DOI: 10.1093/9780198953470.003.0007

dysfunction or mental illness, the focus was more on individual treatment and therapy and less on broader social and societal contexts. Feminist critiques towards psychological explanations for domestic violence therefore argued that such perspectives ignored its systemic nature. It was asserted that 'men beat women because society and its institutions encourage and allow woman-assault',[7] highlighting the implications of victim-blaming narratives which claimed that women 'enjoy' violence.[8] Prosecuting acts of abuse in domestic and intimate relationships through the law was therefore considered a means through which to challenge the structural and societal ideals that permitted them.[9]

There have been mixed views within feminist scholarship about defining acts of domestic violence as criminal, with some feminists optimistically finding that it was essential to replace 'man's law' with 'law that reflects the female reality'.[10] Others however, doubted whether partnering with a 'male' institution was the best way to promote women's interests, worrying that this move may substitute one form of oppression with another.[11] Because of the attribution of State inaction to systemic patriarchy, the criminal justice system's failure in responding to domestic violence cases was taken as a reflection of men and masculine ideals controlling institutions, leading to a reluctance to move towards mandatory criminal intervention. And while fully engaging with this debate is beyond the scope of this book, it raises a question about whether the relative shift from psychological to legal explanations and responses to domestic abuse may implicate an uneasy merger of the two disciplines, particularly with regard to the construction of victim-subjects of domestic violence. As discussed in Chapter 2, the disciplines of law and psychiatry both share a tendency towards using gendering strategies in the creation of discursive subject positions. However, relevant scholarship from both disciplines may also share a gap, in that the two do not engage with how the constructed subjectivities of one may be used as a gendering strategy for another. This book has attempted to answer this question, amongst others.

[7] Woods (n 3) 12.
[8] K Horney, 'The Problem with Female Masochism' (1935) 22(1) Psychoanalytic Review 241, 242.
[9] L Lerman, *Prosecution of Spouse Abuse: Innovations in Criminal Justice Response* (Center for Women Policy Studies 1981) 26, 27.
[10] Brownmiller (n 4) 388.
[11] C Mackinnon, 'Feminism, Marxism, Method and the State: An Agenda for Theory' (1983) 8(4) Feminist Theory 635.

Drawing upon perspectives and approaches commonly bracketed under feminist post-structuralism, this book provided a socio-legal analysis of domestic violence cases in Pakistan to examine how gendering practices construct victim-subjects, framing them at times as 'bad' women and at other times as 'mad' women. By adopting a process-based structure to shadow the stories and narratives of women complainants as they move through various stages of the judicial system, it advanced four thematic investigations which served to address *why* the subjectivity of women victims of abuse is shaped in particular ways, and *how* these subjectivities are captured and negotiated within the Pakistani legal system. This chapter accordingly opens with a summary of the key arguments developed over the course of the book, which stipulate that character allegations are used by legal actors to (a) silence victims through gendered narratives, (b) police victims through gatekeeping approaches, (c) script victims through lawyerly practices, and (d) enact victims through anticipatory practices. It goes on to draw on these findings to deconstruct the victim-subject of domestic violence by identifying four recurring and cross-cutting conclusions that relay the ways in which character allegations mould the subjectivity of women complainants and alter their narratives during the legal process, and how this relates to the secondary victimization of complainants in the Pakistani legal system. The book will then conclude with final reflections, presenting a vision for the way forward as one of duality; such that it acknowledges the limitations of the law, while retaining 'cautious optimism'[12] about the transformative potential of legal reform to prioritize the safety of women, clear pathways for justice, and ultimately improve systemic legal responses in cases of domestic violence.

Deconstructing victim-subjects

A key aspect of feminist post-structuralism, as discussed in Chapter 2, is the assumption that reality is not simply reflected, but rather actively constructed by temporarily fixing meanings that are shaped by discourses. This ongoing process continually (re)produces various forms of subjectivities and power relations, influencing both bodies and minds.[13] Gendering

[12] V Munro, *Law and Politics at the Perimeter: Re-evaluating Key Debates in Feminist Theory* (Hart 2007) 72.
[13] See J Butler, *Gender Trouble: Feminism and the Subversion of Identity* (Routledge 1990); and M Foucault, *The History of Sexuality* (Vol 1, Penguin 1981).

strategies operate in a similar manner, with societal and institutional practices shaping what it means to be a woman, as well as what qualifies as a 'good' woman or a 'sane' woman. As Weedon and Hallak posit, these practices 'constitute discursive fields to produce meanings, subject positions and subjectivity'.[14] This theorizing suggests that the term 'subject' can refer both to the process of becoming a subject and to becoming subjected to power structures through repeated performances of gendered language, gestures, and roles.[15] Exploring gendering strategies in the construction of victim-subjects of domestic violence accordingly provided a valuable framework through which to understand the roles that rhetoric and discourse play across different vernaculars, and the ways in which constructed meanings and subjectivities come to appear as 'natural'[16] and legitimized in institutional structures and forms of knowledge.[17]

Operating within this framework, this book argued that the first way in which character allegations are used as a gendering strategy is through narratives that aim to silence women (Chapter 3). Here, silencing refers to the institutional and societal gendered discourses which employ silence as a mechanism in situations of disagreement. Particularly, it was argued that framing of women as 'bad' and/or as 'mad' is a silencing technique that works to produce subjectivities that suppress opposition to dominant constructions of gendered normativity. By drawing on literatures that engage with the victim-survivor paradox, this chapter reflected on how labels can shape subjects, and went on to relate these ideas to the use of gendered narratives and allegations pertaining to a woman's character and mental state. Further, I looked at how perceptions concerning silent, 'passive' victims and loud, 'active' victims are encapsulated amongst the politics of respectability, which may similarly inform the silencing techniques that are used to manage 'dissenting' women and help construct them as unfavourable victim-subjects that are not to be heard. By bringing the voices and narratives of women to the forefront, this chapter also explored the different considerations of what 'justice' may mean for complainants of domestic

[14] C Weedon and A Hallak, 'Feminist Poststructuralism: Discourse, Subjectivity, the Body and Power' in J Angouri and J Baxter (eds), *The Routledge Handbook of Language, Gender and Sexuality* (Routledge 2021) 437.

[15] J Butler, *Bodies That Matter: On the Discursive Limits of 'Sex'* (Routledge 1993) 124.

[16] S Crowley, *Toward a Civil Discourse: Rhetoric and Fundamentalism* (University of Pittsburgh Press 2006) 63.

[17] L Hutcheon, 'Postmodernism, Poststructuralism, and Feminism' (1985) 6(3) Canadian Woman Studies 36.

violence, and highlighted their agency in those negotiations as they move through various stages of the Pakistani legal system.

The discussion then followed the experiences and interactions of women victims at police stations, finding that law enforcement personnel adopt gendering strategies to police women through gatekeeping approaches (Chapter 4). This chapter examined how the gendered constructions of respectability and social control inform the ways in which police officers understand their 'duty' towards protecting the State-endorsed sanctity of the family structure, and employ strategies that subjectivize victims through allegations and claims that minimize their harms and encourage compromise and reconciliation as a way to mask their private truths as 'public secrets'.[18] It also served to illustrate how policing processes embed practices which focus more on policing culturally disputed ideas of domestic violence, and less on punishing or deterring perpetrators of that violence. This in turn helps to understand why some women may 'disappear' from the legal system during this process and why many cases of domestic abuse are found scattered across family courts, although they should, by way of legislation, belong under criminal jurisdiction.

The book subsequently looked at how character allegations are used as a gendering strategy to script victims through lawyerly practices as they travel through the courts (Chapter 5). In examining how character allegations are introduced and navigated by lawyers in the courtroom, I contended that women are framed as 'bad' and/or 'mad' in legal documents and arguments through the use of pre-drafted boilerplate suits that are employed in a one-size-fits-all approach. The chapter went on to illustrate how lawyers build on these scripted narratives by using oral tactics that engage in performative and restrictive questioning practices, in conjunction with the presentation of peculiar forms of evidence and the strategic use of suggestibility. These gendering strategies and practices are employed by legal actors to shape how women complainants are perceived in the courts, in a way that not only subjectivizes the woman but also secures her within the field of that subjectification, setting her up to be viewed by the judiciary through the lens of the allegations applied to her.

And finally, in examining courtroom practices and the role of the judiciary, I argued that victim-subjects are enacted through anticipatory performances (Chapter 6). Here, I looked more closely at how legal actors

[18] See P Baxi, 'Justice Is a Secret: Compromise in Rape Trials' (2010) 44(3) Contributions to Indian Sociology 207.

perform to the judge as audience, and investigated the distorting effects that may come to form when litigation is carried out as a scripted performance for spectators. Through a relational analysis, I assessed how the ideas of 'playing to the judge' and 'playing the victim' anticipate judicial reactions and discretions, and outlined the effect that this has on how victims of domestic violence are perceived in the courtroom and, indeed, the role that this plays in how domestic violence cases are adjudicated. Additionally, this chapter examined the interplay between performance and language, to find that complainants can be subjectivized through a reframing of their narratives which can minimize their harms, and in some cases eradicate the commission of an offence altogether. Particularly, it contended that judges and lawyers selectively use language to bring about desired outcomes and 'legal truths' which may then lead to the constructed subjectivities of victim-subjects of domestic violence being circulated in courtrooms as forms of legal knowledge.

Further, the choice to structure this book in a process-based approach helped demonstrate how various stages of the legal process are entangled with each other. These entanglements are prominent in that they reflect how the challenging and negative experiences of women victims at early stages of the legal process may inform whether and how their complaints and cases progress to later stages. For example, the practices and decisions relating to policing can impact whether a victim's case is prosecuted, and comparably, the practices and decisions of legal actors during litigation can impact how her case is adjudicated. As seen in Chapter 4, this came to form through the analysis of women who 'disappear' during the police process, and the policing strategies and procedures which deter (and at times obstruct) women from filing criminal complaints. As a result, women's cases are often redirected to the family courts. And as seen in Chapter 5, the lawyerly practices adopted in cases of domestic violence may discourage women from continuing their cases by, for example, proposing compromises and out-of-court settlements in exchange for the withdrawal of their cases.

Similar to the ways in which each stage of the legal process is entangled with the next one, there are a number of recurring and cross-cutting themes that can be identified by drawing on the findings of empirical chapters. The first is that character allegations work to minimize and mitigate women's harms.[19] In Chapter 3, this was illustrated by the ways in which victims

[19] See for example, H Douglas, 'The Criminal Law's Response to Domestic Violence: What's Going On?' (2008) 30(3) Sydney Law Review 439.

were framed as 'bad' or 'mad' by family members and others to invalidate their harms, in conjunction with the idea that they should be grateful that the harm perpetrated upon them was not worse. By imagining hypothetical situations that could have had more adverse effects on the victim, these allegations serve to reduce the perceived severity of the harm, and therefore the blameworthiness of the act. Additionally, in Chapter 4, police officers routinely dismissed women's complaints based on ideas relating to the 'female psyche' and suspicions that women were trying to manipulate police officers by bringing false, misrepresented, or exaggerated claims of abuse and violence. Here too, character allegations serve to minimize or mitigate women's harms. In Chapter 5 this came to form more prominently through lawyerly practices which aimed to insinuate that women's testimonies were a product of their untoward mental state, by, for example, proposing that victims of acid crimes were covering their faces with *dupattas* in court not to retain their modesty or due to the disfigurement caused by the attack, but because there was no injury to begin with. Further, in both Chapter 4 and Chapter 6, I found that language was selectively used to minimize harm by reframing gender-based violence under the broad umbrella of 'lady harassment issues' by police officers, and by reframing acts of domestic violence as 'a family matter' or a 'dispute of family nature' in the courtroom. This serves to lessen the criminality and wrongdoing of the offences and acts in question.

Second, character allegations can help the presentation of alternative legal 'truths'[20] by impacting the perceived credibility, reliability, and blameworthiness of the victim. In Chapter 3, women victims of domestic violence recalled that their perpetrators reframed their narratives of abuse and violence by alleging that their testimonies were the product of their unsound minds. For example, in a case where a woman had been raped and coerced into getting married, the accused alleged that she had a psychological issue and reframed the narrative to say: 'So what if I did sex, I am her husband it is my right.'[21] Similarly, a victim who was burnt by her husband was claimed to be a 'psycho' who had doused herself in petrol.[22] Such allegations serve to not only reduce the credibility and reliability of the victim as a legal subject, but also reduce the blameworthiness of her perpetrator.

[20] See for example, S Zaman and M Zia, 'How Much Rape Is Rape? Understanding Normative Assumptions within Rape Victimology in Pakistan' in N Hussain (ed) *Disputed Legacies: The Pakistan Papers* (Zubaan Books 2019) 155.

[21] Interview with lawyer, Karachi, 19 July 2022.

[22] Interview with victim, Karachi, 12 January 2022.

Further, as demonstrated in Chapter 4, gendered understandings of rationality are embedded within police practices which require women's accounts of violence and abuse to be corroborated by a man, leading to numerous instances where the man's word was taken as legal fact and the woman's truth was unattended to. And in both Chapter 5 and Chapter 6, I discussed how lawyers engaged in performative tactics (such as through the Restitution of Conjugal Rights decree) and made use of restrictive questioning tactics together with peculiar forms of evidence to build on scripted narratives which contended that women were of 'bad' character or of unsound mind as a means to present an alternative legal truth. Here, character allegations were used to reframe courtroom narratives and discredit women's versions of events.

Third, character allegations assist in maintaining secrecy.[23] As seen in Chapter 3, this was illustrated in the way that either the threat of character allegations, or the allegations themselves, helped to ensure women's silence and deter public disclosure of the acts of violence perpetrated upon her.[24] This idea was even more prominent in Chapter 4, where police officers advised victims to refrain from discussing familial disputes in public spaces, as 'the more these sort of things are hidden . . . the better it is'.[25] Additionally, amidst the circulation of character allegations, lawyers and judges alike were seen to encourage victims to compromise with their aggressors and withdraw their cases. This too helps to maintain secrecy. Further, in Chapter 5, character allegations were used by the accused and his lawyers as a way to 'pressurize the victim . . . to negotiate with them and reach an out of court settlement'.[26] Similarly, Chapter 6 illustrated that in response to the framing of women as 'bad' and 'mad' during legal proceedings, judges themselves often advised victims: 'just keep going the way you have, it will be easier for you.'[27] Through practices that envelope character allegations as a way to maintain secrecy, perpetrators are able to isolate victims of domestic violence and suppress their stories, thereby also avoiding accountability for the acts of abuse they committed.[28]

[23] Baxi (n 18).
[24] See L Theismeyer, 'Introduction' in L Theismeyer (ed) *Discourses and Silencing: Representation and the Language of Displacement* (John Benjamins 2003) 11.
[25] Interview with lawyer, Lahore, 13 June 2022 [b].
[26] Interview with legal aid personnel, Islamabad, 7 June 2022 [a].
[27] Interview with lawyer, Karachi, 19 July 2022.
[28] See LJ Herman, *Trauma and Recovery* (Basic Books 1992).

Fourth, and perhaps most pertinently, character allegations serve to manage and control 'dissenting' women.[29] In Chapter 1, I recalled that during my own divorce hearings I was warned by my lawyer that the other party may try to 'assassinate my character', and was taken aback when, in response to my suit, it was alleged that I had a 'mental issue'. I also mentioned that I remember thinking at the time that such allegations probably serve the same purpose, but I fell short of identifying what that purpose is. In response to that question, the most prominent cross-cutting theme across the empirical chapters is that character allegations serve to control women, with the themes of 'silencing', 'policing', 'scripting', and 'enacting' victim-subjects contributing towards that aim. This is aligned with discussions in Chapter 2, where institutional gendering strategies premised on the social control of women were described as the social processes and methods that make individuals conform to certain sets of gendered norms and expectations, through which moral and social orders are made possible.[30] Examples from each of the empirical chapters help illustrate how character allegations serve to control 'dissenting' women. In Chapter 3, women's narratives emphasized the kinds of allegations that were used to frame them as disobedient, 'bad' women in need of control. In other instances, those women perceived as 'dissenting' were deemed 'mad', in an attempt to frame their complaints as originating from their troubled minds, and in an effort to pressurize them to recede their complaints. Similarly, in Chapter 4, I outlined how law enforcement may adopt a functional purpose in facilitating the State's gendered nationalist discourse through an analysis of the gatekeeping approaches often employed by the police. In Chapter 5, the moral regulation of women was particularly prominent in findings that related to the one-size-fits-all approach to character allegations in boilerplate text of pre-drafted suits, as well as the way in which abortion pills, contraceptive pills, and birth control pills—typically associated with the 'bad' woman trope—were strategically used as 'evidence' for the 'psy' label applied to the complainant. And in Chapter 6, findings relating to the adjudication of domestic violence cases support the notion that legal actors and

[29] See A Dhanda, 'Psychologising Dissent: Psychiatric Labelling and Social Control' in A Dhanda and A Parashar (eds), *Engendering Law: Essays in Honour of Lotika Sarkar* (Eastern Book Company 2007) 321; and M Wetherell, 'Positioning and Interpretative Repertoires: Conversation Analysis and Poststructuralism in Dialogue' (1998) 9(3) Discourse and Society 387.

[30] See M Innes, *Understanding Social Control: Deviance, Crime and Social Order* (Open University Press 2003); and S Cohen, *Visions of Social Control* (Polity Press 1985).

the judiciary share the 'essential nationalist ideology', delivering a cultural message to remind women that private violence is still sanctioned in some forms, because it ensures the management of gender and sexuality.[31]

By deconstructing the victim-subject of domestic violence, then, it appears that character allegations share a tendency to minimize harms, present alternative legal truths, maintain secrecy, and ultimately serve to control women. As a result, character allegations can lead to numerous secondary victimization outcomes for women complainants in the Pakistani legal system. 'Secondary victimization' is a term used to describe the additional harms or sense of betrayal that is experienced by victims of abuse when the responses and provisions that they receive from formal institutions and/or informal support networks are inappropriate.[32] In other words, these are 'injustices that occur to victims after a trauma'.[33] As seen through numerous examples in the preceding discussion, the additional harms come forth through the invalidation of a woman's expectations of being provided with belief and/or protection, when she is instead made to face victim-blaming attitudes and practices that minimize or disregard her victimization in the social and legal systems she is trying to navigate.[34] This often manifests in interactions with members of institutional systems,[35] such that women victims feel guilty, violated, distrustful, and reluctant to seek further help.[36]

The overview of complaint processes, investigatory procedures, and evidential practices in Chapter 4, for example, helps to illustrate how victims of domestic violence encounter secondary victimization in police settings. At first contact with law enforcement personnel, women often face disbelief when they are told that their complaints cannot be investigated unless they are able to produce a male guardian to corroborate her testimony. They are also viewed with suspicion when they bring their own evidence of abuse (such as clothes or photographs) and are met with victim-blaming

[31] See L Abu-Odeh, 'Crimes of Honour and the Construction of Gender in Arab Societies' (2011) 2(1) Comparative Law Review 27.

[32] SL Brown, *Counselling Victims of Violence: A Handbook for Helping Professionals* (Hunter House 2007).

[33] J Hattendorf and TR Tollerud, 'Domestic Violence: Counselling Strategies that Minimise the Impact of Secondary Victimisation' (1997) 33(1) Perspectives in Psychiatric Care 14, 17.

[34] See L Laing, 'Secondary Victimisation: Domestic Violence Survivors Navigating the Family Law System' (2017) 23(11) Violence Against Women 1314.

[35] R Campbell and S Raja, 'Secondary Victimisation of Rape Victims: Insights from Mental Health Professionals Who Treat Survivors of Violence' (1999) 14(3) Violence and Victims 261.

[36] R Campbell, R Dworkin and G Cabral, 'An Ecological Model of the Impact of Sexual Assault on Women's Mental Health' (2009) 10(3) Trauma, Violence and Abuse 225, 234

responses which question their characters and/or their relationship with the perpetrator. Additionally, victims are often told that the only evidence considered 'good' in cases of domestic violence is a medico-legal examination. However, societal constraints and a lack of available women medico-legal officers may lead to victims feeling violated when they are told to be examined by men. This contributes to their reluctance to proceed with the case as well.

It is similarly relevant to note that while literature on secondary victimization predominantly focuses on setbacks and failures within social and legal services, including both criminal justice institutions[37] and family law systems,[38] this book demonstrates that it is equally important to assess realities relating to secondary victimization through interpersonal relationships, particularly in domestic violence cases. This is because secondary victimization, as per the analysis presented in empirical chapters, can often be enacted not only by police or legal personnel, but by individuals in interpersonal relationships with the victim as well. In Chapter 3, women were victimized by family members and community members after they spoke out about their experiences of domestic abuse.[39] This included victim-blaming comments that normalized the abuse[40] and allegations of mental instability by husbands, parents, and other family members.[41] Similarly, women victims felt coercion and pressure to withdraw cases of domestic violence not only from legal actors, but from the their families and communities as well. As a victim of an acid crime recounted, 'even in my family, there was no support . . . the community and neighbourhood were also not happy that I had taken the case [to court]. They said that it gives the community a bad name.'[42] In this case, her father did not inform her nor seek

[37] For example, see D Patterson, 'The Linkage between Secondary Victimisation by Law Enforcement and Rape Case Outcomes' (2011) 26(2) Journal of Interpersonal Violence 328. Additionally, see K Rich and P Seffrin, 'Police Officers' Collaboration with Rape Victim Advocates: Barriers and Facilitators' (2013) 28 Violence and Victims 681.

[38] EA Rivera, CM Sullivan and AM Zeoli, 'Secondary Victimisation of Abused Mothers by Family Court Mediators' (2012) 27 Journal of Family Violence 321.

[39] As one interviewee said, 'Here, the woman who speaks loudly, or who speaks of her rights, we do not like her. People in our society will say, see how she talks, she probably runs her mouth with her husband too, no wonder he has to hit her, or no wonder he has to control her.' Interview with victim support personnel, Lahore, 15 June 2022.

[40] Interview with victim, Lahore, 14 June 2022 [a]; Interview with victim, Karachi, 12 January 2022 [b].

[41] Interview with victim, Karachi, 12 January 2022 [d]; Interview with victim, Karachi, 12 January 2022 [b].

[42] Interview with victim, Islamabad, 8 June 2022 [a].

her consent before withdrawing the legal case on her behalf and reaching an out-of-court settlement with her perpetrator.

Perhaps it is because of such secondary victimization outcomes that Pakistani women preferred to refer to themselves as 'victims' rather than as 'survivors'[43]—because doing so conveys that the trauma and harms they experienced were not limited to the acts of domestic abuse and violence, but included (and at times were intensified) by the secondary victimization they faced both within their communities and when navigating the justice system.

Reflections and way forward

In closing this book, it is pertinent to return to the beginning. While I first introduced and used Smart's theorizing of gendering strategies as a stepping-off point, I further developed her ideas through engagement with interdisciplinary literatures to arrive at a conceptual framework, and indeed, a conclusion that is different from Smart's de-centring law thesis.[44] Smart's descriptive thesis, relating to the constructive aspects of the law, discusses the disciplinary tendency of legal power which produces and constrains the behaviour of individuals through surveillance and normalization techniques. By exploring the construction of victim-subjects of domestic violence through gendered character allegations, this thesis similarly aligned with the analysis in this book. In her prescriptive thesis, however, Smart discourages the use of feminist reform strategies through the law, advocating for non-legal strategies instead.[45] This conclusion is less compatible with the arguments developed in this book, which rather look at the strategic potential of poststructuralist approaches to 'pursue a deconstructivist agenda within legal arenas and discourses'.[46] As stated by

[43] See '"I am not a survivor, I am a victim": How labels shape subjects' in Chapter 3; Interview with victim, Karachi, 12 January 2022 [a]; Interview with victim, Lahore, 14 June 2022 [a].

[44] C Smart, *Feminism and the Power of Law* (Routledge 1989); Also see V Munro, 'Legal Feminism and Foucault—A Critique of the Expulsion of Law' (2002) 28(4) Journal of Law and Society 546.

[45] Smart (n 44); also see V Munro, 'Feminist Critiques of the Rule of Law' in J Meierhenrich and M Loughlin (eds), The Cambridge Companion to the Rule of Law (Cambridge University Press 2021) 340; ML Fineman, 'Challenging Law, Establishing Difference: The Future of Feminist Legal Scholarship' (1990) 42 Florida Law Review 25.

[46] R Sandland, 'Between Truth and Difference: Poststructuralism, Law and the Power of Feminism' (1995) 3 Feminist Legal Studies 3, 14.

Lacey, what is needed 'is not an abandonment of the legal and political project, but rather the development of more sophisticated understandings of legal practices, their strengths as well as their evident and important limitations'.[47] In challenging the continued conception and construction of victim-subjects of domestic violence in the legal realm, this book has attempted to do just that. It has outlined how the law can indeed be used as a tool of agency, protection, and justice for women,[48] while also cautioning against the disciplinary subjective forms of patriarchal power operating within the law.

By presenting accounts of harmful legal practices concerning domestic violence cases in Pakistani courts, positioned against the backdrop of desired legal reform through recent legislative developments, this book offers empirical insights and critical theorizations that identify shortcomings relating to where and how the legal system fails women, 'while retaining cautious optimism about the potential for change offered by legal reform'.[49] The efforts of civil society organizations and national women's movements in Pakistan, alongside international human rights discourses, have contributed to significant legislative advancements in this area. However, the narratives detailed in preceding chapters provide compelling evidence of the need to further engage with the law and improve systemic legal responses to violence against women. The vision for the law in this context is therefore one of duality: where the law can and should be engaged with as a tool for protection, agency, and justice, while simultaneously recognizing and challenging it as a site of patriarchal power. This recognition allows for a nuanced approach to feminist legal reform which goes beyond simply demanding inclusion and protection within existing legal structures and instead seeks to reshape the law's underlying assumptions about gender, power, and subjectivity. The deconstructivist agenda, then, is one that reveals how legal discourse constructs gendered subjects and actively works to challenge these constructions. It does not abandon the legal project, but seeks to transform it by harnessing the law's ability to offer safeguards while confronting its tendency to normalize gendered

[47] N Lacey, 'Closure and Critique in Feminist Jurisprudence: Transcending the Dichotomy or a Foot in Both Camps?' in *Unspeakable Subjects: Essays in Feminist Legal and Social Theory* (Hart 1998) 180.

[48] For example, see 'What is justice really? Locating agency in negotiations' in Chapter 3.

[49] V Munro, *Law and Politics at the Perimeter: Re-evaluating Key Debates in Feminist Theory* (Hart 2007) 72. Also see C MacKinnon, 'The Power to Change' in *Women's Lives, Men's Laws* (Harvard University Press 2005) 103.

ideals and undermine women's experiences through character allegations and other such strategies and mechanisms. The following sections accordingly attempt to offer a vision for the way forward by addressing two areas highlighted at the beginning of this book that have relevance and applicability both within and beyond Pakistan: the reimagining of adversarial court processes, and the iterative relationship between domestic abuse and mental health.

Adversarial court processes

In Chapter 1, I questioned whether gendering practices and narratives are an inevitable product of adversarial legal processes, where challenging the accused's credibility is the default focus of defence strategies,[50] or whether the courtroom can be imagined as a space that recognizes and values stories grounded in lived experiences rather than boilerplate character tropes. This requires legal systems to not just include women within existing frameworks but rather adopt practices that aim to dismantle the gendered assumptions that underpin legal reasoning. As per the findings of this research, two areas of potential engagement, then, are the use and application of pre-drafted boilerplate suits, and the peculiar forms of evidence circulating in courtrooms in cases relating to domestic violence.

The cases analysed in this book demonstrate that the first predominant claim made by the accused in response to allegations of domestic abuse is that the woman is of 'bad' character, specified as 'immoral' and/or 'disobedient'. The former dampens her credibility, and the latter infers that she is not liable to relief.[51] The practice of questioning a woman's credibility through gendered narratives is neither new nor surprising in adversarial court systems. As discussed in Chapter 2, an amendment to the criminal laws in 2016[52] omitted a clause in the *Qanun-e-Shahadat* Order (Law of Evidence) which stipulated that 'when a man is prosecuted for rape or an attempt to ravish, it may be shown that the prosecutrix was of generally immoral character'.[53] This was an important step in line with legal

[50] D Smith, 'The Disordered and Discredited Plaintiff: Psychiatric Evidence in Civil Litigation' (2009) 31(3) Cardoza Law Review 749.
[51] See S Riaz and S Begum, 'Non-Maintenance Creates a Right of Separation: A Comparative Study of Courts' Practices and Shariah Law' (2021) 4(1) IQAN 21.
[52] See s 16, Criminal Law Amendment (Offences Relating to Rape) Act 2016 [PAK].
[53] Article 151(4), Qanun-e-Shahadat Order (Law of Evidence) 1984 [PAK].

developments in numerous jurisdictions, which aimed to curtail evidence of a victim's sexual behaviour that was introduced by the defence to suggest that sexually active women are less credible witnesses.[54] Popularly termed 'rape shield' laws in sexual offence cases, these provisions prohibit the admittance of evidence or questioning about the sexual history of the complainant, whether with the accused or a third party.[55]

As evidenced throughout this book, however, evidence of the 'bad' or 'immoral' character of victims continues to be prevalently used in litigative practices in Pakistan, despite efforts to disallow character evidence in courtrooms. For example, a more recent judgment in a rape case stated that the victim was 'a lady of *easy virtue* and hence corroboration of her statements was needed'.[56] It additionally posited that 'when a victim is *enjoying bad character* then these things . . . are important to believe her version'.[57] During fieldwork, it was suggested that the incorporation of character allegations into the aggressive litigation strategies employed by the defence counsel are a means to try and 'break' or 'butcher' the victim in courtrooms.[58] This testament came to form strongly during an interview with a judge, who stated that the attitude of defence lawyers is to 'hang her [the victim] from the gallows',[59] as well as in interviews with multiple lawyers who spoke of 'putting her [the victim] through the wringer.[60] Further, as seen in Chapter 5, defence lawyers employ restrictive questioning strategies and oral tactics to intimidate and harass women complainants, with the use of (false) character allegations leading to additional harms for victims. In consequence, many victims choose to withdraw their legal cases, as their expectations in relation to the recognition of their harms, as well as for protection from those harms, are invalidated. This sentiment was also reflected in Chapter 6, where judges and legal actors posited that the use of physical

[54] C McGlynn, 'Rape Trials and Sexual History Evidence: Reforming the Law on Third-Party Evidence' (2017) 81(5) The Journal of Criminal Law 367, 369.

[55] ibid. In England and Wales, for example, this is regulated by the Youth Justice and Criminal Evidence Act of 1999.

[56] Judgment, Sessions Court [2017] OSC 124 as cited in FY Bokhari, 'Accountability for Rape: A Case Study of Lodhran' (2018) Centre for Human Rights, University College Lahore 1, 41 [emphasis added].

[57] ibid [emphasis added].

[58] O Smith and T Skinner, 'Observing Court Responses to Victims of Rape and Sexual Assault' (2012) 7 Feminist Criminology 298, 304.

[59] Interview with family judge, District and Sessions Courts, Karachi, 5 August 2022.

[60] Interview with lawyer, Karachi, 5 January 2022 [a]. A similar sentiment came to form in numerous other interviews, such as: Interview with lawyer, Islamabad, 9 June 2022 [c]; and Interview with lawyer, Lahore, 16 June 2022 [a].

violence by husbands was justified if the wife was being 'disobedient',[61] and further exacerbated by the idea that legal actors use character allegations relating to immorality to play to the judge's discretion and sensibilities that are informed by societal beliefs and 'old' contrivances of power, leading to judges often viewing women complainants not as victims of domestic violence, but as aggressors.

McGlynn finds that the ongoing use of character allegations in cases relating to violence against women is because the focus has shifted from 'probative credibility' to 'moral credibility',[62] with the latter referring to evidence that shows the complainant to be 'so morally inferior' that she does not 'deserve the court's sympathy'.[63] She argues that while restrictions may be introduced on identifiable acts or practices relating to sexual history evidence, evidence regarding the broader sexual character of women victims continues to be admitted in courts. This makes references to women's lifestyle, way of dressing, and personal habits which are more vague than specific instances of sexual history, making it much more difficult to control and much more likely to invite moral judgements that can influence determinations of credibility and blameworthiness within courtrooms.[64] Comparably, the introduction of evidence relating to 'personal habits' was arguably most visible in Chapter 5, where medications presented in support of character allegations typically related to women's sexuality, in the form of emergency contraceptive pills and birth control pills (also referred to as 'period medicine'[65]). These medications were presented alongside suggestions that 'only a woman of questionable mind and questionable character would feel the need to take medication of *such nature*',[66] indicating the need for procedural safeguards that prevent the use of information that is not directly connected to the facts of the case. This could be facilitated, for example, by requiring the defence to provide a clear demonstration of how such 'evidence' pertains to the case at hand, rather than simply serving as a vehicle for moral judgements.

[61] See for example, S Bucha and A Aqeel, 'Battered Lives' *Newsline* (March 2002) <https://newslinemagazine.com/ magazine/battered-lives/> accessed 3 January 2023; and Interview with lawyer, Lahore, 17 June 2022 [a].

[62] McGlynn (n 54).

[63] A McColgan, 'Common Law and the Relevance of Sexual History Evidence' (1996) 16 Oxford Journal of Legal Studies 275, as cited in McGlynn (n 54).

[64] McGlynn (n 54) 371. See also M Burman, 'Evidencing Sexual Assault: Women in the Witness Box' (2009) 56 Probation Journal 379, 384.

[65] See *SR Abbas v SS Sattar* [2015] YLR 489 as discussed in Chapter 2.

[66] Interview with lawyer, Lahore, 15 June 2022 [c] [emphasis added].

Further, as discussed in Chapter 5, the majority of character allegations and 'psy' labels are included in boilerplate pre-drafted suits that are easily and readily available for filing in response to claims of domestic violence. In family law particularly, a significant portion of legal practitioners seek the services of draftsmen at the courts who provide them with standardized documents that do not make necessary adjustments to reflect the specific facts of the case. The reliance on boilerplate text diminishes the quality and indeed the individuality of legal representation and leads to a high prevalence of copy-paste approaches to legal practice. Regulating the use of such standardized legal practice is not an easy task, particularly given the prevailing role of draftsmen in the courts. As one lawyer said, 'it is a proper business'.[67] Reflecting on interviews with practitioners, however, there is an acknowledgement of these practices by some judges, and an ambivalence towards these practices by some lawyers. And it is perhaps within that acknowledgement and ambivalence that we find potential to challenge the system. For lawyers, this could be through mentorship of junior colleagues, and by fostering a culture of accountability within their own firms. For judges, the implications of boilerplate practices can be mitigated by setting higher standards for case filings within their own courts.

In addition, the problematic recording of court proceedings, as mentioned in Chapter 6, leads to an inaccurate capturing of women's narratives in the courtroom. While proceedings are often done in Urdu or another local language, the court transcript does not record the questions and responses accurately as proceedings are not only translated into English, but also summarized for ease by the court clerk—both of which are as per the clerk's interpretation of those proceedings. As mentioned by a lawyer during an interview, this means that for a lot of what the victim says, 'that value is gone and her story is gone—the context and the actual words that she is saying, all of that disappears'.[68] Similarly, the harmful narrative strategies of defence lawyers and the (at times rather problematic) comments made by judges are not captured either. This can be particularly concerning in instances such as those discussed above, where medicine or pharmacy receipts are introduced to the court as evidence for the 'psy' label applied to the victim and she confirms taking that medicine. Due to how the proceedings are transcribed, the record might deductively state that she 'admitted to

[67] Phone interview with lawyer, Rawalpindi, 13 July 2022.
[68] Interview with lawyer, Karachi, 11 August 2022 [a].

taking medication' without specifying its type.[69] This omission means that the context or relevance of the medicine to her mental state is not included, which, in turn, produces documentary evidence of proceedings that do not reflect the litigative practices used to subjectivize women complainants. Ensuring the accurate and detailed recording of court processes can therefore assist in identifying and challenging gendering strategies, particularly in relation to the level of familiarity that judges have with newer laws, and the gendered implications of evidentiary burden.

As such, reimagining the adversarial courtroom as a space where multifaceted stories and narratives can be spoken and heard requires a shift—both in societal and cultural perceptions and in legal practices—towards more nuanced understandings of lived experiences that acknowledge the emotional and psychological complexities that often accompany cases of domestic violence.

The relationship between domestic abuse and mental health

The expansion of domestic violence definitions to include psychological and emotional abuse reflects an important and necessary change in how the law acknowledges and responds to the reality of victims' harms. Having been historically largely understood solely in terms of physical violence (with the level of physical harm being the primary measure of abuse), the incorporation of a broader scope of abusive behaviour within domestic violence definitions provides a more comprehensive framework to address it.[70] The theorizing of 'coercive control' as a model of abuse, for example, developed from evidence which suggests that the most common type of abuse is often invisible.[71] It has been argued that broadening the legal definition of domestic abuse to include what Stark defines as 'the strategic course of self-interested behaviour designed to secure and expand gender-based privilege

[69] For a detailed discussion about this, see '"A dispute of family nature": Language in the courtroom' in Chapter 6.

[70] See K Candela, 'Protecting the Invisible Victim: Incorporating Coercive Control in Domestic Violence Statutes' (2016) 54 Family Court Review 112; MA Dutton and LA Goodman, 'Coercion in Intimate Partner Violence: Toward a New Conceptualization' (2005) 52(11–12) Sex Roles 743.

[71] E Stark, 'Coercive Control' in N Lombard and L McMillan (eds) *Violence against Women: Current Theory and Practice in Domestic Abuse, Sexual Violence and Exploitation* (Jessica Kingsley Publishers 2013) 17.

by establishing a regime of domination in personal life'[72] would enable legal responses to be better equipped to address the varied impacts of abusive relationships and provide complainants with the resources they need to recover.[73] This definition allows for the acknowledgement of facets of women's lived experience that are often obscured by the violence model; for instance, that the oppression is ongoing rather than episodic, and that the harms are multifaceted and not just physical.[74] The UK's Serious Crime Act of 2015 is one example of recent laws where acts of coercive control, such as isolation and emotional abuse, are now treated as criminal offences,[75] demonstrating that the inclusion of psychological and emotional abuse in domestic violence legislation recognizes the iterative relationship between domestic abuse and mental health.[76]

In line with these developments, each of the relevant provincial domestic violence laws in Pakistan specify psychological and emotional abuse as falling within their respective ambits.[77] Similar to understandings of broader coercive control in relationships, the Sindh and Balochistan laws identify 'a pattern of degrading and humiliating conduct'[78] to be well within the scope of domestic abuse. The Punjab and KP laws, however, take a slightly different approach, defining psychological and emotional abuse on the basis of the impact it has on the victim—specifying that acts which result in mental health illnesses or disorders such as 'anorexia, suicidal attempts or clinically proven depression'[79] are considered to be acts of domestic violence. And while these definitive expansions are crucial to acknowledge the full scope of abusive relationships, and indeed speak to the well-documented links between domestic abuse and mental health,[80]

[72] ibid 21.

[73] ME Johnson, 'Redefining Harm, Reimagining Remedies, and Reclaiming Domestic Violence Law' (2008) 42 UC Davis Law Review 1107.

[74] Stark (n 71) 21.

[75] See K Fitz-Gibbon and others, 'The Criminalization of Coercive Control: The Benefits and Risks of Criminalization from the Vantage of Victim-Survivors' in H Douglas, K Fitz-Gibbon, L Goodmark and S Walklate (eds), *The Criminalization of Violence Against Women: Comparative Perspectives* (Oxford University Press 2023) 21.

[76] C Humphreys and R Thiara, 'Mental Health and Domestic Violence: "I call it symptoms of abuse"' (2003) 2(1) The British Journal of Social Work 209.

[77] The scope of the laws, and understandings and definitions of acts of domestic violence covered under respective provincial legislation, are outlined in Chapter 1.

[78] See s 5(f), Sindh Domestic Violence (Prevention and Protection) Act 2013; s 4(m), Balochistan Domestic Violence (Prevention and Protection) Act 2014.

[79] See s 2(1)(r), Punjab Protection of Women against Violence Act 2016; s 2(1)(p)(ii), Khyber-Pakhtunkhwa Domestic Violence against Women (Prevention and Protection) Act 2021.

[80] Humphreys and Thiara (n 76); S Oram, H Khalifeh and L Howard, 'Violence against Women and Mental Health' (2017) 4(2) Lancet Psychiatry 159.

these laws reflect an incongruity in how evidence for the same would be perceived in the courts. For example, given that the Punjab and KP laws require mental health illnesses to be an *outcome* of the abuse, if women bring forward proof of that diagnosis before a judge, would that be seen as proof of the abuse she experienced, or would it fuel defence narratives that aim to construct her as a 'mad' woman?

This book has documented the incorporation and use of 'psy' labels as a (newer) defence strategy in response to claims of domestic abuse to dampen the credibility of the complainant. As discussed above, the fact that the most common 'evidence' presented in court by the defence to support claims of mental unsoundness was medication for sexual health rather than mental health suggests a procedural gap in how such claims are substantiated within the law. This issue is compounded by a lack of judicial oversight in relation to the relevance of these medications to the allegations at hand, and a lack in determining any potential links to mental health outcomes as specified in domestic abuse legislation. Additionally, it resonates with broader concerns about how the evolving 'psy' disciplines influence legal knowledges, particularly in gendered contexts. Even as legal standards evolve, these practices are reminiscent of gendered assumptions that may still shape judicial reasoning, such as Wigmore's notion of women's 'unchaste mentality' from the 1940s that illustrates the influence of 'psy' disciplines on the legal credibility of women, and which, we hope, would find little support today:

> Modern psychiatrists have amply studied the behaviour of errant young girls and women coming before the courts in all sorts of cases. Their psychic complexes are multifarious, distorted partly by inherent defects, partly by diseased derangements or abnormal instincts, partly by bad social environment, partly by temporary physiological or emotional conditions.[81]

There is therefore an identifiable need to establish a higher threshold of evidence when claims relating to women's mental state are introduced to refute allegations of domestic abuse in court settings. Claims of mental unsoundness must be substantiated in accordance with the burden of proof, rather than relying solely on vague references to medication or 'psy' labels.

[81] JH Wigmore, *A Treatise on the Anglo-American System of Evidence in Trials at Common Law* (3rd edn, Little Brown and Company 1940) 921.

This could include, for example, detailed medical records and expert testimony. It is pertinent to note, however, that even in instances where there is evidence to suggest that the complainant is battling a mental illness as an outcome of the domestic abuse perpetrated, the nature of that illness may not necessarily have any substantial bearing on the case at hand. For example, a woman may be diagnosed with depression, which, despite being a recognized mental illness, may not have an impact on her ability to recount events accurately[82] (in cases of domestic violence), or her ability to be a good mother[83] (in cases of custody) as claimed by the defence. The decisions of judges, based on 'common sense',[84] are likely to overestimate both their own understandings of mental illnesses and the impact of mental health factors on the circumstances of the case—particularly in the absence of expert testimony and in the presence of gendered narratives and insinuations. The substantiation of claims using 'psy' labels must therefore be accompanied by a clear indication of the relevance of that claim to the specific legal issue under consideration.

Further, as mentioned previously, given the discursive impact of 'psy' labels on the subjectivity of victims, the harms identified as outcomes of domestic abuse by complainants may simultaneously be used by the defence to position her as an unreliable and uncredible litigant. It is therefore not surprising that, as seen in Chapter 5, complainants' lawyers choose not to introduce to the court medical evidence relating to the clinically diagnosed mental health impact that domestic abuse had on the victim. This is because the diagnosis would be seen as proof of the 'psy' label applied to the victim as a gendered character allegation, instead of as proof for the violence that she experienced. A member of victim support personnel put it succinctly: 'that prescription is a stain [on the victim], better not to bring it up.'[85] This illustrates yet again a troubling tension between the use of 'psy' labels to undermine women's claims and the complex relationship between domestic abuse and mental health, where the former may cause or aggravate symptoms of the latter.[86] Indeed, the deployment of 'psy' labels and mental health as a narrative gendering strategy can then also be said to be doing

82 See D Smith, 'The Disordered and discredited plaintiff: Psychiatric evidence in Civil Litigation' (2009) 31(3) Cardoza Law Review 749.

83 See AS Geva, 'Judicial Determination of Child Custody When a Parent Is Mentally Ill: A Little Bit of Law, a little Bit of Pop Psychology, and a Little Bit of Common Sense' (2012) 16(1) UC Davis Journal of International Law and Policy 78.

84 ibid 61.

85 Interview with victim support personnel, Lahore, 15 June 2022.

86 Humphreys and Thiara (n 76); Oram and others (n 80).

a disservice to that complex relationship. As seen above, this means not only that aspects of victim's needs and harms are being kept off the official record, but also that those needs and harms are not acknowledged within the legal system. This indicates that simply amending legal definitions of domestic abuse to explicitly include psychological and emotional harms is not sufficient. What is needed is a reassessment of how these definitions are perceived and applied in practice, so that a victim is able to acknowledge her mental health outcomes of domestic abuse without having them weaponized by the other party in attempt to overshadow her testimony. As Cooper and Sweet argue, the weaponizing of mental health[87] is a critical aspect of power and control in intimate relationships and relies on three strategies that echo the legal tactics explored in this book. The first is the 'denigration' of a victim's mental soundness by using gendered stereotypes that characterize 'emotional instability as an inherently feminine trait'; the second is the use of gendered language to recast a victim's reactions to abuse as irrational; and the third is the leveraging of a victim's mental health diagnosis (if there is one) or claims that a victim's actions fit the criteria of a mental illness (if there isn't one).[88] This, too, is reflective of the expansive need to move beyond an episodic approach to domestic violence—where the use of character allegations that frame women as 'bad' and/or as 'mad' are recognized as part of a larger pattern of abuse which simply shifts the site of that abuse from the home to the courtroom.

A quote from Thomas Szasz resonates:

> [T]his, then, is the essential communicational dilemma in which many weak or oppressed persons find themselves vis-à-vis those who are stronger or who oppress them: if they speak softly, they will not receive a hearing; if they raise their voices literally, they will be considered impertinent; and if they raise their voices metaphorically, they will be diagnosed as insane.[89]

[87] CE Cooper and PL Sweet, '"Daddy Issues" and Diagnoses: Gendered Weaponisation of Mental Health in Intimate Relationships' (2024) Violence Against Women 2 <https://doi.org/10.1177/10778012241277894> accessed 2 October 2024.

[88] ibid.

[89] T Szasz, *The Myth of Mental Illness: Foundations of a Theory of Personal Conduct* (Harper and Row 1961) 119.

Bibliography

Literature

Abbott HP, *The Cambridge Introduction to Narrative* (2nd edn, Cambridge University Press 2018) 3, 44.
Abu-Odeh L, 'Crimes of Honour and the Construction of Gender in Arab Societies' (2011) 2(1) Comparative Law Review 27.
Adams PJ, 'Interventions with Men Who are Violent to Their Partners: Strategies for Early Engagement' (2012) 38 Journal of Marital and Family Therapy 458.
Adikaram AS, '"Good Women" and "Bad Women": How Socialisation of Gendered Behavioural Norms Influences Sri Lankan Working Women's Interpretation of Sexual Harassment at Workplaces' (2014) 1(1) South Asian Journal of Human Resources Management 61.
Afifi T, MacMillan H, Cox B, Asmundson G, Stein M and Sareen J, 'Mental Health Correlates of Intimate Partner Violence in Marital Relationships in a Nationally Representative Sample of Males and Females' (2009) 24(8) Journal of Interpersonal Violence 1398.
Alcoff L, 'The Problem of Speaking for Others' (1991) 20(Winter) Cultural Critique 5.
Alden A, *Disorder in the Court: Morality, Myth and the Insanity Defence* (The University of Alabama Press 2018) 3, 20.
Alexander MJ, 'Erotic Economy as a Politics of Decolonization' in MJ Alexander and CT Mohanty (eds), *Feminist Genealogies, Colonial Legacies, Democratic Futures* (Routledge 1997) 65.
Ali PA, Naylor PB, Croot E and O'Cathain A, 'Intimate Partner Violence in Pakistan' (2015) 16(3) Trauma, Violence and Abuse 299.
Ali SS, 'Law, Islam and the Women's Movement in Pakistan' in SM Rai (ed), *International Perspectives on Gender and Democratisation* (Palgrave Macmillan 2000) 41.
—— 'Testing the Limits of Family Law Reform in Pakistan: A Critical Analysis of the Muslim Family Laws Ordinance 1961' [2002] International Survey of Family Law 317.
—— *Modern Challenges to Islamic Law* (Cambridge University Press 2016) 33.
Ali TS, Nargis A, Mogren I and Gunilla K, 'Intimate Partner Violence in Urban Pakistan: Prevalence, Frequency, and Risk Factors' (2011) 3 International Journal of Women's Health 105.
Allen H, *Justice Unbalanced* (Open University Press 1987) 30.
Amsterdam AG and Bruner J, *Minding the Law* (Harvard University Press 2002) 110.
Andersson M, Mellgren C and Ivert AK, 'How Victims Conceptualise Their Experiences of Hate Crime' (2018) DoC Malmo University 4.

Ashfaq A and Shafiq Z, 'Contested Images of "Perfect Women" in Pakistani Television Dramas' (2018) 55(1) Journal of the Research Society of Pakistan 60.

Back L and Puwar N, 'A Manifesto for Live Methods: Provocations and Capacities' (2012) 60(1) Sociological Review 6.

Baker NV, Gregware PR and Cassidy MA, 'Family Killing Fields' (1999) 5(2) Violence Against Women 164.

Baker W, *America's Crisis of Values* (Princeton University Press 2005) 3.

Baldwin J, 'Research on the Criminal Courts' in R King and E Wincup (eds), *Doing Research on Crime and Justice* (Oxford University Press 2007) 375.

Ballweg ML, 'Blaming the Victim: The Psychologizing of Endometriosis' (1997) 24(2) Obstetrics and Gynaecology Clinics of North America 441.

Bard M and Berkowitz B, 'Training Police as Specialists in Family Crisis Intervention: A Community Psychology Action Program' (1967) 3 Community Mental Health Journal 315, 317.

Barett M, *The Politics of Truth: From Marx to Foucault* (Polity Press 1992).

Barlas A, *Believing Women in Islam: Unreading Patriarchal Interpretations of the Quran* (University of Texas Press 2002) 188.

Baxi P, 'Justice Is A Secret: Compromise in Rape Trials' (2010) 44(3) Contributions to Indian Sociology 207.

—— *Public Secrets of Law: Rape Trials in India* (Oxford University Press 2013) 191.

Berti D and Bordia D, 'Introduction' in D Berti and D Bordia (eds), *Regimes of Legality: Ethnography of Criminal Cases in South Asia* (1st edn, Oxford University Press 2015) 1.

Bhabha H, 'Of Mimicry and Man: The Ambivalence of Colonial Discourse' (1984) 28 Discipleship: A Special Issue on Psychoanalysis 125.

—— *The Location of Culture* (Routledge 1994) 124.

Bhanbhro S, Wassan M, Shah M, Talpur A and Wassan A, 'Karo Kari: The Murder of Honour in Sindh Pakistan, an Ethnographic Study' (2013) 3(7) International Journal of Asian Social Science 1467.

Bhatti N, Jamali MB, Phulpoto NN, Mehmood T and Shaikh FM, 'Domestic Violence against Women: A Case Study of District Jacobabad, Sindh Pakistan' (2011) 7(12) Asian Social Science 154.

Bohner G, 'Writing about Rape: Use of the Passive Voice and Other Distancing Text Features as an Expression of Perceived Responsibility of the Victim' (2001) 40(4) British Journal of Social Psychology 515.

Brown SL, *Counselling Victims of Violence: A Handbook for Helping Professionals* (Hunter House 2007).

Brownmiller S, *Against Our Will: Men, Women and Rape* (Simon and Schuster 1975) 15.

Burgess RG, 'Keeping a Research Diary' (1981) 11(1) Cambridge Journal of Education 77.

Burman M, 'Evidencing Sexual Assault: Women in the Witness Box' (2009) 56 Probation Journal 379, 384.

Butler J, *Gender Trouble: Feminism and the Subversion of Identity* (Routledge 1990).

—— *Bodies That Matter: On the Discursive Limits of 'Sex'* (Routledge 1993) 124.

—— 'Performative Agency' (2010) 3(2) Journal of Cultural Economy 147.

—— 'Is Judaism Zionism?' in E Mendieta and J Vanantwerpen (eds), *The Power of Religion in the Public Sphere* (Columbia University Press 2011) 72.

Campbell R and Raja S, 'Secondary Victimisation of Rape Victims: Insights from Mental Health Professionals Who Treat Survivors of Violence' (1999) 14(3) Violence and Victims 261.

Campbell R, Adams AE, Wasco SM, Ahrens C and Sefl T, '"What has it been like for you to talk with me today?": The Impact of Participating in Interview Research on Rape Survivors' (2010) 16(1) Violence Against Women 60.

Campbell R, Dworkin R and Cabral G, 'An Ecological Model of the Impact of Sexual Assault on Women's Mental Health' (2009) 10(3) Trauma, Violence and Abuse 225.

Campbell S, 'Relational Remembering: Suggestibility and Women's Confidential Records' in CM Koggel, A Furlong and C Levin (eds), *Confidential Relationships: Psychoanalytic, Ethical and Legal Contexts* (Rodopi 2003) 152.

Candela K, 'Protecting the Invisible Victim: Incorporating Coercive Control in Domestic Violence Statutes' (2016) 54 Family Court Review 112.

Casper ST and O'Donnell K, 'The Punch-Drunk Boxer and the Battered Wife: Gender and Brain Injury Research' (2020) 245 Social Science and Medicine 1.

Chadwick R, 'On the Politics of Discomfort' (2021) 22(4) Feminist Theory 556.

Charmaz K, *Constructing Grounded Theory: A Practical Guide through Qualitative Analysis* (SAGE 2006).

Cheema SA, 'Islamisation of Restitution of Conjugal Rights by the Federal Shariat Court of Pakistan: A Critique' (2019) 58(4) Islamic Studies 535.

Chesler P, *Women and Madness* (Doubleday 1972) 56.

Christie N, 'The Ideal Victim' in EA Fattah (ed), *From Crime Policy to Victim Policy* (Palgrave Macmillan 1986) 18, 19.

Clark EV, *Word Choice and Conceptual Perspective* (Koninklijke Nederlandse Akademie Van Wetenschappen 1998) 5.

Cohen S, *Visions of Social Control* (Polity Press 1985).

—— *Folk Devils and Moral Panics* (Routledge 2004) 1.

Collins D, 'Islamization of Pakistani Law: A Historical Perspective' (1987) 24(3) Stanford Journal of International Law 567.

Cooper CE and Sweet PL, '"Daddy Issues" and Diagnoses: Gendered Weaponisation of Mental Health in Intimate Relationships' (2024) Violence Against Women 2 <https://doi.org/10.1177/10778012241277894> accessed 2 October 2024.

Corrigan P and Sayer D, *The Great Arch: English State Formation as Cultural Revolution* (Basil Blackwell 1985) 4.

Cotterill J, 'Collocation, Connotation, and Courtroom Semantics: Lawyers' Control of Witness Testimony through Lexical Negotiation' (2004) 25(4) Applied Linguistics 513.

Crowley S, *Toward a Civil Discourse: Rhetoric and Fundamentalism* (University of Pittsburgh Press 2006) 63.

Davar BV, 'From Mental Illness to Disability' (2008) 15(2) Indian Journal of Gender Studies 265.

Davies B, 'Subjectification: The Relevance of Butler's Analysis for Education' (2006) 27(4) British Journal of Sociology of Education 425.

Davies M and Munro V, 'Editors' Note' in M Davies and V Munro (eds), *The Ashgate Research Companion to Feminist Legal Theory* (1st edn, Routledge 2013) 1.

Davis AY, Dent G, Meiners ER and Richie BE (eds), *Abolition. Feminism. Now.* (Haymarket Books 2022).

Delgado R, 'Storytelling for Oppositionists and Others: A Plea for Narrative' (1988) 87 *Michigan Law Review* 2411.

Denzin NK, 'Triangulation 2.0' (2012) 6 Journal of Mixed Methods Research 80, 82.

Dev S and Kamath V, 'Gender Justice and Women Empowerment: Legal Measures in India' (2016) 41(2) Journal of Sharma 140.

Dhanda A, 'Psychologising Dissent: Psychiatric Labelling and Social Control' in A Dhanda and A Parashar (eds), *Engendering Law: Essays in Honour of Lotika Sarkar* (Eastern Book Company 2007) 321.

Douglas H, 'The Criminal Law's Response to Domestic Violence: What's Going On?' (2008) 30(3) Sydney Law Review 447.

Dunn JL, '"Victims" and "Survivors": Emerging Vocabularies of Motive for "Battered Women Who Stay"' (2005) 75(1) Sociological Inquiry 3.

Dutton MA and Goodman LA, 'Coercion in Intimate Partner Violence: Toward a New Conceptualization' (2005) 52(11-12) Sex Roles 743.

Dyregrov K, Dyregrov A and Raundalen M, 'Refugee Families' Experience of Research Participation' (2000) 13(3) Journal Of Traumatic Stress 413.

Epstein D and Goodman L, 'Discounting Women: Doubting Domestic Violence Survivors' Credibility and Dismissing Their Experiences' (2019) 167(1) University of Pennsylvania Law Review 406, 433.

Ernst W, 'Idioms of Madness and Colonial Boundaries: The Case of the European and "Native" Mentally Ill in Early Nineteenth-Century British India' (1997) 39(1) Comparative Studies in Society and History 172.

—— *Colonialism and Transnational Psychiatry: The Development of an Indian Mental Hospital in British India 1925–1940* (Anthem Press 2013) 43.

Fairclough N, *Discourse and Social Change* (Polity Press 1992) 3, 4.

Fasihuddin, 'Police and Policing in Pakistan' (2010) 2(3) Pakistan Journal of Criminology 131.

Fikree FF, Razzak JA and Durocher J, 'Attitudes of Pakistani Men to Domestic Violence: A Study from Karachi, Pakistan' (2005) 2(1) Journal of Men's Health and Gender.

Fineman ML, 'Challenging Law, Establishing Difference: The Future of Feminist Legal Scholarship' (1990) 42 Florida Law Review 25.

Finkel NJ, *Commonsense Justice: Jurors' Notions of the Law* (Harvard University Press 1995).

Fitz-Gibbon K, Walklate S, Meyer S and Reeves E, 'The Criminalization of Coercive Control: The Benefits and Risks of Criminalization from the Vantage of Victim-Survivors' in H Douglas, K Fitz-Gibbon, L Goodmark and S Walklate (eds), *The Criminalization of Violence against Women: Comparative Perspectives* (Oxford University Press 2023) 21.

Flower L and Ahlefeldt MS, 'The Criminal Trial as a Live Event: Exploring How and Why Live Blogs Change the Professional Practices of Judges, Defence Lawyers and Prosecutors' (2021) 43(8) Media, Culture and Society 1480.

Foucault M, *Madness and Civilization: A History of Insanity in the Age of Reason* (trans R Howard, Random House 1965) 269.
—— *Discipline and Punish: The Birth of the Prison* (A Sheridan tr, 2nd edn, Random House 1977) 135.
—— *The History of Sexuality* (Vol 1, Penguin 1981).
Frigon S, 'A Genealogy of Women's Madness' in RE Dobash, RP Dobash and L Noaks (eds), *Gender and Crime* (University of Wales Press 1995) 20.
Gayatri S, 'Can the Subaltern Speak?' in C Nelson and L Grossberg (eds), *Marxism and the Interpretation of Culture* (University of Illinois Press 1988) 271.
Geva AS, 'Judicial Determination of Child Custody When a Parent Is Mentally Ill: A Little Bit of Law, a Little Bit of Pop Psychology, and a Little Bit of Common Sense' (2012) 16(1) UC Davis Journal of International Law and Policy 78.
Gill AK and Brah A, 'Interrogating Cultural Narratives about "Honour"-Based Violence' (2014) 21(1) European Journal of Women's Studies 72.
Gove WR and Tudor JF, 'Adult Sex Roles and Mental Illness' (1972) 78(4) American Journal of Sociology 812.
Greeson M and Campbell R, 'Rape Survivors' Agency within the Legal and Medical Systems' (2011) 35(4) Psychology of Women Quarterly 582.
Habib RI, Liaquat S, Aslam MA and Akhtar N, 'Schizophrenia—a Mental Disorder or Not? An Analytical Study of the Judgment of the Supreme Court of Pakistan in Safia Bano Case' (2019) 39(3) Pakistan Journal of Social Sciences 795.
Hacking I, *Rewriting the Soul: Multiple Personality and the Sciences of Memory* (Princeton University Press 1995) 267.
Hafez S, *An Islam of Her Own: Reconsidering Religion and Secularism in Women's Islamic Movements* (New York University Press 2011) 5.
Hajjar L, 'Religion, State Power and Domestic Violence in Muslim societies: A Framework for Comparative Analysis' (2004) 29(1) Law and Social Inquiry 1.
Hall S, *The Toad in the Garden: Thatcherism among the Theorists. Marxism and the Interpretation of Culture* (University of Illinois Press 1988) 51.
Hamadeh N, 'Islamic Family Legislation: The Authoritarian Discourse of Silence' in M Yamani (ed), *Feminism and Islam: Legal and Literary Perspectives* (Ithaca Press 1996) 331, 337.
Haraway D, 'Situated Knowledges: The Science Question in Feminism and the Privilege of Partial Perspective' (1988) 14(3) Feminist Studies 575.
Hartley C, 'He Said, She Said: The Defense Attack of Credibility in Domestic Violence Felony Trials' (2001) 7(5) Violence Against Women 510.
Hassan SM, 'Problems Faced by Women in Police Stations: Need for Police Reforms in Pakistan' (2015) 7(1) Pakistan Journal of Criminology 95.
Hastrup K, 'Writing Ethnography—State of the Art' in J Okely and H Callaway (eds), *Anthropology and Autobiography* (Routledge 1992) 116.
Hattendorf J and Tollerud TR, 'Domestic Violence: Counselling Strategies that Minimise the Impact of Secondary Victimisation' (1997) 33(1) Perspectives in Psychiatric Care 14, 17.
Hemmings C, 'Telling Feminist Stories' (2005) 6(2) Feminist Theory 115.
—— *Why Stories Matter: The Political Grammar of Feminist Theory* (Duke University Press 2011).

Herman LJ, *Trauma and Recovery* (Basic Books 1992).

Hesse-Bieber SN, 'Feminist Research: Exploring, Interrogating, and Transforming the Interconnections of Epistemology, Methodology, and Method' in SN Hesse-Bieber (ed), *Handbook of Feminist Research: Theory and Praxis* (SAGE 2011) 2.

Hockett JM and Saucier DA, 'A Systematic Literature Review of "Rape Victims" versus "Rape Survivors": Implications for Theory, Research and Practice' (2015) 25 Aggression and Violent Behaviour 1.

Holz S and Bano A, 'Navigating Respectability in Patriarchal Contexts: Ethical Dilemmas of Women Researchers in Pakistan' (2022) 53 International Quarterly for Asian Studies 553.

Honkatuki P and Keskinen S, 'The Social Control of Young Women's Clothing and Bodies: A Perspective of Differences on Racialization and Sexualization' (2018) 18(1) Ethnicities 142.

Horney K, 'The Problem with Female Masochism' (1935) 22(1) Psychoanalytic Review 241, 242.

Hume M, 'Questioning Violence: Meanings, Myths and Realities' (2009) 28 Bulletin of Latin American Research 22.

Humphreys C and Thiara R, 'Mental Health and Domestic Violence: "I call it symptoms of abuse"' (2003) 2(1) The British Journal of Social Work 209.

Hunter R, 'Law's (Masculine) Violence: Reshaping Jurisprudence' (2006) 17(1) Law and Critique 40.

Hutcheon L, 'Postmodernism, Poststructuralism, and Feminism' (1985) 6(3) Canadian Woman Studies 36.

Innes M, *Understanding Social Control. Deviance, Crime and Social Order* (Open University Press 2003).

Irvine A, Drew P and Sainsbury R, '"Am I not answering your questions properly?" Clarification, Adequacy and Responsiveness in Semi-Structured Telephone and Face-To-Face Interviews' (2013) 13(1) Qualitative Research 87.

Ishaque S and Khan MM, 'The Best Interests of the Child: A Prevailing Consideration within Islamic Principles and a Government Principle in Child Custody Cases in Pakistan' (2015) 29(1) International Journal of Law, Policy and Family 86.

Jalal A, 'The Convenience of Subservience' in D Kandiyoti (ed), *Women, Islam, and the State* (Temple University Press 1991) 77.

Jalil A, Mahmood QK, Usman A and Ahmad A, 'Qualitative Analysis of Feminine Morality and Visible Personality Characteristics among Young Adults' (2020) 54 Quality and Quantity 887.

Jamal A, 'Piety, Transgression and the Feminist Debate on Muslim Women: Resituating the Victim-Subject of Honour-Related Violence from a Transnational Lens' (2015) 41(1) Journal of Women in Culture and Society 59.

Jamshed J, Jan J, Muhammad AA and Baig K, 'Mental Illness and Criminal Justice System of Pakistan: Analysis of the Landmark Judgement in Safia Bano Case' (2023) 11(1) Pakistan Journal of Humanities and Social Sciences 102.

Jawad HA, *The Rights of Women in Islam: An Authentic Approach* (Palgrave Macmillan 1998) 78, 81.

Jenks C, *Transgression* (Routledge 2003) 2.

Johnson ME, 'Redefining Harm, Reimagining Remedies, and Reclaiming Domestic Violence Law' (2008) 42 UC Davis Law Review 1107.
Jones K, 'The Politics of Credibility' in L Antony and C Witt (eds), *A Mind of One's Own: Feminist Essays on Reason and Objectivity* (Routledge 2002) 159.
Kafka F, 'Before the Law' in N Glazer (ed), *The Complete Stories* (Schocken Books 1971) 3.
Kamal D, 'Networked Struggles: Placards at Pakistan's Aurat March' (2022) 30 Feminist Legal Studies 219.
Kandiyoti D, 'Bargaining with Patriarchy' (1988) 2(3) Gender and Society 274.
Kapur R, 'Human Rights in the 21st Century: Take a Walk on the Dark Side' (2006) 28 Sydney Law Review 665.
Karmen A, *Crime Victims: An Introduction to Victimology* (Wadsworth Belmont 2010) 140.
Kelly L, Burton S and Regan L, 'Beyond Victim or Survivor: Sexual Violence, Identity and Feminist Theory and Practice' in L Adkins and V Merchant (eds), *Sexualising the Social* (Palgrave Macmillan 1996) 77.
Kennedy J, 'The Citizen Victim: Reconciling the Public and Private in Criminal Sentencing' (2019) 13 Criminal Law and Philosophy 91.
Khan A and Hussain R, 'Violence against Women in Pakistan: Perceptions and Experiences of Domestic Violence' (2008) 32(2) Asian Studies Review 239.
Khan A and Kirmani N, 'Moving beyond the Binary: Gender-Based Activism in Pakistan' (2018) 30 Feminist Dissent 156.
Khan LA, Khan MA and Hussain A, 'The Good Woman Is the Silent One: A Feminist Critique of Proverbial Stance on Gendered Talk' (2021) 12(1) Pakistan Journal of Applied Social Sciences 57, 66.
Khan S, *Zina, Transnational Feminism, and the Moral Regulation of Pakistani Women* (UBC Press 2006) 56.
—— 'Reconfiguring the Native Informant: Positionality in the Global Age' (2005) 30(4) Signs: Journal of Women in Culture and Society 2017.
Khan TS, *Beyond Honour: A Historical Materialist Explanation of Honour Related Violence* (Oxford University Press 2006) 229.
Khurshid A, 'Does Education Empower Women? The Regulated Empowerment of *Parhi Likhi* Women in Pakistan' (2017) 48(3) Anthropology and Education Quarterly 252.
Krause P, Szekely O, Bloom M, Christia F, Daly SZ, Lawson C, Marks Z, Milliff A, Miura K, Neilson R, Reno W, Souleimanov EA and Zakayo A, 'COVID-19 and Fieldwork: Challenges and Solutions' (2021) 54(2) Political Science and Politics 264.
Lacerda T, 'Victim: What Is Hidden Behind This Work?' (2016) 10 International Journal of Transitional Justice 179.
Laing L, 'Secondary Victimisation: Domestic Violence Survivors Navigating Family Law Systems' (2017) 23(11) Violence Against Women 1314, 1322.
Lakkimsetti C, 'Stripping Away at Respectability: #MeToo India and the Politics of Dignity' (2021) 33(3) Feminist Formations 303.
Leisenring A, 'Confronting "Victim" Discourses: The Identity Work of Battered Women' (2006) 29 Symbolic Interaction 307.

Lewis R, Dobash RP, Dobash RE and Cavanagh K, 'Protection, Prevention, Rehabilitation or Justice? Women's Use of the Law to Challenge Domestic Violence' (2000) 7(1) International Review of Victimology 179, 184.

Liebling A, 'Doing Research in Prison: Breaking the Silence?' (1999) 3 Theoretical Criminology 147.

Lodrick Z, 'Psychological Trauma: What Every Trauma Worker Should Know' (2007) 4(2) British Journal of Psychotherapy Integration 18.

Mackinnon C, 'Feminism, Marxism, Method and the State: An Agenda for Theory' (1983) 8(4) Feminist Theory 635.

MacLean L, Meyer M and Estable A, 'Improving Accuracy of Transcripts in Qualitative Research' (2004) 14(1) Qualitative Health Research 113, 115.

Madigan L and Gamble LC, *The Second Rape: Society's Continued Betrayal of the Victim* (Lexington Books 1991) 102.

Mahmood QK, Ahmad I and Bhutta MH, 'Vigilantism and the Police: Assessing the Perception of Pakistani Women about the Gender-Related Ineffectiveness of the Police and the Preference for Vigilante Acts in Lahore' (2013) 5(1) Pakistan Journal of Criminology 43.

Mahoney M, 'Victimisation of Oppression? Women's Lives, Violence and Agency' in MA Fineman and R Mykitiuk (eds), *The Public Nature of Private Violence* (Routledge 1994) 59.

Marsh DT, 'Parental Mental Illness: Issues in Custody Determinations' (2009) 23(1) American Journal of Family Law 28.

Masika R and Bailur S, 'Negotiating Women's Agency through ICTs: A Comparative Study of Uganda and India' (2015) 19(1) Gender, Technology and Development 43, 63.

Mason J, *Qualitative Researching* (2nd edn, SAGE 2002) 149.

McClintock A, 'Family Feuds: Gender, Nationalism and the Family' (1993) 44 Feminist Review 63, 66.

McColgan A, 'Common Law and the Relevance of Sexual History Evidence' (1996) 16 Oxford Journal of Legal Studies 275.

McGlynn C, 'Rape Trials and Sexual History Evidence: Reforming the Law on Third-Party Evidence' (2017) 81(5) The Journal of Criminal Law 367.

Michael RB, Garry M and Kirsch I, 'Suggestion, Cognition and Behaviour' (2012) 21(3) Current Directions in Psychological Science 151.

Michelson E, *Decoupling: Gender Injustice in China's Divorce Courts* (Cambridge University Press 2022) 237.

Miles MG and Huberman AM, *Qualitative Data Analysis* (2nd edn, SAGE 1994).

Miller T and Bell L, 'Consenting to What? Issues of Access, Gatekeeping and "Informed" Consent' in T Miller, M Birch, M Mauthner and J Jessop (eds), *Ethics in Qualitative Research* (Sage Publications 2005) 53.

Millett K, *Sexual Politics* (Virago Press 1971) 35.

Mills C, *Decolonizing Global Mental Health: The Psychiatrization of the Majority World* (Routledge 2014).

Moodley S, Subramaney U and Hoffman D, 'A Qualitative Study of Mentally Ill Women Who Commit Filicide in Gauteng, South Africa' (2019) 10 Front Psychiatry 757.

Mullally S, 'As Nearly as May Be: Debating Women's Human Rights in Pakistan' (2005) 14 Social and Legal Studies 341.
—— *Law and Politics at the Perimeter: Re-evaluating Key Debates in Feminist Theory* (Hart 2007).
Munro V, 'Legal Feminism and Foucault—A Critique of the Expulsion of Law' (2002) 28 (4) Journal of Law and Society 546.
—— *Law and Politics at the Perimeter: Re-evaluating Key Debates in Feminist Theory* (Hart 2007)
—— 'Feminist Critiques of the Rule of Law' in J Meierhenrich and M Loughlin (eds), *The Cambridge Companion to the Rule of Law* (Cambridge University Press 2021) 340.
Munro V and Aitken R, 'From Hoping to Help: Identifying and Responding to Suicidality amongst Victims of Domestic Abuse' (2020) 26(1) International Review of Victimology 29.
Mumtaz K and Shaheed F, *Women in Pakistan: Two Steps Forward, One Step Back?* (Zed Books 1987) 72.
Naeem F, Ayub M, Javed Z, Irfan M, Haral F, and Kingdon D, 'Stigma and Psychiatric Illness. A Survey of Attitude of Medical Students and Doctors in Lahore, Pakistan' (2006) 18(3) Journal of Ayub Medical College 46.
Narayan K, 'How Native Is a "Native" Anthropologist?' (1993) 95(3) American Anthropologist 671.
Narayan U, 'The Project of Feminist Epistemology: Perspectives of a Non-Western Feminist' in CR McCann and SK Kim (eds), *Feminist Theory Reader: Local and Global Perspectives* (Routledge 2003) 308.
Nario-Redmond MR and Branscombe NR, 'It Could Have Been Better or It Might Have Been Worse: Implications for Blame Assignment in Rape Cases' (1996) 18(3) Basic and Applied Psychology 349.
Nasir JJ, *Guardianship in Relation to Marriage in His Book, The Status of Women under Islamic Law and under Modern Islamic Legislation* (Graham and Trotman 1994).
Nayar PK, *Postcolonialism: A Guide for the Perplexed* (Continuum 2010) 28.
Ng KH, *The Common Law in Two Voices: Language, Law and the Post-Colonial Predicament in Hong Kong* (Stanford University Press 2009) 254.
Niaz U, 'Human Rights Abuse in Family' (1994) 3 Journal of Pakistan Association of Women's Studies 33.
—— 'Contemporary Issues of Pakistani Women: A Psychosocial Perspective' (1997) 6 Journal of Pakistan Association of Women's Studies 29.
—— 'Women's Mental Health in Pakistan' (2004) 3(1) World Psychiatry 60.
Nightingale A, 'A Feminist in the Forest: Situated Knowledges and Mixing Methods in Natural Resource Management' (2003) 2(1) ACME International E-Journal for Critical Geographies 79.
Nyazee I, *Outlines of Islamic Jurisprudence* (3rd edn, Advanced Legal Studies Institute 2005) 40.
Olivia Smith O and Skinner T, 'Observing Court Responses to Victims of Rape and Sexual Assault' (2012) 7 Feminist Criminology 298, 304.
Omar S, 'Dissolution of Marriage: Practices, Laws and Islamic Teachings' (2007) 4(1) Policy Perspectives 91.

Oram S, Khalifeh H and Howard L, 'Violence against Women and Mental Health' (2017) 4(2) Lancet Psychiatry 159.
Pagelow MD, *Woman-Battering: Victims and Their Experiences* (SAGE Publications 1981) 19.
Papendick and Bohner G, 'Passive Victim—Strong Survivor? Perceived Meanings of Labels Applied to Women Who Were Raped' (2017) 12(5) PLoS ONE 2.
Patterson D, 'The Linkage between Secondary Victimisation by Law Enforcement and Rape Case Outcomes' (2011) 26(2) Journal of Interpersonal Violence 328.
Peter F, 'Gender and the Foundations of Social Choice: The Role of Situated Agency' (2003) 9(2) Feminist Economics 13, 27.
Peters JS, 'Legal Performance Good and Bad' (2008) 4 Law Culture and the Humanities 181.
—— *Law as Performance: Theatricality, Spectatorship, and the Making of Law in Ancient, Medieval and Early Modern Europe* (Oxford University Press 2022).
Poornima S, 'Medicine in Colonial Andhra: A Study in the Production of Medical Knowledge Systems, 1880–1930' (University of Hyderabad, CAMH Archive 1995) 36.
Porter R, *Madness* (Oxford University Press 2003) 12.
Potter N, *Mapping the Edges and the In-between: A Critical Analysis of Borderline Personality Disorder* (Oxford University Press 2009) 167.
Potter J and Wetherell M, *Discourse and Social Psychology* (SAGE 1986).
Quilter J, 'Re-framing the Rape Trial: Insights from Critical Theory about the Limitations of Legislative Reform' (2011) 35(1) Australian Feminist Law Review 23.
Ramon S, 'Intersectionalities: Intimate Partner Domestic Violence and Mental Health within the European Context' (2015) 4(2) A Global Journal of Social Work Analysis, Research, Polity, and Practice 76.
Rashid A and Rashid U, 'Constitutional and Legal Guarantees for Transgender in Pakistan: Reforms and Failures in Law' in G Guney, D Davies and P Lee (eds), *Towards Gender Equality in Law* (Palgrave Macmillan 2022) 79.
Rashid M, 'Giving Men Choices: A Rozan Project with the Police Force in Pakistan' in A Grieg (ed), *Partners in Change: Working with Men to End Gender-Based Violence* (INSTRAW 2002) 68.
Rasul S, 'Gender and Power Relationships in the Language of Proverbs: Image of a Woman' (2015) 9(2) FWU Journal of Social Sciences 53.
Riaz S and Begum S, 'Non-Maintenance Creates a Right of Separation: A Comparative Study of Court's Practices and Shariah Law' (2021) 4(1) IQAN 21.
Rich K and Seffrin P, 'Police Officers' Collaboration with Rape Victim Advocates: Barriers and Facilitators' (2013) 28 Violence and Victims 681.
Ring S, 'On Delay and Duration: Law's Temporal Orders in Historical Child Sexual Abuse Cases' in S Beynon-Jones and E Grabham (eds), *Law and Time* (Routledge 2018) 93.
Rivera EA, Sullivan CM and Zeoli AM, 'Secondary Victimisation of Abused Mothers by Family Court Mediators' (2012) 27 Journal of Family Violence 321.
Robinson DN, *Wild Beasts and Idle Humours* (Harvard University Press 1996) 20.
Rosenhan DL, 'On Being Sane in Insane Places' (1973) 179(4070) Science 250.

Rosenthal R, 'Suggestibility, Reliability and the Legal Process' (2002) 22(3) Developmental Review 337.

Rouse S, 'The Outsider(s) Within: Sovereignty and Citizenship in Pakistan' in P Jeffery and A Basu (eds), *Resisting the Sacred and the Secular: Women's Activism and Politicised Religion in South Asia* (Kali for Women 1999) 54.

—— *Shifting Body Politics: Gender, Nation, State in Pakistan* (Women Unlimited 2004).

Roy S, 'Melancholic Politics and the Politics of Melancholia: The Indian Women's Movement' (2009) 10(3) Feminist Theory 341.

—— (ed) *New South Asian Feminisms: Paradoxes and Possibilities* (Palgrave Macmillan 2012).

Rua Wall I, 'The Ordinary Affects of Law' (2019) 19(2) Law Culture and the Humanities 1.

Saeed K, Gater R, Hussain A and Mubbashar M, 'The Prevalence, Classification and Treatment of Mental Disorders among Attenders of Native Faith Healers in Rural Pakistan' (2000) 35(10) Social Psychiatry and Psychiatric Epidemiology 480.

Saeed M and Griffin G, 'Researching a Sensitive Topic in an Unstable Environment: Fieldwork Dilemmas in the Khyber-Pakhtunkhwa Province of Pakistan' (2019) 19(3) Qualitative Research Journal 248.

Saeed R, 'Law and Coloniality of Empire: Colonial Encounter and Normative Orderings in the Indian Sub-Continent' (2016–17) 19 Yearbook of Islamic and Middle Eastern Law 103.

Saigol R, *Symbolic Violence: Curriculum, Pedagogy, and Society* (Society for Advancement of Education 2000).

—— 'His Rights/ Her Duties: Citizen and Mother in the Civics Discourse' (2003) 10(3) Indian Journal of Gender Studies 379.

Sarantakos S, *Social Research* (4th edn, Palgrave Macmillan 2013).

Schafran LH, 'Credibility in the Courts: Why Is There a Gender Gap?' (1995) 34 Judges Journal 40.

Schechner R, *Theatre and Anthropology* (University of Pennsylvania Press 1985) 36.

Scheppele KL, 'Foreword: Telling Stories' (1988) 87(8) Michigan Law Review 2079.

Schwobel-Patel C, 'The Ideal Victim of International Criminal Law' (2018) 29(3) The European Journal of International Law 714.

Seedat F, *Sex and the Legal Subject: Women and Legal Capacity in Ḥanafī Law* (PhD dissertation, McGill University 2013).

Semmens N, 'Methodological Approaches to Criminological Research' in P Davies, P Francis and V Jupp (eds), *Doing Criminological Research* (2nd edn, Sage Publications 2011) 72.

Serisier T, *Speaking Out: Feminism, Rape and Narrative Politics* (Palgrave Macmillan 2018).

Setia A, Marks M and An S, 'Double Standards in Perceived Traits of Women Labelled Victims versus Survivors' (2020) 24(5) Sexuality and Culture 1562.

Shah R, Khan S, Farid S and Shah A, 'Delaying Tactics used by Lawyers in Dispensation of Civil Justice in Lower Courts of Pakistan' (2014) 6(2) Pakistan Journal of Criminology 113.

Shahbaz M, *Saday Akhaan [Our Proverbs]* (Aziz Book Depot 2004) 155.

Sheehy EA, 'Evidence Law and "Credibility Testing" of Women: A Comment on the E Case' (2002) 2(2) Queensland University of Technology Law and Justice Journal 157.
Sherwin RK, 'The Narrative Construction of Legal Reality' (2009) 6 Journal of the Association of Legal Writing Directors 88, 93.
Shulamit R and Chase SE, 'Interviewing Women' in J Holstein and JF Gubrium (eds), *Inside Interviewing – New Lenses, New Concerns* (1st edn, Sage Publications 2003) 222.
Shultz L, 'The Wife Assaulter' (1960) 6(1) Journal of Social Therapy 103.
Siddique O, *Pakistan's Experience with Formal Law: An Alien Justice* (Cambridge University Press 2013) 137.
Skjelsbaek I, 'Victim and Survivor: Narrated Social Identities of Women who Experienced Rape during the War in Bosnia-Herzegovina' (2006) 16 Feminism and Psychology 373.
Smart C, *Feminism and the Power of Law* (Routledge 1989) 11.
—— 'The Woman of Legal Discourse' (1992) 1(1) Social and Legal Studies 29, 34.
Smith DM, 'The Disordered and Discredit Plaintiff: Psychiatric Evidence in Civil Litigation' (2009) 31 Cardoza Law Review 788.
Smith O, 'Researching English Sexual Violence Trials using Court Observation Methods' in *SAGE Research Methods Cases* (SAGE Publications 2020)
Smith O and Skinner T, 'How Rape Myths Are Used and Challenged in Rape and Sexual Assault Trials' (2017) 26(4) Social and Legal Studies 447.
Spivak GC, 'Can the Subaltern Speak' in C Nelson and L Grossberg (eds), *Marxism and the Interpretation of Culture* (Macmillan Education 1988) 271.
Stark E, 'Do Violent Acts Equal Abuse? Resolving the Gender Parity/ Asymmetrical Dilemma' (2010) 62 Sex Roles 210.
—— 'Coercive Control' in N Lombard and L McMillan (eds), *Violence against Women: Current Theory and Practice in Domestic Abuse, Sexual Violence and Exploitation* (Jessica Kingsley Publishers 2013) 17.
Stoetzler M and Yuval-Davis N, 'Standpoint Theory, Situated Knowledge and the Situated Imagination' (2002) 3(3) Feminist Theory 315.
Stoler AL, *Race and the Education of Desire: Foucault's History of Sexuality and the Colonial Order of Things* (Duke University Press 1996).
Stubbs J, 'Domestic Violence and Women's Safety: Feminist Challenges to Restorative Justice' in H Strang and J Braithwaite (eds), *Restorative Justice and Family Violence* (Cambridge University Press 2002) 52.
Szasz T, *The Myth of Mental Illness: Foundations of a Theory of Personal Conduct* (Harper and Row 1961) 119.
Tambe A, 'Reckoning with the Silences of #MeToo' (2018) 44(1) Feminist Studies 197.
Tanwir M, Fennell S, Lak HR and Salman S, 'Not Accepting Abuse as the Norm: Local Forms of Institutional Reform to Improve Reporting on Domestic Violence in Punjab' (2019) 20(7) Journal of International Women's Studies 129, 140.
Taussig M, *Defacement: Public Secrecy and the Labour of the Negative* (Stanford University Press 1999) 2.
Temple B and Young A, 'Qualitative Research and Translation Dilemmas' (2004) 4 Qualitative Research 161, 171.

Thiesmeyer L, *Discourses and Silencing: Representation and the Language of Displacement* (John Benjamins 2003).
Thompson M, 'Life after Rape: A Chance to Speak' (2000) 15 Sexual and Relationship Therapy 329.
Thummapol O, Park T, Jackson M and Barton S, 'Methodological Challenges Faced in Doing Research with Vulnerable Women: Reflections from Fieldwork Experiences' (2019) 18(1) International Journal of Qualitative Methods 1.
Tiersma P, *Legal Language* (Chicago University Press 1999) 159.
Toor S, 'Gender, Sexuality, and Islam under the Shadow of Empire' (2011) 3(9) The Scholar and Feminist Online 22.
Towns AJ and Adams PJ, '"I didn't know whether I was right or wrong or just bewildered": Ambiguity, Responsibility and Silencing Women's Talk of Men's Domestic Violence' (2016) 22(4) Violence Against Women 496, 500.
Tuerkheimer D, 'Incredible Women: Sexual Violence and the Credibility Discount' (2017) 166(1) University of Pennsylvania Law Review 14.
Turley SL, 'To See Between: Interviewing as Legal Research Tool' (2010) 7(1) Journal of the Association of Legal Writing Directors 283.
Ussher J, *The Madness of Women: Myth and Experience* (Taylor and Francis Group 2005).
Van Dijk J, 'Free the Victim: A Critique of the Western Conception of Victimhood' (2009) 16(1) International Review of Victimology 1.
Varma LP, 'History of Psychiatry in India and Pakistan' (1953) 4(1) Indian Journal of Psychiatry 26.
Waheed M, 'Domestic Violence in Pakistan: The Tension between Intervention and Sovereign Autonomy in Human Rights Law' (2004) 29(2) Brooklyn Journal of International Law 962.
Wahlbeck K and Aromaa E, 'Research on Stigma related to Mental Disorders in Finland: A Systemic Literature Review' (2011) 42(1) Psychiatria Fennica 87.
Wakefield A, 'Undertaking a Criminological Literature Review' in P Davies, P Francis and V Jupp (eds), *Doing Criminological Research* (2nd edn, Sage Publications 2011) 69.
Walklate S, *Gender, Crime and Criminal Justice* (2nd edn, Willan Publishing 2004) 180.
—— *Imagining the Victim of Crime* (Open University Press 2006) 27.
Watkins D, 'Recovering the Lost Human Stories of the Law: Finding Mrs Burns' (2013) 7(1) Law and Humanities 71.
Watkins D and Burton M (eds), *Research Methods in Law* (Routledge 2013) 15.
Weare S, '"The Mad", "the Bad", "the Victim": Gendered Constructions of Women Who Kill within the Criminal Justice System' (2013) 2 Laws 337.
Weedon C and Hallak A, 'Feminist Poststructuralism: Discourse, Subjectivity, the Body and Power' in J Angouri and J Baxter (eds), *The Routledge Handbook of Language, Gender and Sexuality* (Routledge 2021) 437.
Werbner P and Yuval-Davis N, 'Introduction: Women and the New Discourse of Citizenship' in P Werbner and N Yuval-Davis (eds), *Women, Citizenship and Difference* (Zed Books 1999) 6.
Wetherell M, 'Positioning and Interpretative Repertoires: Conversation Analysis and Poststructuralism in Dialogue' (1998) 9(3) Discourse and Society 387.

Wiener C, 'From Social Construct to Legal Innovation: The Offence of Controlling or Coercive Behaviour in England and Wales' in M McMahon and P McGorrery (eds), *Criminalising Coercive Control: Family Violence and the Criminal Law* (Springer 2020) 159.
Wigmore JH, *A Treatise on the Anglo-American System of Evidence in Trials at Common Law* (3rd ed. Little Brown and Company 1940).
Winter S, Diamond M, Green J, Karasic D, Reed T, Whittle S and Wylie K, 'Transgender People: Health at the Margins of Society' (2016) 10042 The Lancet 390, 394.
Wolf S, 'Talking to Migrants: Invisibility, Vulnerability, and Protection' (2021) 26(1) Geopolitics 207.
Woodbury H, 'The Strategic Use of Questions in Court' (1984) 48(3-4) Semiotica 197.
Woods L, 'Litigation on Behalf of Battered Women' (1979) 5(1) Women's Rights Law Reporter 7, 12.
Y Qassem, 'Law of the Family (Personal Status Law)' in N Bernard-Maugiron and B Dupret (eds), *Egypt and its Laws* (Kluwer Law International 2002) 19, 25.
Younas F, Naseem M and Mustafa M, 'Patriarchy and Social Media: Women Only Facebook Groups as Safe Spaces for Support Seeking in Pakistan' (Information and Communication Technologies and Development Conference, 17 June 2022, New York).
Young K, Fisher J and Kirkman M, 'Women's Experiences of Endometriosis: A Systematic Review and Synthesis of Qualitative Research' (2015) 41 Family Planning, Reproduction and Health Care 225.
Yung CR, 'Rape Law Gatekeeping' (2017) 58(1) Boston College Law Review 206.
Yuval-Davis N, *Gender and Nation* (Sage Publications 1997).
Zaccour S, 'Crazy Women and Hysterical Mothers: The Gendered Use of Mental-Health Labels in Custody Disputes' (2018) 31(1) Canadian Journal of Family Law 57.
Zaman S and Zia M, 'How Much Rape Is Rape? Understanding Normative Assumptions within Rape Victimology in Pakistan' in N Hussain (ed), *Disputed Legacies: The Pakistan Papers* (Zubaan Books 2019) 155.
Zia A, *Sex Crime in the Islamic Context: Rape, Class and Gender in Pakistan* (ASR Publications 1994) 15.
—— 'My Body, Allah's Choice: Islamic Laws and Sexual Autonomies in Pakistan' (2022) 23(2) Australian Journal of Asian Law 95, 99.

Organizational Reports and Policy Papers

Acid Survivors Foundation, 'Acid/Burn Violence Statistics 2018' (ASF, 2018) <https://asfpakistan.org/wp-content/uploads/2020/07/ASF-Data-2007-2018-FINAL.pdf> accessed 2 June 2023.
—— 'Acid Violence in Pakistan: A Situational Analysis' (ASF, 2015) <https://asfpakistan.org/wp-content/uploads/2017/02/SAAV-report-2015.pdf> accessed 2 June 2023.
Ali K and Inam M, *Domestic Violence Policy Brief* (National Commission of Human Rights Pakistan 2023).

Bokhari FY, 'Accountability for Rape: A Case Study of Lodhran' (2018) Centre for Human Rights, University College Lahore 1, 41.

Burman M, Jamieson L and Nicholson J, *Impacts of Aspects of the Law of Evidence in Sexual Offence Trials: An Evaluation Study* (Edinburgh: Scottish Government 2007).

Burney S, 'Crime or Custom? Violence against Women in Pakistan' (1999) Human Rights Watch 48.

Committee on the Elimination of Discrimination against Women (CEDAW), 'Fifth Periodic Report submitted by Pakistan' (2018) CEDAW/C/PAK/5 2.

Dennerstein L, Astbury J and Morse C, *Psychosocial and Mental Health Aspects of Women's Health* (WHO Geneva 1993).

Gilani Research Foundation Survey, 'Opinion Poll: Social Behaviour and others' (*Gallup Pakistan*, 2 March 2017) <http://gallup.com.pk/wp-content/uploads/2017/03/2-March-2017-English-1.pdf> accessed 3 November 2020.

Hayat K, *State of Human Rights in 2001* (Human Rights Commission of Pakistan 2002).

Karmaliani R, Asad N, Khan KS, Bawani S, Ali TS, Jones N, Gupta T, Allana A, Maqbool H and Walker D, 'Understanding Intimate Partner Violence in Pakistan through a Male Lens' (Overseas Development Institute, March 2017) <https://cdn.odi.org/media/ documents/11398.pdf> accessed 4 June 2023.

Lerman L, *Prosecution of Spouse Abuse: Innovations in Criminal Justice Response* (Center for Women Policy Studies 1981) 26, 27.

National Institute of Population Studies, 'Pakistan Demographic and Health Survey 2017–2018' (NIPS and ICF, 2019) <https://dhsprogram.com/pubs/pdf/FR354/FR354. pdf> accessed 3 June 2023.

Prosecutor General, 'Veracity of Witness or Reliability' *Government of Punjab* <https:// pg.punjab.gov.pk/veracity_of_witness_or_reliability> accessed 20 October 2022.

Suddle MS, 'Reforming Pakistan Police: An Overview' (2003) United Nations Asia 94.

UN Women, 'Acid Attacks' (27 January 2011) <http://www.endvawnow.org/en/ articles/607- acid-attacks.html> accessed 2 June 2023.

United Nations, 'Good Practices in Legislation on "Harmful Practices" against Women' (2009) EGM Meeting, Department of Economic and Social Affairs <https://www.un.org/womenwatch/daw/egm/vaw_legislation_2009/Final%20report%20E GMGPLVAW.pdf> accessed 20 July 2023.

World Economic Forum, 'Global Gender Gap Report 2024' (2024) <https:// www3.weforum.org/docs/WEF_GGGR_2024.pdf> accessed 26 September 2024.

Zia M, 'A Pilot Study on Honour Killings in Pakistan and Compliance of Law' (2011) Aurat Publication and Information Service Foundation.

—— 'Understanding Domestic Violence within the Legal Framework of Pakistan' (2018) Legal Aid Society 18.

Zia M, David SO and Randhawa S, 'Gap Analysis on Investigation and Prosecution of Rape and Sodomy Cases' (2021) Legal Aid Society 69.

Print Journalism and Media

Ahmad I, 'Islamabad Police Baton Charge Aurat March Participants' *The Nation* (9 March 2023) <https://www.nation.com.pk/09-Mar-2023/islamabad-police-baton-charge -aurat-march-participants> accessed 15 March 2023.

Ali K, 'Marriage Age Laws Un-Islamic: CII' *Dawn News* (12 March 2014) <https://www.dawn.com/news/1092571> accessed 1 June 2018.

Anis M, 'Govt Orders Probe into Objectionable Activities of Aurat March' *The News International* (15 March 2021) <https:// www.thenews.com.pk/print/804425-govt-orders-probe-into-objectionable-activities-of-aurat-march> accessed 4 April 2021.

Asad M, 'Loopholes Persist in "Honour Killing" Bill' *Dawn News* (24 July 2016) <https://www.dawn.com/news/1272833> accessed 10 July 2023.

Baloch SM, 'Pakistan Court Acquits Man Who Killed Sister after Parents' Pardon' *The Guardian* (14 February 2022) <https://www.theguardian.com/world/2022/feb/14/ pakistan-court-acquits-man-waseem-azeem-who-killed-sister-after-parents-pardon> accessed 1 June 2023.

Bucha S and Aqeel A, 'Battered Lives' *Newsline* (March 2002) <https://newsline magazine.com/magazine/battered-lives/> accessed 3 January 2023.

Buckwalter-Poza R, 'Troubled History of Domestic Violence Legislation in Pakistan' *Huffpost* (10 July 2010) <https://www.huffpost.com/entry/troubled-history-of-domes_b_753400> accessed 2 February 2021.

The Daily Times, 'Pakistani Journalist Shot Dead by Husband for Not Quitting Job' (27 November 2019) <https:// dailytimes.com.pk/508366/pakistani-journalist-shot-dead-by-husband-for-not-quitting-job/> accessed 20 March 2021.

Danish N and Rabbani F, 'Men Pelt Stones at Aurat March Islamabad Participants' *Samaa TV* (8 March 2020) <https://www. samaa.tv/news/pakistan/2020/03/men-pelt-stones-at-aurat-march-islamabad-participants/> accessed 5 April 2021.

Dawn News, 'Woman Killed for Texting' (27 June 2018) <https://www.dawn.com/news/1423071/woman-killed-for-texting> accessed 22 March 2021.

—— 'Govt Recommends Referring Domestic Violence Bill to Council of Islamic Ideology' (6 July 2021) <https://www.dawn.com/news/1633531> accessed 19 July 2023.

—— 'Layyah Woman Killed by In-Laws over Delay in Cooking' (10 July 2024) <https://www.dawn.com/news/1844881> accessed 2 September 2024.

The Express Tribune, 'Mistrustful Man Kills Wife for Leaving House sans Permission' (05 December 2021) <https://tribune.com.pk/story/2332545/mistrustful-man-kills-wife-for-leaving-house-sans-permission> accessed 06 December 2021.

—— 'In Pakistan, Passion for Higher Studies Costs Woman Her Life' (16 September 2019) <https:// tribune.com.pk/story/2057291/1-passion-higher-studies-costs-woman-life> accessed 15 March 2021.

Gabol I, 'Religious Parties Denounce Law Protecting Women from Abuse As "Un-Islamic"' *Dawn News* (15 March 2016) <https://www.dawn.com/news/1245835> accessed 11 July 2023.

Hanif S, 'Husband Axes Wife to Death in Badin for "Taking Too Long"' *Dawn News* (23 June 2016) <https://www. dawn.com/news/1266741> accessed on 1 April 2021.

Hayat A and Akbar A, 'KP Assembly Unanimously Passes Resolution against Aurat March' *Dawn News* (20 March 2019) <https://www.dawn.com/news/1470834> accessed 2 April 2021.

Khaleej Times, 'Man Murders Wife over Cold Dinner in Pakistan' (30 November 2017) <https://www.khaleejtimes.com/international/pakistan/man-murders-wife-over-cold-dinner-in-pakistan> accessed 21 March 2021.

Khan R, '"Lightly Beating" Wife Is Permissible, Says CII's Proposed Women Protection Bill' *Dawn News* (26 May 2016) <https://www.dawn.com/news/1260803> accessed 2 June 2018.

Mehboob S, 'Where Pakistan's Domestic Violence Law Fails' *The Express Tribune* (7 August 2022) <https://tribune. com.pk/story/2369842/where-pakistans-domestic-violence-law-fails> accessed 18 July 2023.

Mushtaq R and Haider SB, 'Why Violence against Women Continues Unabated despite Presence of Laws' *Geo News* (24 October 2022) <https://www.geo.tv/ latest/448066-why-violence-against-women-continues-unabated-despite-presence-of-laws> accessed 10 June 2023.

Naya Daur, 'Over 82 per cent of Rapists are Fathers or Brothers of Victim: PTI MNA' (15 September 2020) <https://nayadaur.tv/2020/09/over-82-per-cent-of-rapists-are-fathers-or-brothers-of-victim-pti-mna/> accessed 28 July 2023.

The News, 'Woman Files Case of "Marital Rape" against Husband' (16 September 2018) <https://www.thenews.com.pk/print/369113-woman-files-case-of-marital-rape-against-husband> accessed 20 July 2023.

Perraudin F, 'Alleged "Honour" Killing Victim Was Murdered, Pakistani Police Confirm' *The Guardian* (3 August 2016) <https://www.theguardian.com/uk-news/2016 /aug/03/alleged-honour-killing-victim-samia-shahid-murdered-pakistani-police-confirm> accessed 26 June 2023.

Shah N, 'Honour Killings: Code of Dishonour' (19 November 1998) *The Weekly Review, Dawn News.*

Shah WA, 'View from Courtroom: KP Domestic Violence Bill a Diluted Version of Previous Drafts' *Dawn News* (11 January 2021) <https://www.dawn.com/news/1600820> accessed 13 February 2022.

Siddique O, 'The Language of Justice' *The Express Tribune* (27 February 2022) <https://tribune.com.pk/story/342487/the-language-of-justice> accessed 26 January 2022.

Siddiqui N, 'Motorway Rape Occurred because Victim Travelled "Late Night Without Husband's Permission", CCPO tells Senate Panel' *Dawn News* (28 September 2020) <https://www.dawn.com/news/1582117> accessed 26 October 2022.

Sirajuddin, 'Peshawar Court Orders Registration of FIR against Aurat March' *Dawn News* (26 March 2021) <https://www.dawn.com/news/amp/1614730> accessed 4 April 2021.

Zaman S, 'Pakistan's Progressive Transgender Law faces Opposition 4 Years Later' *Voice of America* (28 September 2022) <https://www.voanews.com/a/pakistan-s-progres sive-transgender-law-faces-opposition-4-years-later-/6768168.html> accessed 26 January 2023.

Interviews (Pakistan)

Interview with lawyer [a], 5 January 2022, Karachi

Interview with lawyer [b], 5 January 2022, Karachi

Interview with lawyer [c], 5 January 2022, Karachi
Interview with lawyer [d], 5 January 2022, Karachi
Interview with lawyer, 6 January 2022, Karachi
Interview with lawyer, 8 January 2022, Karachi
Interview with victim support personnel [a], 12 January 2022, Karachi
Interview with victim support personnel [b], 12 January 2022, Karachi
Interview with victim support personnel [c], 12 January 2022, Karachi
Interview with victim [a], 12 January 2022, Karachi
Interview with victim [b], 12 January 2022, Karachi
Interview with victim [c], 12 January 2022, Karachi
Interview with victim [d], 12 January 2022, Karachi
Interview with lawyer, 14 January 2022, Karachi
Interview with lawyer, 15 January 2022, Karachi
Interview with victim support personnel, 7 June 2022, Islamabad
Interview with victim support personnel [b], 7 June 2022, Islamabad
Interview with victim [a], 7 June 2022, Islamabad
Interview with victim [b], 7 June 2022, Islamabad
Interview with victim [c], 7 June 2022, Islamabad
Interview with victim [d], 7 June 2022, Islamabad
Interview with police, 7 June 2022, Islamabad
Interview with victim [a], 8 June 2022, Islamabad
Interview with victim [b], 8 June 2022, Islamabad
Interview with victim [c], 8 June 2022, Islamabad
Interview with victim [d], 8 June 2022, Islamabad
Interview with victim [e], 8 June 2022, Islamabad
Interview with lawyer [a], 9 June 2022, Islamabad
Interview with lawyer [b], 9 June 2022, Islamabad
Interview with lawyer [c], 9 June 2022, Islamabad
Interview with lawyer [d], 9 June 2022, Islamabad
Interview with lawyer [e], 9 June 2022, Islamabad
Interview with lawyer [f], 9 June 2022, Islamabad
Interview with victim support personnel, 13 June 2022, Lahore
Interview with lawyer [a], 13 June 2022, Lahore
Interview with lawyer [b], 13 June 2022, Lahore
Interview with victim [a], 14 June 2022, Lahore
Interview with victim [b], 14 June 2022, Lahore
Interview with victim [c], 14 June 2022, Lahore
Interview with victim support personnel, 14 June 2022, Lahore
Interview with lawyer, 14 June 2022, Lahore
Interview with lawyer [a], 15 June 2022, Lahore
Interview with lawyer [b], 15 June 2022, Lahore
Interview with lawyer [c], 15 June 2022, Lahore
Interview with lawyer [d], 15 June 2022, Lahore
Interview with victim support personnel, 15 June 2022, Lahore
Interview with lawyer [a], 16 June 2022, Lahore
Interview with lawyer [b], 16 June 2022, Lahore

Interview with lawyer [c], 16 June 2022, Lahore
Interview with lawyer [a], 17 June 2022, Lahore
Interview with lawyer [b], 17 June 2022, Lahore
Phone interview with victim support personnel, 27 June 2022, Sukkur
Phone interview with lawyer, 28 June 2022, Sialkot
Phone interview with lawyer, 1 July 2022, Peshawar
Interview with judge, 4 July 2022, Karachi
Interview with victim, 4 July 2022, Karachi
Interview with lawyer, 4 July 2022, Karachi
Phone interview with lawyer, 8 July 2022, Hyderabad
Phone interview with lawyer, 13 July 2022, Islamabad
Interview with lawyer, 19 July 2022, Karachi
Interview with victim support personnel, 19 July 2022, Karachi
Phone interview with lawyer, 28 July 2022, Lahore
Interview with lawyer, 1 August 2022, Karachi
Phone interview with police, 1 August 2022, Gilgit
Interview with police [a], 2 August 2022, Karachi
Interview with police [b], 2 August 2022, Karachi
Interview with police [c], 2 August 2022, Karachi
Interview with victim, 4 August 2022, Karachi
Interview with judge, 5 August 2022, Karachi
Interview with lawyer [a], 11 August 2022, Karachi
Interview with lawyer [b], 11 August 2022, Karachi
Interview with medico-legal officer, 14 August 2022, Karachi

Police Reports (Pakistan)

FIR 05/22 Karachi West
FIR 13/22 Karachi Central
FIR 16028/21 Gilgit
FIR 232/21 Ahmad Nagar
FIR 242/20 Islamabad
FIR 266/22 Karachi West
FIR 322/22 Karachi West
FIR 338/22 Karachi Central
FIR 412/22 Karachi West

Index

For the benefit of digital users, indexed terms that span two pages (e.g., 52–53) may, on occasion, appear on only one of those pages.